A TIME TO SING

Dorothy Kirsten

A Time to Sing

With the Collaboration of Lanfranco Rasponi

Foreword by Robert Jacobson, Editor-in-Chief, *Opera News*

DOUBLEDAY & COMPANY, INC.
Garden City, New York
1982

Library of Congress Cataloging in Publication Data

Kirsten, Dorothy, 1915–
A time to sing.

Includes index.
1. Kirsten, Dorothy, 1915–   . 2. Singers—United
States—Biography. I. Rasponi, Lanfranco. II. Title.
ML420.K479A3   782.1'092'4   [B]
AACR2
ISBN: *0-385-14744-9*
Library of Congress Catalog Card Number 81-43395

*In memory of my beloved parents
and of Grace Moore*

Acknowledgments

To my devoted husband, Jack, whose patience and understanding supported me greatly while I sadly neglected him.

To my secretary, Vicki, for her loyalty these many years and her tireless efforts in gathering the tons of material through which we revived this story.

To my friend Irving Stone, who convinced me I could write my own book.

To my friend Madeline Arnold, who followed my career, studied every detail of my costumes, and presented me with a complete collection of my image in miniature dolls.

To my teacher Ludwig Fabri who gave me the fine vocal technique with which I have enjoyed singing these many wonderful years.

To Lanfranco Rasponi for his contributions.

To my editors, Ken McCormick and Louise Gault, for their encouragement and enthusiasm, which kept me inspired.

Contents

Foreword

by Robert Jacobson, Editor-in-Chief, *Opera News*

The first time I ever laid eyes on Dorothy Kirsten was at the stage door of the Chicago Civic Opera House. It was after a matinee of *Carmen* with two other great American singers of her generation, Risë Stevens and Richard Tucker. Dorothy was arriving for the evening performance of *La Traviata*, the finale to the Metropolitan Opera's spring tour week in the Windy City. She was swathed in honey-colored mink, and just about the most glamorous human being ever.

Nowadays, to be American and glamorous seems anachronistic, but Dorothy grew up at a time when her mentor Grace Moore, Gladys Swarthout, Risë Stevens, and others personified operatic glamour—a world all their own, ready to entice the public. It was what brought people into the theatre and kept them coming back for more. I like what Dorothy told me on the occasion of her twenty-fifth anniversary at the Met: "Singers aren't idols anymore. They're too close to the public. When they go on the talk shows, they become too familiar, too much the good Joe and the girl next door. I've tried to maintain the image of the prima donna all through the years, wherever I was."

That blond glamour often defined Dorothy's repertoire—her Barbara Stanwyckish Minnie in Puccini's *La Fanciulla del West* (a still definitive performance in every way), her glamorous Floria Tosca (played in dark wig to go with *bruna Floria,* but a more compelling Tosca is hard to imagine), her fragile but strong and beautiful Cio Cio San (as complete a performance of this hapless heroine as one can hope for), her radiant Marguerite in *Faust* (back to blondness again), her alluring Manon Lescaut (has anyone ever looked more ravishing than Dorothy in the Act II boudoir?) or her beauteous Violetta in *La Traviata.* I never saw her as Louise or as Fiora in *L'Amore dei Tre Re* or as Massenet's Manon, but pictures capture a woman of devastating looks, charm, grace. And her singing? That word beauty again comes to mind. Beauty of pure tone, beauty of phrasing, beauty of line. Take Louise's "Depuis le jour" on record or in countless concerts and gala evenings. The soaring French idiom fit her like a glove, the radiant soprano hand in hand with the elegant, linear French style. Listening to Dorothy, I've always thought of tradition, of all those great ladies who came out of Mathilde Marchesi's school—Calvé, Eames, Garden, Melba, Sanderson. With her high placement, purity, refinement, Dorothy remains a throwback to the tenets of Garcia and Ronconi, Marchesi's own teachers.

Dorothy is all woman, prima donna—a term she likes. She is probably the first to admit to loving roles in which she can dominate as the singular feminine force onstage. Is that why we were never privileged to share her Liù in *Turandot*, to fill out the Puccini picture? And with artists one loves—and I confess to loving Dorothy Kirsten—one becomes greedy. How tragic not to have had her Thaïs, for who better could have taken the sinner-saint role out of mothballs and made it glow in the theatre, as witnessed in her definitive final scene recorded with Robert Merrill. Or what about Desdemona in *Otello*, Alice Ford in *Falstaff*, or some Mozart outings—the Countess in *Le Nozze di Figaro*, Donna Elvira in *Don Giovanni*—or even the light Wagner of *Die Meistersinger*'s Eva, or Strauss's Arabella and, eventually, his Marschallin?

But Dorothy has maneuvered her career with that commodity rare in these times: caution. How many times, over how many dinners, have I heard her tell about saying that one word, "No." Rudolf Bing must have been sick and tired of hearing it come from her lips. Initially, he envisioned her as Rosalinde in his *Fledermaus*, but she waited over a decade to air it at the Met. He asked for Fiordiligi in *Così Fan Tutte* and Elizabeth in *Don Carlo* and any number of juicy parts. But Dorothy stuck to her guns. Just after we first met—and what a thrill to know that creature who had been a bundle of honey fur some years earlier—she had been asked by Bing to look at Marie in *Wozzeck*. I arrived with score, recording, background articles for her study. We put on Marie's first scene, and after just a few moments the verdict was in: No! And she probably was right. Dorothy has probably refused more roles than she has sung, but this made celebrating her thirtieth anniversary with the Met possible. Not only could she celebrate with a stunning New Year's Eve *Tosca*, she could do it with full command of her vocal resources and a freshness of tone that singers of half her experience could envy.

Prima donnas are wonderful creatures, and Dorothy always sees herself as such. Letters from California arrive signed, "Your favorite prima donna," "Your diva," and she means it. I like that. Dorothy gives opera that sense of style, of glamour—that slightly unattainable goddess who sings, performs and vanishes until the next magical evening. In true diva fashion, she's not happy about going to the theatre, unless she's singing. In the mid-1960s when Maria Callas made her celebrated return to the Met for two historic Toscas, the late Francis Robinson prevailed on Dorothy to attend the second performance. Under duress, she finally agreed and went. Her verdict? "She doesn't do anything I don't do." So speaketh a diva.

The long-running Kirsten image has been perpetuated in many

ways. Like such predecessors as Farrar, Moore, and others, she has not limited herself to opera. There have been films, radio, television, popular music, operetta, records, and attention paid to publicity. Even at the time of her thirtieth year at the Met, she could climb into a New York taxicab and be instantly recognized by the driver. She has traveled this country far and wide, singing recitals and concerts in faraway places that never could hear a live opera. Dorothy brought them a strong dose of glamour and pizzazz they will never forget. She traded quips with Sinatra and Crosby on the radio (while mastering the pop idiom to a T), and while she may have offended the opera purists, she developed a large, loyal public fascinated by the aura that surrounds her.

Everyone has different associations with Dorothy—the prima donna of *The Great Caruso* with Mario Lanza (she was already a huge star because of the film when she traveled to the Soviet Union), "The Railroad Hour" with Gordon MacRae, "Kraft Music Hall" with Nelson Eddy, Lucky Strike's "Light Up Time" with Sinatra, glorious season after season with her real operatic home, the San Francisco Opera where her repertoire extended to Poulenc's *Dialogues of the Carmelites* and Walton's *Troilus and Cressida*. And, of course, the Met, the dream of every American singer.

I feel fortunate to have known and heard Dorothy at a still impressionable age. She has taught me a lot about opera, about its professionalism, about its responsibilities, about the stupidity of useless antics, about performing values, about believing in one's abilities and about exercising wisdom and care that leads to longevity and a mellowing of one's resources, about seriousness and dedication to the artistic life. Her attitudes sometime seem like those of a prehistoric creature in our age of anxiety, our time of novelty for its own sake, of singers reeling off course in terms of repertoire and pacing, of irresponsibility and carelessness to colleagues, the public, even oneself. Dorothy has never been careless. There may have been rough times, disagreements, misjudged decisions, but she moved step by step with intelligence and sureness, combining well-honed craft, art, and single-mindedness.

I've always felt that Dorothy could have reaped more out of her career—but at the same time it could have meant less in the long run. Early on, she was accused of a certain coolness, aloofness, reticence. Perhaps that kind of start made it possible for her to let loose throughout the 1960s and 1970s in truly memorable performances—dramatic, full-throated, dynamic. In this book, she writes of mistakes, of wrong turns. But she can look back on a long, illustrious career during which she built and then commanded the respect of everyone in her profes-

sion along with all those who pay their money, sit out front and observe her. She's cool, calm, collected. She knows her opera, and it has
always been a source of surprise and delight to see her in the dressing
room before a performance of a role she may have sung hundreds of
times, to see her studying the notes and words just as a beginner
would. It has been a joy to watch her do certain roles time and time
again, and never sound tired or look stale in them. Once after a particularly riveting performance of *Tosca*, I commented on a superb new
piece of "business" with Scarpia (Cornell MacNeil) in Act II, using
his proffered glass of wine and a furious gesture by the lady that
knocked it out of his hand—so good that it was either ingeniously
planned or a glorious accident. "Well," she shrugged, "we've *always*
got to do something new."

All of us have fond memories of Dorothy. For me, she'll always be
that Girl of the Golden West—or in her case, the Golden Girl of the
West—entering on that swell of Puccini, firing her pistol, the cowgirl
settling down the rowdy miners in Act I, the expert cheater at poker
in Act II, the athletic horsewoman of Act III. In November 1964 that
memorable, historic team of Kirsten, Corelli, and Colzani hit the stage
in Philadelphia, and the next year the Met recreated it, and brilliantly.
Puccini's wonderful opera found a brand-new life in such hands. Any
other soprano with her lyric instrument would have been dashed on
the rocks of such a demanding, dramatic role—Puccini's Brünnhilde,
she calls it. But Dorothy, typically, waited to sing it. And when she
did, she was ready. She knew its every nook and cranny, and she made
it her own.

Too bad big-time opera did not hit television at the peak of her career, for how wonderful it would be to have her masterful portrayals
captured for all time. Too bad she made so few recordings—whatever
exists is cherished. Too bad she never conquered Europe, as she did
Russia. Well, too bad in all our lives. But cheers for an authentic
American diva who loves being just that—Dorothy Kirsten, Prima
Donna.

A TIME TO SING

Farewell But Not Good-bye

hen I was a little girl I never dreamed of being a singer; for that matter, a future on the stage never even crossed my mind. To think that one day I would be standing on the most important opera stage in the world, filled to the brim with emotion, tears streaming down my face, my arms full of flowers, enjoying a standing ovation, was just preposterous. But there I was, on New Year's Eve 1975, celebrating a wonderful career of thirty years with the Metropolitan Opera. The house was jammed with my friends and fans from all over the country, and I was the happiest prima donna in the world.

I had chosen the glamorous role of Tosca for my celebration and asked the management to engage as Scarpia the great Tito Gobbi. John Alexander was my Mario, and no diva could have been surrounded with a more perfect cast of colleagues for this grand occasion.

I don't think I have ever felt happier singing than I did that night, for the warmth of the audience coming across the footlights was more inspiring than I could ever describe. Like a squirrel storing his food for the winter, I was drinking in the elixir of that exquisite sound to help me keep warm and remember it forever.

It was a night of emotionally difficult decisions for me too, for I was fighting with myself to slow down my busy career and had almost decided to announce that very night that this would be my last performance at the Met. My husband had been patient for many years and had recently admitted that he hoped I would spend more time at home. But when it came time to go before my audience and make my parting speech, I seemed to have little control over what I was saying, and heard myself blubbering through my tears, "Farewell, my friends, farewell but not good-bye."

After the performance, the directors of the opera asked me if I had really meant what I said. I replied, "Of course," and I'm so glad I did. Since that wonderful night they have called me back several times. How sweet it is to feel so highly regarded.

I love an emergency, and the feeling of saving a difficult situation has always been special to me. These unforeseen circumstances happen in every opera company, and I have had my share of calls for help from both the Metropolitan and San Francisco operas. When either of these two major companies call, my husband knows I'll be off again.

Many times it has been difficult to rearrange engagements and plans that may have been long standing, but over the years our friends have come to realize that my work is extremely important to me, and I am graciously forgiven, with their blessings.

When I was going to New York or San Francisco for my regular seasons with the companies, I usually had some time at home to prepare my roles and send my costumes ahead. Years ago that was no problem, because we stored them at the Met from season to season. In recent years mine have all been kept at home in trunks, and as I prefer always to wear my own, that presents a problem. Being called to fly as soon as possible because someone is ill is always a hectic exercise. Wigs, jewelry, props and costumes are packed in suitcases, and we pray nothing important is forgotten. My make-up kit is always kept ready, and in it is the rabbit's left hind foot that Grace Moore, the great American prima donna, gave me on the night of my debut at the Metropolitan Opera.

The last time my secretary, Vicki, and I flew out of Los Angeles early in the morning for an emergency at the Metropolitan, I remember it as a long and miserable flight. Flying has been my cross to bear all my life, and I need to do a lot of it living in California. Although I have many good friends in the airlines, no one seems to have been able to convince me over all these long years that I am safer in the air than riding in an automobile.

We were to land in Newark. The Met had called me late the night before to tell me that the Essex House, my hotel in New York for many years, was oversold, and though sorry, could not accommodate me. They were trying several other hotels and by the time we arrived there would be a message with their chauffeur, who was to pick us up at the airport.

The opera was *Tosca* again. This time Cornell MacNeil and Carlo Bergonzi, with whom I had sung many times, were to be my colleagues, although we had never appeared together in this opera at the Met. I asked for a rehearsal with as much of the cast as possible. It was arranged, and I was rushed directly to the opera house upon my arrival. *Tosca* is an opera that requires a great deal of "stage business," and the action between the baritone and soprano in the second act can make or break the success of the performance. I had heard that Cornell was working with Tito Gobbi and becoming a great Scarpia. The role seemed so right for him, and I was looking forward to working out some of my own ideas for our scenes together.

My colleagues were great and there was complete cooperation. MacNeil had absorbed so much of Gobbi's interpretation that at times I felt I was singing with Tito himself. How gratifying it was to see this fine American baritone develop so well in this difficult role. Bergonzi too was fired up, and I knew it was going to be an exciting performance. The news of my return had spread like wildfire through the musical grapevine, and the reception when I first appeared on the stage was absolutely overwhelming. The entire company was so affectionate in welcoming me back that I was deeply touched.

Since my thirtieth-anniversary gala evening, this marked the third time I was called back to the Metropolitan; twice to sing *La Bohème*, and this time *Tosca*. I was swept away each time by an enveloping wave of nostalgia. After all, opera is an inseparable part of me, and I do not believe anyone, unless he or she has personally experienced it, can fully understand the impact of gradual twilight on a career such as mine. Since I have dedicated more than half of my life to this form of art, it has taken deep root within me. As I sang "Vissi d'arte" (I have lived for art) that night, so many emotions filled me. During the countless curtain calls at the end, as I gathered up the many flowers thrown on the stage, I could hardly see through my tears again and could not help but wonder, "When will my last performance be in this beloved opera house of mine?" My colleagues must have sensed my feelings, for they kept pushing me forward to the stage alone. When the lights were finally turned on, even though there were still many people hanging over the orchestra pit, I was completely spent.

This volume of reminiscences gives me the opportunity to tell the story of my life or, at least, most of it. For the aspiring singer, I hope to convey not only how my career came to be, but how, unlike so many others, I have been able to continue singing for this long span of time, maintaining my voice and the physical strength to support it.

Wading through the enormous amount of material that Vicki Hillebrand, my secretary of more than thirty years, has kept makes me wonder how I ever crowded so much into one lifetime. Reliving it all through this writing has been a most exhausting but gratifying experience.

Poor Dad—Not Another Girl!

The wonderful thing about being born American is the fine tradition that goes into the making of one. My father's family for several generations were born American with ancestors of Norwegian and German origin. Mother had a mixture of Irish, English and Scottish parents, making their children a combination of five different nationalities. Dad's side was strictly Protestant, while Mother's family was half Catholic. There were four children. First, a girl named Ethel Irene, another Eleanor Frances, then Dorothy Adelle, and finally a boy, George, Jr.

My mother, Margaret Irene Beggs, was the daughter of a famous conductor and bandmaster, James J. Beggs. She was living in Brooklyn Heights, New York, at the time she met my father, George William Kirsten, a building contractor in New Jersey.

My father's wish for a son was well known to Mother and after the appearance of two daughters he was understandably anxious for a boy. When Mother was expecting again several years later, Dad prepared to celebrate, hoping this would be the time. He had promised his sister, who lived only a few blocks away, that when the child was born she would hear three shots from his gun if his wish had come true, and only one if it had not. But my entrance into this world as a healthy nine-and-a-half-pound screaming child with a cry that, I am told, could be heard all over the neighborhood, so overwhelmed my father that he just kept shooting. He forgave me for being another girl and graciously welcomed me into the family. My poor aunt was so alarmed at hearing him continue to shoot that she was sure our delicate sweet mother had borne twins.

The family was living in Montclair, New Jersey, when I was born on July 6, 1915, and Mother delivered her only son, George William Kirsten, Jr., a year and a half later.

Both my parents were handsome, loving, affectionate, and broad-minded within certain limits. Dad was a disciplinarian and Mother, though always siding with him, was a patient pacifier. I lost my mother on October 12, 1951, the night I made my debut in *Tosca* with the San Francisco Opera Company, and Father died about ten years later, lonely and miserable without her. They had celebrated more than fifty years of marriage and deeply loved each other. We were a closely knit family, and though we children enjoyed a certain degree of independence, the watchful eyes of our parents were always with us. Avenues of discussion were patiently left open and our problems were carefully examined, but deep respect for our parents' judgments came to us all naturally.

Playing with dolls never interested me, but I loved the outdoor life and was more attracted to sports. During my high school days, the gymnasium was one of my favorite places, and I played center on the girls' basketball team. However, that unfeminine pastime was not very popular with my parents.

High school in general seemed a waste of time to me. I hated geography, and history, too, was a bore. I had been attracted to drawing in my early school days and did well but never again gave it a thought. Although math was my best subject, I took a secretarial course instead. The result was a passing mark, but when I finished school I forgot the shorthand promptly; and as for the typewriter, I am still a hunt-and-peck performer at the keys.

The area in which we lived was surrounded by trees and the wild flowers were lovely in the spring. We all loved to skate and the small lakes nearby became our skating rinks in the winter. The family often gathered around to play and sing; Mother at the piano, Dad with his mandolin, and George with his trumpet. We girls all studied the piano and it was a happy musical family.

Thoughts of the theatre never entered my mind in those days, but subconsciously I must have known I wanted to be an actress. This struck me after one of my childish escapades. Fearing my father's reaction to my newest transgression, when I heard his footsteps returning home that night I pretended to faint dead away on the kitchen floor. Mother had a great sense of humor, and the memory of her standing over me is still clear in my mind, for she laughed, saying, "Dorothy, that was a great fall. You have the makings of a real actress." I've often wondered if that was the seed that took hold in my brain.

Several years later, while visiting my aunt a few blocks away, I noticed some people preparing what looked like a circus ring and setting up for a show in the lot across the way. Amid the various vehicles were two beautiful dapple-gray horses, and I could not resist wandering nearer. As I approached, a man beckoned me to come in. He told me that he and his wife had retired from the circus and were on the road doing their own show. Intrigued by these show people, I quickly made friends and visited them as often as possible, not telling my parents for fear they would halt this exciting adventure.

My new friends soon found out that I loved horses and offered to teach me to ride bareback circus style (standing). I had the time of my life, and after I lost my fear of falling, I began to learn tricks while galloping around the ring. My friends were careful to see that I wore a type of training belt. A rope was securely fastened to the back of it and then through a ring at the top of a high pole in the middle of the circle. When I faltered or lost the gait, the man in the ring pulled the rope and I would fly through the air like Peter Pan. How I ever got away with this folly was a mystery, because I soon began skipping classes. It was not long before I was sure enough of myself to ride without the belt, but that was not enough for my circus friends. They had high hopes for me and were anxious to teach me other acts. By this time they were performing each evening and I was still working with them afternoons. There were always children around and sometimes a few grownups who would applaud my efforts, which delighted me.

Alas, a friend of my aunt told her she thought she had seen her niece with those "circus people." Disbelieving this incredible news, my aunt arrived on the scene to see me in action, and that was the end of my circus career. But the performer survived and my aspirations toward the entertainment field began.

The Depression had taken its toll of the family funds and when my father, not well, had to slow down his work, we all began to feel the pressure. My young brother and I were almost ready to break out of the nest and if we were to have a career, there was no doubt we would need help. Both sisters had found their niche in a large insurance company after finishing high school, but my parents were particularly anxious for their only son to learn a profession and have a good education. Fortunately, our grandfather took care of that, and George, Jr., was sent off to study in New York at the Ernest Williams School of Music.

As the economic situation became increasingly problematic, I knew that once my schooling was finished, I had to find a way to fend for myself. One day while discussing my future with Mother, I told her of my feelings that college was not the way I wanted to go. I too would find work somewhere until I decided what I wanted to do with my life. My parents could do nothing but give me their blessings and painfully admit they could offer no help.

Looking back, I know that this was the best thing that could have happened to me. I had received my first big challenge, and it was gratifying to learn that I could succeed on my own; that those things we come by easily are not nearly as satisfying as those attained by struggle and hard work.

Out I went to hunt for a job. Fortunately, I soon found one with the New Jersey Bell Telephone Company. Who could have predicted that one day that very same company would be engaging me to sing on their radio program, "The Telephone Hour."

I worked there long enough to put aside some money, but no one will ever know what a restless time that was. The work bored me, but I was making a good salary and helping at home, which was important.

On weekends, it was a real treat to get away with friends to the Jersey Coast; swim all day, bake in the sun, and eat steamed clams by the bucket. But when the fun was over, I realized I was wasting a lot of time and getting nowhere. I wanted to study dance, but not particularly ballet. Acting was another dream, but how did I go about that? Being a small-town girl I had no connections and no idea how to make them. I wanted to perform, only that was certain.

One day I was lolling on the beach, telling my tale of woe to one of my music-loving friends, and he startled me by saying, "Dorothy, why don't you try Broadway? You have a lovely voice, the figure for it, and there you can act as well." That avenue to the stage had not occurred to me. Singing was fun, but I had never aspired to a serious career in it. However, my friend had sparked a new idea and before I left for home that weekend, I had the name of a singer in New York who would find a teacher for me. At last I had the "bit in my teeth" and things moved fast.

The teacher was found, and no audition was necessary after the account of a "beautiful voice" that my friend's friend gave him. My parents approved with reservations, and all I needed to get started was to quit my job and go!

Fortunately for me the teacher did nothing to harm my young voice, but he also did nothing to develop a technique. While he wasted my time, thank goodness my voice remained sweet and quite pure. Later I realized that though he had been a singer at one time, he was more of a coach than a vocal teacher.

While I was living in New York, I began to feel the pressure of no income as my savings ran out. Knowing this, the maestro offered to teach me twice a week without fee if I would act as his secretary. That arrangement worked out fine for a while, but when other duties were forced upon me it was very uncomfortable. I had become, in fact, his housekeeper.

But there were other advantages to this encounter which kept me there and made it worthwhile. I learned one day that there was a fine dancer named Ruth Moltke living in the same apartment house. She was said to have been one of the original Wigman Dancers, a well-known group in Germany, and was teaching aesthetic dancing in New York. Working in her class was a delight and I can think of no dance that teaches body movement more beautifully. I have always felt that this work was an asset to my career, teaching me how to walk on the stage as well as the many concentrated moves that add greatly to an artist's presence.

During that period I met two people who became good friends and were very helpful in getting me started in radio, Eddie Albert, who later became famous both on Broadway and in motion pictures, and Grace Albert (her stage name), who was then his partner in a radio show, "The Honeymooners." They were both studying voice in the same studio, and much to my good fortune asked one day if they could set up an audition for me at the Hearst radio station, WINS in New York. I was engaged a few days later and began my radio career at this station.

At last, my first professional step in the entertainment world! I shall always be grateful to Grace and Eddie, for this was the beginning of my long and happy career in radio, which was also the start of all that followed.

The Irishman and the Diva Send Cinderella to Rome

*M*y first engagement at WINS was a fifteen-minute spot every day for five dollars a show, with Henry Silvern, an organist, as my accompanist—ridiculous by today's standards, but I thought it was great in the late thirties. Here I began to build a repertoire of all the show tunes and fell in love with Gershwin and Kern. But the major importance of this show was the exposure it gave me to many people who were to prove so helpful to my young career. J. E. Dinty Doyle, a newspaperman who wrote a column called "Dialing with Doyle" for the *Herald Tribune*, was one of those people. Dinty's office and the radio station were in the same building. Being the warm, friendly Irishman he was, he lost no time in introducing himself. While I was working in a studio close to his office, he visited us, and one day asked me to drop by after the show. Dinty was not beyond making a pass at a young aspiring songstress, but when he discovered that I intended to have a career without "paying" my way, he became my biggest booster in helping me build a name.

At least once a week he wrote flattering things about my voice in his daily column, and it was these notices that led to my being engaged by some of the top groups in radio such as the Ted Straeter Singers. I soon became the top soprano on the "Kate Smith Show." Kate had a natural delivery and I don't believe she ever had a vocal lesson. Her throat was blessed and I never heard "God Bless America" sung with such inner faith and conviction.

I soon became busy with my new work and was at last free from having to work as my teacher's secretary. To be able to live alone in my own little apartment with the privacy I longed for was a dream come true.

Dinty called me Kirsten right from the beginning. I used to feel it was strange until I learned it was meant as a compliment. "Great artists are often called by their last names," he explained, "and that is what you are going to be one day."

I was still singing occasionally at WINS and often stopped in to bring Dinty up to date on my activities. On one of those visits he started to talk about Grace Moore and it became quite obvious that she was his favorite star.

Dinty told me that while he watched me work those first few weeks at the station, he kept thinking about how much alike Grace and I were. Then and there he decided he was going to get me an introduction to her. Grace was singing on the "Chesterfield Presents" radio show with André Kostelanetz at this time, and when Dinty asked me if I would like to meet her, I jumped at the chance.

On March 30, 1938, Dinty and I presented ourselves backstage and were ushered into Miss Moore's mobile dressing room. When he knocked on her door, the smile that greeted Dinty told me he was very welcome, and as he beckoned me forward I saw that I was too. Grace Moore was a warm, outgoing and generous woman, and our "chemicals" seemed to mix beautifully right from the start. I knew this was an extremely important moment in my life and my career.

After a short interview it became obvious that Dinty had talked to her at length about me. I did not have the slightest idea that I could become an opera singer. Though I had already sung operetta I was satisfied that this brief exposure and my short experience on Broadway would be my career, but Grace and Dinty had other ideas. I was told by the diva that she would expect me to prepare two arias: Mimi's aria from the first act of *La Bohème*, and Musetta's from the same opera. A date was then set for two weeks later in Grace's apartment where I would sing for her. I was thrilled but stunned. Never had I sung an aria in my life, and for that matter I knew very little about opera. My work was cut out for me. Grace suggested a coach and, though I had a few commitments, we worked hard on these arias.

I was disappointed two days before the eagerly awaited audition when Miss Moore's secretary telephoned to tell me that there would have to be a postponement as the prima donna had to leave town. She would be calling in the near future to set up another appointment. My heart sank. I waited and waited, trying to be patient, and consoled myself with the belief that fate was on my side as it was giving me more time to perfect those arias.

Knowing that probably more would be expected of me with this delay, I listened to recordings and tried my best to imitate the pronunciation of the words, which were so foreign to me. A friend had a translation made and in the meantime I was also becoming more and more intrigued with it all. The call finally came two months later, and my date with the great lady was set for May 31, 1938, 6 P.M., at the Waldorf Towers in New York.

Dinty had promised to escort me, and Grace said she would have

her accompanist there. We arrived early, and at exactly six o'clock we
knocked on her door. Her husband, Val Parera, admitted us with an
anxious look on his face. He explained that Grace was late and he was
really concerned. She was usually very prompt, he told us, and it was
unlike her not to have at least telephoned. We sat for almost an hour,
nervously making small conversation, when the door opened and there
stood Grace, disheveled, with a tear in her coat and ripped hose. She
told us of being hit by another car while getting out of her taxicab.
Assuring us that she was fine, she apologized for keeping me waiting
and insisted that she still wanted to hear me sing. By that time I was a
wreck and my heart was beating so fast I was sure everyone in the
room could hear it. Dinty, sensing my dilemma, and fearing disappointment as well, said sternly, "It's your big chance, kid. Don't blow
it!"

Grace asked to be excused and disappeared "to clean up," as she
said. Fortunately, it gave me time to recover my composure; at least
enough to stop my fast heartbeat. Back she came all too soon looking
refreshed, and with a broad smile signaled the accompanist she was
ready. Knowing that all this was unnerving, Grace simply said,
"Relax, Dorothy, I'm all right now," and before I knew it I was singing my heart out to her.

I shall never forget that evening. Grace looked at Dinty when I had
finished singing and said, "We'll make her a star. She has it!" I can
hear those words yet.

Introducing me to Grace Moore was the finest thing Dinty could
have ever done for me. I was lucky to have this wonderful Irishman as
my friend. He had recognized the potential in me, but it was Grace
who led me on the way with unfailing instinct.

The evening was over and I was Grace Moore's protégée.

The following day a press conference was arranged and our picture
together hit every paper. A wire service picked up the story, which
sent the news across the country, and I was launched. I still did not
know what all this would mean to me, but I was in seventh heaven,
and we were all excited. Plans would now be made and I was to wait
for instructions.

Again I waited. I heard nothing for several weeks. Although my
faith in Grace was still strong, my colleagues of the radio shows knew
all about my tentative prospects and the delay was embarrassing. Just
about the time I was thinking it had all been a lovely dream, I received
a call from Grace's secretary. "Would you like to go to Italy to study
with Beniamino Gigli's teacher? Can you be ready to sail soon?"
There would be a friend of Grace's, a Polish baritone, George Czapli-
ski, who would chaperone me to Italy (I had never been abroad). He

would get me settled and introduce me to my teacher. Suddenly I was happy again.

That it was all meant to be is easy to say several decades later. Certainly, I must say that once I began to glimpse what was behind the doors of this unknown magical future I became more determined than ever to enter them. This sounded like the greatest adventure of my life!

Within a few days it developed that our Polish baritone had been advised by his consulate that if he left the country at this time it was certain he would be drafted into the Army and unable to get out of Poland to return to America. Of course that made it impossible for him to go, but I was determined to take advantage of this great opportunity, even though my parents were worried about my traveling alone. My independence in New York for some time was a good argument and at last I was able to convince them I could take care of myself.

I did not know how frightened I would be when I found myself alone on the *Vulcania* on my way to Italy. I was hoping that I could sit alone in the dining room and survey the situation in order to get my wits together and stop that horrible lonely feeling. I was already so homesick I could hardly stand it. But hunger took over and, as if to warn me of other such dangers ahead, one of my table partners turned out to be a well-known newspaperman and a real Lothario, who chased me around throughout the trip.

Our arrival in Naples was just after Italy's takeover of Albania. As I boarded the train to Rome it became clear to me that there were hundreds of drunken soldiers surrounding me and not another woman in sight. I was terrified, and just at the right moment a familiar face appeared—my newspaperman! I fell into his arms, and never have I been so glad to see someone I knew, even him. As the train made its way north I found it difficult but necessary to stay awake.

Fortunately, just before I was to leave I had taken a crash course in Italian, working every day with a private teacher. I was not yet fluent in the language but understood several of the remarks of the soldiers as they stared at this blond American girl traveling alone. Young Italian girls did not travel unescorted.

Upon my arrival in Rome, I was to be met by a friend of Grace's. I was eagerly looking forward to meeting an American woman who would speak my language and help me get settled after my frightening experiences. Instead, I was met by a young girl who appeared to be very bored and resentful of this job entrusted to her, making me feel I was decidedly in the way. She was more interested in the boy who accompanied her and paid little attention to me. With this experience I was once again on the edge of tears. Grace would have been furious. I never told her.

I was anxious to get to the pensione or anywhere I could find to regain my composure. We finally gathered my things and got into a taxicab. They took me to the Villa Fiorita and obviously could not wait to drop me off at the entrance, and having "done their duty," off they went. They promised to call the next day to see if I needed help, but I never heard from them again. Now I had the added problem of finding my teacher.

Grace wanted me to stay in a small hotel such as the Fiorita where I would quickly learn the language. Although I had studied so hard before leaving, my spirits were low and the trip from Naples so shattering that it was next to impossible to concentrate on a new language those first few days.

The Fiorita was charming but I was exhausted on arrival. I locked myself in my room and cried my eyes out. Moreover, I had no taste for food that day and the temptation to return home crossed my mind several times, but my pride would never allow it.

Fortunately, that evening my prayers were answered. A gentleman who had been on board the same ship also was a resident of the Villa Fiorita. He told me later that he had seen my dilemma on board as I tried to get away from the newspaperman and was concerned. When he saw me arrive at the hotel and noticed I had not been down for food that whole day, he was determined to knock on my door. I hesitated to answer until I heard someone say, "May I speak to you, Miss Kirsten?" I quickly responded, and there stood the man who had been at the next table in the dining room of the *Vulcania*, and his was a very welcome face. We dined together and I relaxed. That evening he got the whole story and I gladly accepted his offer to help me. Ben Stern became my first real friend in Italy and this was only the beginning of his many kindnesses.

It was Ben who took me to the studio of my new teacher and, because of my bad start at the Villa Fiorita, helped me find another pensione near my teacher's studio. The change was good and I was quite comfortable, thanks to him.

My Italian improved so rapidly that I was called upon by the manager of my new pensione to interpret for the English and American tourists staying there. This bolstered my ego and I no longer felt like the frightened American girl in this strange country. I had begun my studies with Maestro Astolfo Pescia and was also working with a new Italian teacher.

Grace had established a financial arrangement to pay for my expenses with a bank in Rome where she deposited the equivalent of five thousand dollars in lire. Although I used only part of that money, she never asked me to sign a contract or requested a percentage of my fees if I succeeded. Before I left I promised her that I would keep books on every single cent and that when I began to work I would pay her back as soon as possible.

Grace's memoirs were published shortly after I returned from Italy and was well on my way in my career. When I received my copy from her there was a note attached that said, "Dorothy dear, turn to page 142. This is my gift to you with love." When I turned to that page I was surprised and deeply touched to read that because of my success and her pride in me, her gift was a complete clearance of my debt to her.

Interrupted Interlude on Capri and a Rough Journey Home

The day I arrived at Astolfo Pescia's studio, I was introduced to a young, handsome Sicilian tenor, Ugo de Caro. He was the son of a wealthy shoe manufacturer, had a magnificent natural tenor voice, lived with the Pescias and was the maestro's protégé. We worked together a great deal, and our romance, which is covered in another chapter, was inevitable.

While I was in Rome, Ugo was a great guide and every chance we had away from our studios, we went sightseeing and visiting the many important attractions of that fascinating city. Only a few weeks after I arrived, one of the exciting social events we attended was a colorful wedding, followed by a huge banquet. The bride was an American girl I had met on the *Vulcania,* and she was coming to Italy to marry a rich young Italian. Bruno Mussolini, Il Duce's son, was the best man and the place was filled with medal-bedecked celebrities and movie stars. The bride had told me that it would be exciting and gay and it certainly was.

Another evening I spent in Rome soon after arriving was exciting but hardly gay. Phyllis Piquett, an American who was also studying with Pescia, and I decided to go on our own to a *festa* which was taking place at a small ancient town just outside of the Italian capital. We did not realize what we were getting ourselves into (we were completely unaware of certain Italian customs). At the *festa* a young man suddenly pinched me. I was so shocked that I turned and socked him as hard as I could. This created great excitement; crowds gathered and suddenly the police appeared. We were surrounded by jabbering Italians, laughing uproariously at us. When the police heard what all the commotion was about they too simply laughed and one of them smilingly said, "Signorina, you will be sorry many years from now, when this sort of thing no longer happens to you." By then my anger had subsided and we all laughed self-consciously, but Phyllis and I made for the first *carozza* available and returned to our hotel, never again venturing unescorted into the streets of Rome after dark.

Maestro Astolfo Pescia was a big man. He towered over most of his pupils, was volatile and very demanding. I had heard about the old Italian maestros who easily became enraged and would throw a book at you. Though I felt he was quite capable of such action, personally, I never witnessed any such behavior. After I had studied with him for a while, I discovered that Pescia had not been Gigli's vocal teacher but his coach. The great tenor had actually studied with Enrico Rosati.

As I became aware that he was rapidly developing my voice to a much larger size, I began to wonder if this transformation was all happening too quickly. But I was enjoying the new bigger sound and fortunately I did know enough not to force it. With my scant knowledge of technique at this point, however, I was quite unaware that the sound was spreading and not properly focused. Nevertheless, the maestro had been effective in enlarging my voice without damage and for that I was grateful.

All was progressing beautifully, and we were quite oblivious of the ominous signs of war on the horizon until the American tourists began to leave the country and my hotel started to look quite empty. Rome became restless and my family's letters began to show their concern about my being in Europe. The maestro, worried about losing his students, suddenly suggested we all move to his villa in Capri. "We will live on the vegetables in my garden and continue our work untouched by all the furor in Rome. Italy will never go to war." In the meantime, Mussolini was shouting to millions from his balcony. It was fascinating and frightening, but we would escape all this, and because I wanted to be an opera singer, I moved with the others to Villa California in Anacapri.

The maestro's villa was all he had said it would be: comfortable, beautiful gardens of flowers and vegetables high above the exquisitely blue Mediterranean Sea, and all very romantic. It was a most inspiring atmosphere in which to study.

Grace was following every detail of my progress through my letters. When I wrote that the maestro had me working on Massenet's *Manon*, she was very disturbed and a long letter arrived stating that I should be studying Italian opera in Italy and French opera in France, in order to learn the style and language properly. How right she was. But Pescia was firm in what he wanted me to study and there was no way I could say "no" to him. I had not yet learned what was to become eventually my credo and philosophy; the art of saying "no." I loved the Massenet opera, however, and with that preliminary study of it, I was sure I would sing it one day.

Capri is a fascinating island with beautiful grottos and tiny cobblestone roads. I wish I had been painting then, as I remember all the picturesque sites.

Near the maestro's villa was a little store I used to visit frequently to buy my own bottle of wine. One day I met an old gentleman who invited me to see his small vineyard and introduced me to his private stock. Full of questions about America, he was an avid listener and we became good friends. As time went on he became alarmed with the stories of possible war and told me he had buried his wine out in the vineyard for fear of invasion. He shared his best vintage with me for a few lire, perhaps twenty-five cents, and when my jug was empty I would trot back to my friend who would disappear among the vines, only to return with a big smile on his kind face and my jug full of that beautiful Lacrima d'Oro (Tear of Gold) wine.

My radio was a precious item during this period. It was the only one in the villa, and knowing it was forbidden, presumably for military reasons, we had to keep it out of sight. With everyone becoming more concerned about war, we listened anxiously for the news.

Ben Stern, who had been so helpful in getting me settled in Rome, once more became my guardian angel. When he left Europe, I asked him to call my family and assure them all was well and I was very happy. From then on they were in touch frequently and exchanged the news in my letters. When the mail stopped, it was to Ben my family turned for help. An excerpt from a letter he sent to the Honorable W. Warren Barbour, a United States senator in Washington, will help to describe some of the problems I was having.

Miss Kirsten has gone to Naples several times for the purpose of obtaining booking back to the United States, without any success. Not only is she not able to obtain booking, but her return ticket, which she purchased in the United States, will not be honored by the Italian Line for passage because they have increased the price an additional $105.00.

The United States Consul at Naples, with whom she is registered, has informed her that there are several thousand applications for passage previous to hers and that he cannot do anything for her. She is 23 years of age, alone, and very much frightened. If the question of additional passage should arise, Dorothy's parents are ready to furnish same, although I personally feel that when an American buys a round trip ticket to Europe, that the

foreign country that accepts that money should at least honor
that passage.

It is absolutely imperative that you use your official influence to
obtain passage for Dorothy immediately, as her parents are almost
frantic.

I will deem it more than a favor if this matter can be brought
to a head at once, and I know that you will have the everlasting
blessings of these two old people.

Grace's last communication had been from Casa Lauretta, her home
in Cannes. She was planning to come to Capri on her way home to
hear me, but now was extremely worried about the situation and
wanted to leave. She knew my parents were also alarmed and insisted I
meet her in Paris and return home with her. Not wanting to concern
them any further, I made plans immediately to go across to Naples
and to get out of Italy and up to Paris as soon as possible. My heart
was breaking with the thought of leaving Capri. But when I tried to
get transportation, I was shocked to hear that the borders were closed
and there was no way I could get to Paris.

Returning to Capri the next morning, I did not know whether to be
happy or sad. My emotions were mixed. I was not really afraid and
yet I loved my family very much and the pressure to come home was
getting to me. The mail service had completely deteriorated by this
time. My parents were unable to communicate with me and were
frantically pulling all strings to have me put on a ship. I was oblivious
to all that was taking place back home.

Life at the Villa California in Anacapri had been a dream. We were
a wonderful group of international students working hard to have a
career. There were twelve in all: two Americans, a Czech, two Polish
boys, two or three Germans, one Frenchman, and an Italian. We dined
at a large table with the maestro at one end and his quiet, beautiful
wife Olga at the other. She had been a fine mezzo-soprano and gave
up her career when she married him. It was a happy family until the
students were called to serve their countries one by one. As they left
us, we wondered who would be next to go. The Germans were first,
and until they left it was hard to believe that these boys with whom
we had been such close friends were now our enemies. Soon after it
was the beautiful Czech with a coloratura voice of pure gold who was
summoned. But the saddest departure was that of the two Polish
tenors who the night before had heard on my radio that Hitler had
just bombed their home, Warsaw. Every parting of friends was a
highly emotional experience. We were students, unaware of the dismal
world surrounding us. Only God knows what happened to them. The

Poles and the Czech girl promised to write, but I never heard from them.

During this depressing time I was running back and forth to Naples, trying through our consulate to get booking on a ship for home. I had sent a telegram to Grace when I could not get through to meet her. Fortunately, she received it, for when I got back to the villa a cable was waiting to tell me that she was on her way home.

There was still no word from my family. But a few days later the word came from the Italian Line in Naples that my American friend Phyllis, her father who had accompanied her, and I were booked on a ship. It was back again to Naples, though we still had no idea how the solution finally came about, as no one at the booking office would tell us. I was so glad that my friends had been brave enough to stay as long as I did so we could come back home together. We breathed a big sigh of relief, but there were a few very important problems to face, the consulate said. First, the Italian Line was sending her ships over only to return empty and thought we should pay another fare. They refused to take lire, wanting only dollars. I had about twenty dollars left of my own. Consequently, my only choice was to sell my belongings, clothes, luggage, books, radio and everything I could to anyone who had American money. When I couldn't quite make it, Phyllis and her father staked me to their last few dollars. Now we were broke but relieved, not knowing the worst was still to come.

The next bad news was an announcement that we were leaving at our own risk. The Italian Line would not be responsible for anything that might happen to the ship! Thank heaven I was not alone, because this really shook us, but we knew there was no turning back.

After we said our good-byes to Capri, the maestro, Olga, our many friends, and Ugo, the boy I deeply loved, we were a sad threesome on our way back to Naples. A shocking sight greeted us as we arrived at the dock. There were thousands trying to board the ship, and when I went to my "private" cabin, I was confronted with three other women who were booked in the same room. One, apparently German, was weeping, and two Italians sat nervously wringing their hands, obviously frightened. I did not stay long enough to discover their problems but imagined that they too were escaping to America just as I was.

Having sold most of my possessions, I was glad to have only one suitcase, and with that in hand I left the ladies in order to find a deck chair. Since the ship was so crowded, this was not easy, but I knew I could never stay in that cabin. After finally finding one and falling into it, I did not move for fear I would lose it. I had staked my claim and that was where I would live for the remainder of the trip.

Exhausted, I have no idea how long I slept that day, but when I awoke I remembered that I had not seen Phyllis or her father since we boarded. Piling my suitcase on the chair, I crossed my fingers that it would still be there and took off to search for them. At last I saw them, their problems no less than mine, and we fell into each other's arms and were hardly out of reach for the rest of the trip.

The ship was carrying at least three times the people it normally did and was dangerously overcrowded; it was painted white from stem to stern with large red crosses on its sides and was lit up like a Christmas tree. Instead of sailing to Gibraltar as we expected, we went north to Genoa. Here we docked but were told to stay aboard. No one could tell us why, or when we would again be on our way to America. That night every cabin on the ship was searched and several people taken off. I was frightened but most of the time pretended to be asleep in my deck chair.

The next morning we sailed again, this time straight down the middle of the Mediterranean. During the trip, I was horrified to see a submarine surface quite close to us, look us over, then disappear into the deep again. After that frightening experience I noticed small groups of people gathering, everyone talking at once, hands gesturing and animated discussions everywhere. I discovered they were getting up a petition to demand that the captain turn back to Naples. There were many planes flying over us but not another ship in sight. People were talking about all those that had been sunk around the Azores and how dangerous it was with all the mines in that area. Nothing came of their request to the captain and the ship kept plowing on. I prayed, as so many others did. We came through the feared area, passing the Azores without incident, thank heaven, and about twelve days later sailed past the Statue of Liberty, which looked more beautiful than ever.

It took fourteen days to reach America. My poor worried family was waiting at the dock. They gladly paid off my debts to Phyllis and her father, and I was never so glad to be on American soil in my life.

Back Home

It was a great relief to be safely home and sleep in a regular bed again after that dreadful experience on the ship. But I was crushed at having to interrupt my exciting work.

Grace was naturally anxious to hear me, and I could hardly wait to sing for her. She was astonished at how much my voice had grown and decided she too would like to work with Maestro Pescia. In the meantime, she had a project in mind to create the "Grace Moore School of Singing," at her home in Newtown, Connecticut, and needed someone to teach voice. Considering Pescia as the ideal answer, Grace decided to bring the maestro over from Italy so he could continue to work with me, give her lessons and also fulfill her latest dream of a school.

Naturally, because of the precarious world situation, although Italy had not yet entered the war, there were many complications in getting a visa. She had to pull all sorts of strings to get him into the United States, but if anyone could manage it, Grace could. Once she put her mind to it, with her determination and personal charm, she was able to succeed in almost anything.

Much to my surprise, Ugo de Caro managed to come over too. He had told me, before my hurried departure from Naples, that no one would be able to stop him from following me. He arrived at the very last moment, just a few weeks before Italy threw in her lot with Germany in 1940. His family had some close American friends who sponsored him. But how he escaped the Italian Army at that late date remained a mystery and was never discussed.

Having lost all my connections with the radio stations, which had by this time acquired many new people, I accepted Grace's invitation to work for her school. Pescia had since found a way to include his protégé Ugo in his deal with her, and he too went to Connecticut. After I was settled in her pretty house and had resumed my lessons, my job was to chaperone some of the youngest students. There were about eight in the class, and Grace had found a place for them to live not far from her home.

The idea of a school was great, but most of the pupils, alas, did not have the kinds of voices which gave any hope of developing into operatic or even concert caliber. I could not blame the maestro for being disappointed with the group he found on his arrival.

The school did not survive long, and Grace eventually lost interest. She too soon realized that there was little hope that anything worth-while would develop. When the school was disbanded, Pescia, know-ing that he could not return to his war-torn country, decided to open a studio in Manhattan, and some of his pupils followed him. With all the singers around New York looking for a good teacher, he did ex-tremely well and settled down to spend the rest of his life in this country. I continued to study opera with him.

When I returned to New York, I began working on interpretation with Queena Mario, who had retired after a long and distinguished ca-reer at the Metropolitan. I was once again doing some radio shows and able to afford continuing my Italian lessons as well as some good coaching by Maurice Abravanel, who eventually became a prominent conductor.

It was around this time that I met another aspiring opera singer, Christine Johnson, who had a luscious mezzo-soprano. Christine and I shared a tiny apartment at the Osborne, Fifty-seventh Street and Sev-enth Avenue, where we were close to Carnegie Hall and most of the action. Though she had only a short career at the Metropolitan, it was Christine who created on Broadway the great song from *Carousel*, "You'll Never Walk Alone," which was a smash hit. We still enjoy a warm friendship after all these years.

During my days in radio and before I went to study in Italy, I had already appeared on Broadway and sung several times in operetta. Therefore, I had a fair amount of presence on the stage. But now that I had returned from Europe with a new sound and a voice twice its original size, my hopes of becoming an opera singer were high.

On August 8, 1940, I made my first professional appearance as a concert singer in Newtown, Connecticut, before an audience of about two hundred people in addition to Grace's invited guests. When I made my entrance the applause was spontaneous and encouraging, but it was terrifying to see all the artists and other important people as-sembled in the audience by Grace, who was obviously anxious to show off her new protégée. My mind flashed back to that awful expe-rience the night I first sang for her when Dinty Doyle said, "It's your big chance, kid. Don't blow it." There was my old friend Dinty, sit-ting among the celebrities, smiling up at me, so I just couldn't "blow it." Taking a few deep breaths and mumbling to myself, "Please, God," I signaled to my accompanist and began to sing the lovely aria

"Ah lo so," from Mozart's *Magic Flute*, which I had prepared so carefully for my debut.

I knew Grace and her husband Val would be there, but I never expected her to invite Lily Pons, André Kostelanetz, Gladys Swarthout, the Lawrence Tibbetts, Désiré Defrère (a leading stage director at the Metropolitan) and Grace's famous manager, Frederic Schang, of Columbia Artists. When I recognized them all sitting right down front, too close for comfort, I nearly died. I'm sure that Grace did the right thing by not telling me in advance the list of her guests because my panic would have been much sooner and much longer. I was grateful that night for my early experience onstage, but the audience was waiting to hear my new voice.

Once I began singing, my nerves settled and I was totally consumed by my assignment. Somehow in our heart of hearts we singers know when we have given our best; I sensed that night I had not let Grace down.

As I finished the first aria I was stunned by all those famous eyes staring up at me, but when the audience was slow in responding, my heart began to sink. Suddenly, Maestro Pescia was on his feet shouting, "Brava!" and the whole audience came alive to give me my first standing ovation. It was several minutes before I could continue, but my debut as a concert singer had been a huge success and now I set my sights on opera, which had always intrigued me most.

My faithful newspaper friend, Dinty Doyle, generously continued to give me many stories in his column through the coming years. With each article he sent me, a little note came that invariably began, "Mademoiselle Wonderful."

My Family Tree

wo other members of our family were famous in the music world. First, my grandfather on Mother's side, James J. Beggs, an Irish-Englishman who lived in an adventurous and exciting time. He was an elegant, colorful, and fascinating old gentleman. Music was his life and he was a strong influence on us all. During the last few years he lived after my grandmother passed away, he left his lovely home in Pine Point, Maine, and came to live with us in New Jersey. He died at the age of ninety-three, but not before he saw me on my way to becoming an opera singer and my brother well started in studying his own favorite instrument, the cornet. The family's musical tradition was continuing in its fourth generation.

Grandfather was a distinguished band conductor and composer with a busy, exciting career. Buffalo Bill, otherwise known as Colonel William Cody, chose him to conduct his band and Grandfather traveled for several years touring the country with Buffalo Bill's shows, one of which, *The Prairie Waif*, co-starred Annie Oakley. The fondest memories I have of him are the times we all sat around to hear him tell the stories of his travels with Buffalo Bill, whom he described as "an odd sort of a Romeo."

He also had become President Teddy Roosevelt's favorite bandleader and conducted his military band for the President's campaigns. It was Grandfather who introduced "There'll Be a Hot Time in the Old Town Tonight" one evening just as Roosevelt was entering a hall to address a rally. His music so pleased the great Teddy that from then on it became his campaign theme song.

Born in Liverpool, Grandfather Beggs came to the United States when he was twenty-five. He was one of the founders of the Associated Musicians of Greater New York, and a prime mover in getting the musicians to join the American Federation of Labor in 1903. In 1913 he became president of the Musicians Union. He served as musical expert for the City of New York, organized his own band, and was in charge of all musical entertainment in the parks and other activities for the city. When he retired at a spry eighty-seven years, he continued to maintain a lively interest in music. The cornet was his pet instrument, but late in life he decided to study the violin, which he practiced four to five hours a day.

Grandfather presented my brother George with his famous gold-plated cornet, which was made especially for him. I know that he would be very proud of his only grandson, for George became a fine musician and later a great teacher.

There was also another side to this extraordinary man; he was a poet. Much of his work was published and one of my favorites is called "Be sure you are right, and go ahead." It became for me a kind of credo and often I would recall it when there were doubts in my mind and problems to solve. I quote my favorite verse:

> Whatever claims your earnest care,
> And fills your mind with fear and doubt,
> Don't waste your time in blank despair,
> But think the matter clearly out,
> There is many a noble purpose fails,
> And worthless schemes obtain instead
> For want of planning out details;
> Be sure you are right, and go ahead.

There were two singers of note in my family. First, a great-aunt, Margaret Neary, after whom my mother was named, who was the leading soprano of the famous Choir of St. Nicholas Cathedral in Liverpool, England, for many years. Second, another great-aunt, Catherine Hayes. As a young girl I often heard my parents speak of her as a famous singer but I was not impressed with her importance at that time. Later, when I began to study voice and realized that I was going to have a singing career, I was anxious to find out more about her. My curiosity led me to my grandfather's brother, Frank Beggs, who was interested in our family tree. He produced the most astonishing account of her in an article called "Strange as It Seems," a section in color of the Brooklyn *Eagle*, January 20, 1952. It contained a picture of Catherine that strongly resembled me. She was blue-eyed, blond, and had the same square features, with an imposing figure. As a singer she was called "The Swan of Erin." Below the picture were the following notes:

> Catherine Hayes appeared in San Francisco on her opening night, during the worst storm in years, yet boxes were bid up to $1,125, seats to $300. . . . She gave 13 more concerts, each during a driving rain, but carried away a fortune!

The next interesting information my great-uncle produced was an old program titled "Miss Catherine Hayes in Concert." Listed was a program of arias and songs for soprano, but, most exciting of all, toward the back of the booklet was the story of her life.

Born in Limerick, Ireland, Katie Hayes was singing in a garden in the country of Limerick when the Bishop, Right Reverend Edmund Knox, while boating on the Shannon River, heard her and was struck by the beauty of her voice. He was fascinated by the girl and determined to discover who was the owner of such an angelic instrument. Accordingly he found that she was a relative of an aged lady who resided in the town mansion of the Earl of Limerick. Katie was shortly after invited to the Episcopal dwelling where she sang for her kind patron and began her musical education.

Soon after this, Bishop Knox, who had formed an even higher opinion of her capabilities, raised the necessary money among friends for her further training and sent her to Dublin in 1841 to study with Maestro Sapio, an Italian teacher then a resident there. She remained for two years and it was during this period that having heard her first opera with the great Madame Giulia Grisi and other famous singers that her destiny was cast and she determined to become an opera singer.

In the following year she went to Paris where she worked with Manuel García whom this account claims to have been "the greatest teacher of singing at present living." He was the brother of Maria Felicien Malibran and Pauline Viardot-García and also the teacher of Jenny Lind. Catherine worked with him for two years, and when he told her that she was ready, she traveled to Italy where she had a sensational debut at La Scala of Milan as *Linda di Chamounix* by Donizetti. Of her debut they said, "So absolute was her success, unspeakably triumphant."

Fifteen performances of this opera followed, then Desdemona in Rossini's *Otello*. She sang many operas at La Scala, including *Anna Bolena* and twenty-one performances of Anaide in Rossini's *Mose*. She created the opera *Estella* by Federico Ricci and far too many to mention here. Triumphant appearances in Venice, Florence, Naples and Genoa spread her name throughout Italy, but for some unknown reason the Italians started spelling her name the way it sounds (Hayez) and in that country only it remained this way.

Vienna was her next step and from there she was invited to sing in all the leading opera houses of Europe. Catherine replaced

Jenny Lind, who had retired, and made her first appearance in England at the Royal Italian Opera in Covent Garden. She reaped an even greater triumph at Her Majesty's Theatre than any which she had previously gathered. Catherine was often invited to sing for Queen Victoria and Prince Albert at Windsor Castle and returned to Vienna at the special request of Emperor Franz Joseph who took a personal interest in the opera there.

In the 1850s she toured the United States, and her success in San Francisco was so great that though she was contracted for only one concert, she sang fourteen! The writer of her biography called her, "highly respected as a woman of virtue and intelligence."

The most astounding similarity in our lives was that on November 4, 1845, Great-Aunt Catherine Hayes made her debut at La Scala. One hundred years later, almost to the day, on November 9, 1945, I made my debut with the San Francisco Opera! Our careers paralleled each other in many ways, though hers was more in Europe, where she was born, while mine was in my own country. Also, both our voices were *lirico-spinto*. These remarkable similarities with my Aunt Catherine give me an eerie feeling of reincarnation.

When I began to write this chapter on my family tree I remembered a friend telling me she had heard the great American actress Helen Hayes in a television interview speak of her Aunt Catherine Hayes who was a famous opera singer. When I recalled this odd coincidence, my curiosity was aroused and I decided to find out if the story were true.

Unfortunately, I had never met Miss Hayes but I knew that my longtime friend Frank McCarthy of Twentieth Century-Fox was acquainted with many stars of the theatre and would be able to help me find her. Frank introduced me to a close friend of Miss Hayes, who assured me that she would be delighted to hear from me and gave me her telephone number in New York. Being impulsive by nature, I called her immediately. Helen was charming, and after a hilarious exchange of compliments, I said to her, "Is it true that you had a great-aunt Catherine Hayes who was an opera singer?" She replied in that special Helen Hayes tone, "Yes, indeed I had," and we began to talk about our family ties, whereupon I promptly said, "Hello, Cousin!"

Our conversation was great fun, and we giggled like two teenagers over our exciting new relationship, both promising to be in touch often. In our telephone encounter I had promised to send Helen a copy of Aunt Catherine's biography, which had been in our family for many years. It obviously pleased her very much, and her letter that followed gave me great enjoyment.

August 10, 1980

Dear Coz:

Thank you, thank you, for the Catherine Hayes biography. I have devoured it. . . . Under separate cover, I am sending you the sheet music I mentioned with an engraving of our illustrious ancestor on the front. You, of all people, should have this memento.

I really love having you as a cousin. Imagine, the first famous relative I have ever had! I had plenty through Charlie MacArthur, my husband, but none of my own. Wish he were here to know of my great distinction.

Blessings,
Helen Hayes

(Credit: Steve Berman, courtesy *Opera News*)

Clockwise from top left: With brother George. Concert with George's high school band. My secretary Vicki and me; twenty-fifth anniversary at the Met. (Photo courtesy Metropolitan Opera) Catch of the day, credit the Diva. Jack, seeing me off to Stockholm. Sisters: Eleanor, Ethel, and Dorothy.

Clockwise from top left: My seascape, painted in Maui. Me on the links. Visiting the soldiers. Receiving plaque for volunteer services, voted Navy's favorite artist. With Mimi and Musetta.

Clockwise from top left: Portrait as Manon by Siegfried Kaühnel. Portrait by Sheil. My Las Vegas show. (Credit: John Engstead) My portrait by Wayman Adams.

The Making of a Prima Donna

To he year 1940 was a special one in my professional life. The first opportunity to make my way into the opera world came from Henry Weber, who was at that time General Director of the Chicago Opera Company. I was asked to audition for him at the City Center Theater on New York's West Fifty-fifth Street. It was to be a private hearing, and I was told to prepare two arias. Feeling quite confident, I remember nearly bursting with excitement. Mr. Weber immediately engaged me for two seasons of *comprimario* roles and, though I could hardly believe it, I was on my way to fulfilling my dream.

Comprimario roles require one to be a good musician. They are often short appearances here and there in the opera which hold together the plot and sometimes set it. The expression *comprimario* in Italian signifies "the one who completes," but is used only in theatrical language. Much of the success of the overall production depends upon these roles. I have come to respect enormously those singers, many of whom are my closest friends, who specialize in these assignments in the theatre.

Those days of learning in Chicago were probably the hardest work I have ever experienced while studying to be an opera singer. From early morning till late in the day, whether I had an evening performance or not, I stood at the piano, with Maestro Angelo Canarutto drumming those notes and words into my head. He was a perfectionist and fine conductor who recognized the potential in me and was determined I would one day be a big star. But first, out of respect for my commitments, he saw to it that I sang perfectly every role to which I was assigned. He was a taskmaster and at times I wanted to throw the score at him.

My debut was set for November 9, 1940, in a production of Massenet's *Manon*, starring Helen Jepson, Richard Crooks, and Léon Rothier, the famous basso, in the part of Des Grieux's father. I was Poussette, one of a trio of young courtesans. It was a light soprano part, the girls appearing in two acts, the first, and later in the gambling scene of the third act. Although they do not have much to sing, the assignment is interesting and each of them has a different personality. It was an excellent debut role; not too exposed and yet responsible. Before the performance I received a telegram from Grace that read, "Dear Dorothy, walk gaily and be charming, lively, free. Be yourself and good luck. Always Grace."

I was utterly astonished the next day when all the Chicago critics singled me out in complimentary terms for a role that is usually totally ignored by them. Naturally, these kudos gave me not only enormous satisfaction but confidence for my future assignments.

Then came the role of Flora in *La Traviata*, another courtesan, but a more important role. This glamorous production was headed by lovely Jarmila Novotna, Tito Schipa, and Alexander Sved. These three were big-time stars, and my excitement knew no bounds when, upon arriving at the theatre that night for my performance, I saw that on the marquee, along with their names, the only other one in bright lights was Kirsten. This marked the first time that my name was "out front" of an opera house. Imagine what that did for my ego!

Singing these roles with some of opera's greatest protagonists gave me a wonderful opportunity to observe them closely, which was a lesson in itself. Grace Moore, Helen Jepson, Jarmila Novotna, Lily Pons, and Gladys Swarthout; these were ladies of the opera world, elegant on and off the stage. They always had their own beautiful costumes and year after year managed to keep their figures young and attractive-looking. This set a fine example for the image of the prima donna I was going to be. I cannot help but wonder what has happened to some of our young singers of today who seem to have no interest in such ideals.

The role of Flora demands a talent for acting, and I was already beginning to develop a great interest in the dramatic part of being an opera singer. The story of Camille had always intrigued me, and now I was dreaming of one day being able to sing the leading role of Violetta in *La Traviata* and thus play a favored acting role. Remembering the great Garbo in the film based on that story provided a challenge to which I eagerly looked forward.

Alisa, a sort of duenna to Lucia di Lammermoor, was my next role that year in Chicago, and to be cast in *Lucia* with Lily Pons was a thrill, even though there was little to sing beyond my part in the famous sextet. There was only one Lily, and I don't believe I have ever heard another singer take more liberties with a score. Her coloratura was small but exquisitely produced, a flutelike sound with great warmth. In her prime she had no peer. She was adorable onstage, but got away with murder doing things in her own sweet time.

During a visit with her barely a year before she left us, we were talking about her anxieties before a performance. It was well known by her friends that Lily became so nervous it was impossible to keep her stomach from erupting before her performance which became embarrassing over the years. We had met through Grace Moore and many times I heard her in concert with her famous conductor-husband, André Kostelanetz.

There were more performances with Pons in Chicago when I added Giovanna, the elderly governess in *Rigoletto,* to my repertoire. This gave me a chance to take on a small character role, and then in the same opera switch to a young page with plumed hat, white silk tights, and legs much in evidence. I was young and shy and had never shown my legs on the stage. When some of the company whistled as I arrived to make my entrance, I nearly missed my cue.

The most exciting moment during that Chicago season came in my first appearance with Grace in *L'Amore dei Tre Re,* conducted by its distinguished composer, Italo Montemezzi, who later coached me for the lead in the opera. In the last act Grace, as Fiora, was lying in state in the chapel of the castle. My part was a moving expression of anguish over the sudden murder of my mistress, to whom I had been deeply attached. The sad phrase I had to utter, *"Ho trovato di pianto il mondo pieno"* (I have found the entire world in tears), was to come back to mind painfully when a few years later Grace was killed so tragically. As I stepped close to deliver my brief oration, though the public could not see it, I was aware that her eyes were half open, watching me, and when I had finished, she winked her approval.

A little later I sang again with her, this time as Poussette in another production of Massenet's *Manon,* which was one of her favorite roles. In the gambling scene it was fun to be close to her and observe the obvious joy she had in singing. At a certain moment, attracted by the luxury of the Hotel Transylvanie where the card games are taking place, Manon exclaims, *"Ces ivresses folles, c'est la vie"* (These moments of intoxication, this is life), and Poussette echoes, *"C'est la vie."* A little later they sing in unison, *"Qui sait si nous vivrons demain"* (Who knows if we shall be alive tomorrow). These words haunted me for a long time.

Another great performer with whom I had the chance to appear at that early part of my career was Dusolina Giannini who sang the exhausting lead of Maliella in Wolf-Ferrari's great *verismo* opera, *The Jewels of the Madonna.* I played Concetta, a fiery Neapolitan girl, and I remember the score being a particularly difficult one.

After the first night it was exciting to meet the legendary Rosa Raisa, who had been one of the greatest interpreters of this part and

had made the opera immensely popular in Chicago. She came backstage to congratulate Giannini, and we stood aside watching the retired opera queen make her grand gesture.

Frasquita in *Carmen* was fun, and though it is almost forty years
since I sang the famous quartet, that part was drummed into my memory so thoroughly that I'll wager I could sing it now without a missed
cue. It is a responsible part and an excellent debut role. The music is
lovely to sing, but rather difficult, with lots of ensemble singing where
the voice is heard above the others.

My debut in this part was with Marjorie Lawrence in the lead. It
was not the most successful vehicle for the great Australian soprano;
she was too big and bulky, but a major personality nevertheless. How
sad it is and immensely poignant for me to think that only a year later,
at barely forty years of age, this great lady was struck down by polio
and was forced to spend the rest of her life in a wheelchair. Bravely
she continued to sing, giving recitals, and I am told she even appeared,
seated, as Isolde and also as Venus in *Tannhäuser*.

The experience of singing these *comprimario* roles brought my first
opportunity to work with the great conductor Fritz Reiner. He too
was making his first operatic appearance in Chicago with *Der Rosenkavalier*, and under his direction I was singing the first orphan. This
was a small role, but his reputation of being a taskmaster had reached
me early, and to say I was nervous would be putting it mildly. Because
we were made to repeat everything so many times until he obtained
exactly what he called for, I can still remember every word and
nuance of this charming interlude. What he wanted was three voices
to blend in unison and sound childish, and, believe me, he got it.

When, as an established diva, I was to sing with him as soloist with
the Pittsburgh Symphony several years later, I reminded the maestro
of my early appearance with him in Chicago, curtsying as we did and
singing the part he was so fussy about. He laughed and laughed and
then, with a luminous smile, he said, "Well, congratulations, you are
no longer an orphan but now a Marschallin in your own right."

As I had hoped, in the second year of my contract with the company all the smaller roles were dropped, and I was assigned Musetta in
La Bohème and Micaela in *Carmen*. It was a special event this time to
sing with Grace, who was Mimi. One evening she presented me with a
photo of herself inscribed as follows: "To Dorothy from her watchful
eyes! with every wish that the hopes in them may never die!"

That was 1941. The following year, when I made my debut as a
guest artist with the San Carlo Opera singing Mimi at the Center Theater in New York, Grace was in the audience. On my dressing table I
found another photo of her, this time in costume as Mimi, with the in-

scription, "To the other Mimi and may she be greater." These photos are among my most treasured mementos along with the little ermine muff she gave me three years later when I made my debut with the Metropolitan Opera.

That same season I also had the privilege of singing Musetta with the celebrated prima donna Edith Mason, who had reigned over the Chicago Opera for many years but also had a distinguished career at the Metropolitan and at La Scala with Toscanini. Our *Bohème* together was her last performance of this opera. Fortunately, this great lady immediately took a liking to me and in my future performances never failed to send flowers or a message, often appearing unannounced in my dressing room. I still have a telegram, dated January 1, 1951, from Miss Mason and her famous conductor-husband, Giorgio Polacco, who for many years was a pillar of the Chicago Opera. The message was sent after listening to my broadcast of *Faust* from the Metropolitan. No greater compliment could have been paid me for it read, "We consider you the greatest Marguerite in generations."

For my first Micaela in *Carmen* I was cast with Coe Glade, who was celebrated for her exuberance and sex appeal on stage. I recall being mesmerized by her long, bejeweled eyelashes and wondering whether this was her own idea of the way a Spanish gypsy should look. She is still well remembered today for her incredible flamboyance in all her roles, a trait which the public absolutely adored.

This was by no means the end of my association with the Chicago Opera, but it turned out to be a major stepping-stone toward my goal and I was confident that I was well on my way.

Since 1945, when I was engaged by both the Metropolitan and the San Francisco Opera companies whose seasons always overlapped, it suddenly became important to find out as early as possible which company was going to offer me the most attractive season. What was left of my time was then allotted to the other companies with time out for recitals, radio, orchestral concerts, and study. Fate willed it that I became such a favorite in San Francisco that Gaetano Merola, who was then the director of the company, offered me many new roles, making my Chicago appearances with the opera extremely hard to book. Gradually, with a busy career also at the Metropolitan, I found myself only returning on special occasions. One of them occurred in 1955 when I was engaged to sing Fiora in *L'Amore dei Tre Re*, which had not been heard there since Grace Moore sang it in 1940, my first year with the company.

This performance gave me a golden opportunity to appear with Italy's leading operatic conductor, Tullio Serafin, who had been at the Metropolitan for many years before my time, and later turned the

Rome Opera into a real competitor of La Scala. Serafin was seventy-seven years old when we first met; a fabulous character, gentle but strong-willed, who knew exactly what he wanted. I had the feeling that while he conducted he sang every word with me and truly loved the score. It had long been my ambition to sing with the great maestro because he represented a sort of legend for me. At the Metropolitan, Serafin endeared himself to champions of American opera by conducting the premières of *Emperor Jones, Merry Mount, The King's Henchman,* and *Peter Ibbetson.* He was also the first to introduce *Turandot* to the United States. His reputation as a connoisseur of voices was known to be unequaled and many great singers have been coached by him.

Serafin's reading of *L'Amore dei Tre Re* had more tension and was taken at a brighter pace than when I sang it with its composer, Montemezzi. After the performance he came to my dressing room and said, "*Signorina, lei dovrebbe venire a cantare in Italia*" (Miss, you should come and sing in Italy). It was then that I knew I had pleased him. We talked about my coming, but by that time I was so solidly booked in my own country that it could not be considered, much to my regret.

There is one memory of Chicago that I consider neither fond nor funny. When I was to make my debut there as Mimi in *La Bohème,* only a few years after my apprenticeship seasons, Grace graciously gave me one of her wigs. Of course I was greatly touched and wore it with great pride. It looked lovely in my dressing room, but sometimes stage lights play curious tricks with colors, and as there was no dress rehearsal, the wig was never tested under the lights. Apparently it turned a reddish color. Knowing I had sung well, and after many compliments, I picked up the paper expecting a fine review; but a certain "lady" critic had unkindly headlined her column, "DOROTHY KIRSTEN MAKES DEBUT AS MIMI LOOKING LIKE TOPSY IN A RED WIG."

As a young singer, sensitive and scathed by such poor taste, I was crushed and anything flattering she had written thereafter was meaningless. My colleagues were quick to explain that the "lady" was a frustrated singer who, though successful at her paper because of her provocative writing, was thoroughly disliked by most artists for her caustic and unfair remarks.

I believe I have probably broken in more great tenors on their debut nights in this country than any other prima donna. One of the most pleasant memories occurred on another trip to Chicago in 1946 for the debut of Ferruccio Tagliavini. The opera was again *La Bohème* and Ferruccio was known the world over for his Rodolfo. I considered his voice ideally suited for the role, as it was pure lyric and seemingly effortless from top to bottom. It was a joy to sing many performances with him while he was in this country: *Bohème, Butterfly, Traviata*, and others. He is a serious artist and a great colleague whom I remember fondly.

Chicago also brought me some good friends who were very much a part of those earliest years of my operatic career. Jeanne and Peter Pomier were probably my biggest fans then, and I remember well the good times we shared together. Jeanne eventually traveled with me for several years and was a great companion. Her husband Pete had a fine restaurant at that time and contributed generously to my ravenous appetite after many a hard day at the opera house.

As it so often happens, one thing leads to another. Angelo Canarutto, the conductor and coach who was responsible for teaching me those seventeen roles that first year at Chicago, is also due credit for my first operatic appearances outside of the United States. Canarutto was a relative of the late great Metropolitan Opera conductor Fausto Cleva, and was also highly respected though he never made it to the Met. He was engaged to conduct at the Havana Opera season which in those pre-Castro days was one of the finest south of the border. Many stars were appearing there for excellent fees. Havana was an attractive city then, and though the population may have been poor, they were light at heart and ardent opera lovers.

It was in Havana that I sang my first Musetta, which I was to sing with Chicago the following season. The Rodolfo was Jan Kiepura, and the Mimi was his wife, Martha Eggerth. She was a delightful operetta and film star but simply did not have the vocal means to sing opera.

Performances in Havana began at 5:30 P.M., but then followed what seemed to be an eternal dinner break which I found difficult to contend with. There is nothing more enervating than getting into a role only to break the continuity by having to wait a long period before being able to complete it.

The opera house was beautiful and the public, when pleased, brought the house down. But heaven help the poor singer who cracked on a note or sang off pitch. There was no mercy whatsoever. These people knew their opera and would tolerate no mediocrity. My notices were excellent and the impresario of the company, Georgio d'Andria, became not only a fan but a booster of my career, engaging me later in many opera seasons for which he was responsible.

My other major lyric theatre south of the border was the Teatro de Bellas Artes in Mexico City, where I appeared regularly for several seasons. This handsome building was a tragic error in architecture, for it sinks a little each year and one has to go down several steps in order to enter the stage door. Built in 1932 for both opera and symphony, it has housed some really first-rate seasons. In 1945 I was engaged to sing *Manon Lescaut, La Bohème*, and *La Traviata*.

Ramon Vinay, a Chilean who had been singing baritone roles until that year, had decided to make the transition to tenor. He made his debut in this new vocal estate as Don José in *Carmen* opposite the fine, attractive artist Winifred Heidt. Vinay is a big hunk of a man and immensely attractive to women. One of his admirers became terribly upset over what she believed were torrid love scenes with poor Winifred who, it was reported to me, suffered considerably backstage from the anger of this infuriated jealous fan.

This became a source of worry to me as I was to sing opposite Vinay in *Manon Lescaut* a few nights later. I was warned by my colleagues who had witnessed the assault and knew that I liked to make my love scenes look real that the tenor's passionate admirer might want to repeat her bravado with me. Fortunately, as things turned out, the management wisely got into action and barred the woman from entering the stage door, and I was able to relax for my performance.

Sadly, the Mexican public that had worshiped Vinay as a baritone was not in favor of the change and expressed vociferously its disappointment. The Mexicans were proven wrong, however, because he did make a great success in the heroic tenor repertoire for many years, and though Des Grieux had been too lyric, I was delighted to sing with him again at the Metropolitan as my Julien in *Louise* where his robust tenor was more suited to the role.

In 1946 I returned to Mexico City for a repetition of *La Traviata*, a new production of *Roméo et Juliette*, and to sing my first *Madama Butterfly*.

After singing those first few years in Chicago, I had been pressed to take on *Butterfly*, but fortunately I realized that though I was progressing rapidly in my vocal study, my voice was much too young and not ready to tackle such a demanding role. Eventually, with great care, my teacher and I worked on the score, and now I was ready, eager and confident it would be one of my best and most beloved roles, which it has turned out to be. This was also a fine opportunity for me to break in the opera where I was already well known and had been quite successful before coming to the Met with it.

Because of my busy schedule, unfortunately, I arrived in Mexico City a bit late this time. The city has an uncomfortably high altitude and I did not give myself a chance to become acclimatized, which I certainly regretted. Those rehearsal days were an extreme test of fortitude. If a singer is short of breath, as I certainly was, she has no way to pace herself, but I knew my problem would be only temporary. However, all the gymnastics that are called for in the role of *Madama Butterfly*, such as the necessity of kneeling and rising so much with a very weak stomach, were almost too much for me. Miraculously all the unpleasantness ceased before the first performance and all went well. I had learned a good lesson and from then on I always planned to enjoy lovely Mexico City for a few days before my singing engagement.

Roméo et Juliette, the Gounod opera, was another experience long remembered. The director had insisted on an enormous four-poster bed for Juliette's room. It was beautiful, but not at all practical. In order to accommodate this huge piece of furniture, it had to be put at some distance from the front of the stage. Since it was a difficult scene musically, it was necessary to place the bed in a position where we could see the conductor. My poor Romeo, who was the fine tenor and great colleague Raoul Jobin, had a horrible problem ducking behind the large posts, but that wasn't the worst of it. The bed was so high that we had to use a stool to climb into it. This was placed on the side unseen by the audience. All went beautifully until the point when Romeo was to dash to the bed and take me into his arms. In his exuberance he fairly flew across the room, the stool slipped from under his feet, and Romeo landed squarely on top of Juliette. The audience went wild and surely must have heard my squeal when he hit me. Though we struggled to control ourselves, we didn't miss a note and no one seemed to think it was unplanned. The critics called it a wonderful touch of dramatic realism.

Well-Meaning Tips from People, Mostly Grace Moore

*C*incinnati had an excellent opera company as early as the 1940s. It was an open-air theatre at that time and I enjoyed many performances with them over the years. My debut with the company was as Micaela in *Carmen* with Gladys Swarthout in 1943. Grace Moore was engaged to sing *Tosca* that same year, and I was delighted when she invited me to stay in her suite. It was a special privilege to live close to and have so much time with Grace on that trip, witnessing her routine on the day of performance and the other days. I had always called Grace "Miss Moore," and it was during this time that one day she suddenly said to me, "For heaven's sake, Dorothy, I think it's time you called me Grace." I was delighted and happy to comply.

The Cincinnati Opera attracted many of the biggest stars and some of the finest conductors because it was held during the summer when the larger companies had finished their regular seasons. Grace was a favorite and there has never been a more sensuous, beautiful instrument than hers. As an artist, she hit her stride when the Metropolitan revived *Louise* for her early in 1939 and soon after, *L'Amore dei Tre Re*. The elegant quality of her voice and her vibrant personality ignited the stage when she appeared. Her French diction was far superior to her Italian, and she was never considered an especially good musician. In spite of this, Grace Moore was very special every time she performed, whether in concert, opera, or motion pictures. And offstage, there was never a more sincere, generous, and faithful friend.

Gladys Swarthout was a close friend of Grace's; exquisite in appearance and an irreproachable vocal stylist in concert. The great couturière Valentina, who later designed costumes for me, was responsible for everything Gladys wore, off- and onstage, and never have I seen a more beautiful Carmen. Much to this fine mezzo's disappointment, she was unable to bring to the public the temperament necessary to be great in this tempestuous part. Swarthout sang with the Metropolitan from 1929 until 1937, and though I had never seen her there, I understand her greatest success was considered to be Thomas's *Mignon,* where her lovely technique and fine breath control had an opportunity to reveal themselves best.

The role of Micaela is often assigned to young singers, as it was to me, but actually, as one reads in the annals of opera, in the old days it was more often assigned to the leading sopranos. Kirsten Flagstad, Maria Jeritza, Emma Eames, and Geraldine Farrar sang it at the Met while their voices were still lyric. Grace, who was always a lyric soprano, sang it there in 1928. Vocally it is a sympathetic role that requires a good high B flat and a certain amount of flexibility. The part demands no particular acting skill and after singing it a number of times in my early career I became bored with Micaela and looked for the more dramatically exciting roles. However, I did have a fine success singing the part that season in Cincinnati.

In Grace's performance of *Tosca,* I was stunned when she asked me to sing for her the cantata which appears at the beginning of Act II. This short interlude includes a high C which must be held for several beats, and Grace, at this stage of her career, was terrified of that passage. Of course I obliged and got a great kick out of it.

Tosca was much too heavy for my voice then, but one day I wanted to study the opera. It was later to become one of my most beloved roles. From then on, when I was available, I always sang that cantata for Grace. Although people backstage knew about my small contribution, the public did not, and Grace was more relaxed to sing her difficult second act.

Living with her those two weeks in Cincinnati, I learned a great many of her habits, some of which I eventually adopted as my own. It was Grace who taught me to whisper or send notes the day of performance for it is amazing how even just ordinary conversation can tire the voice. This was especially true with *Tosca,* which demands an enormous amount of vocal power.

Grace used to write many letters on her day of rest, as she was an inveterate letter writer. In her large, attractive handwriting, she kept up a correspondence with friends all over the world. She followed my career closely and for every new role or major concert there would invariably be a message from her, flowers, telegrams, or notes. Her constant attention and interest in my career made me proud that I had not disappointed her. Grace once told me of the many singers she had tried to help and her sad disappointments when they failed. I have kept many of her messages which indicate the pride she felt in my success.

The night of my debut at the Metropolitan she wired:

Dear Dorothy, we both send you our thoughts and blessings on this your great night, may it reach all the joy and the triumph you dreamed of and be the beginning of a great career. We will share in the joy and the pride that means your happiness and success. Love, Grace and Val.

When my career was just beginning, Kirsten Flagstad was a big name and Grace thought it would be wise for me to take a stage name in order to avoid some confusion which she felt might occur. I was quite surprised, realizing that I was still a debutante and Flagstad was already a big star. Wanting to please her, I discussed the suggestion with my family. As I expected, they were hurt and shocked at the idea. Returning to Grace, I tried to make a joke of it. "How could I possibly be taken for this famous diva when the great Norwegian is twice my age and size?"

Grace laughed and the subject was dropped. However, she had undoubtedly made a reasonable point, as I was to discover later. People have occasionally told me how much they enjoyed my Isolde! So for several years while Flagstad was still in this country I tried to explain the difference between us. When it was obvious the person knew nothing about opera or the artists in it, I would simply accept the compliments, wondering if Kirsten Flagstad was ever congratulated for my Violetta.

People have asked me if Grace was my teacher. No, she was not. Nor did she ever interfere with my work in any way. She was my close confidante and friend who was always ready and interested should I ask for her advice.

After graciously giving up the idea of my taking a new name, she suggested one day while I was visiting her in her New York apartment that I change the color of my hair. Hers was a very light bleached blond and mine was a darker blond. She tactfully explained that, were I to brighten it a bit, it would be more attractive onstage. This was a simple procedure, and as her own needed a "do" right now, she was going to show me how I could manage this myself.

It was flattering; my friendship with this great lady had become so personal that she would share her beauty secrets with me. Grace explained that when she was on tour for weeks at a time, she often took care of her hair herself. Once I got the "hang" of it, she said, I could do it too. I was so completely intrigued with the idea that I agreed to let her bleach my hair.

The first time I went back to New Jersey to visit my parents, I thought my mother was going to have a heart attack when she saw me. For a while I'm sure my parents began to think Grace was a bad influence, but that soon passed when later my hairdresser toned it down and Grace wrote a sweet note to them. Two points about which she knew she need not warn me were smoking and drinking, because discipline had been so important in our family life.

When Grace felt I had established myself as a prima donna, she decided to give me a party at the "21" Club to celebrate the occasion. She asked me if there was any one of her friends in particular whom I would like to meet. Straightaway I answered Charles Boyer, whom I had admired so much in pictures. Boyer and his wife came to my party, and I felt immediately the warm relationship between this delightful couple. When his wife died much later and Charles Boyer chose to take his own life rather than live without her, I thought of that lovely encounter the first time we met and was profoundly moved.

At the end of the evening Grace's parting words were so typical of her. "Now, Dorothy, you must do what I say, not what I do." (She meant, don't frequent nightclubs.) Wherever she went her practical point of view and sense of humor were always with her, as was her usual charm.

When I became a member of the Metropolitan Opera Company she would say, "You will learn that talent is not everything. Getting along with certain people is a must, however difficult and tricky they may be. Never compromise on the big things, but be ready to do so on the less important ones." Over the years I have learned how wise she was.

Grace was obviously thrilled that I had succeeded and that her faith in me was fulfilled, but there was one more thing she wanted to do for me. The first few years of my career I was managed by the National Concert and Artists Corporation, with Max Levine as my personal representative. He was a fine man and I appreciated his work. However, before I signed my contract with the Metropolitan, Grace was determined I should be with her own manager, Frederic C. Schang, at Columbia Artists. By the time I came on the scene, Humphry Doulens, also with Columbia and an associate of Schang, had been the personal representative of many of their stars, including Grace. In her opinion there was no better team.

When Grace first spoke to Freddie about me, he told her he was ". . . not interested in youngsters. Let her get lots of experience," he said, "then we'll see." It struck me that such a response was too rough, and I immediately adopted the "I'll show him" attitude. But Freddie is a clever man. He waited until he heard the Metropolitan was interested in me to make his pitch.

On the night of my debut at the New York City Center Opera in Puccini's *Manon Lescaut*, I received a message with my flowers from

Grace that Edward Johnson, the director of the Metropolitan Opera, was coming to hear me. Freddie Schang had also learned of this and told Grace he would be there. She had revealed the fact that I was hurt by his earlier rejection, and Freddie was carefully planning his own performance for that night.

Remembering the promise I made to myself to "show him," in addition to the Met's director being there to look me over, I was strongly motivated to do my darnedest, which I did. It was an exciting and completely successful night, with Freddie Schang throwing bouquets of sweetheart roses on the stage, filling my arms, and a note which said, "I am throwing myself at your feet." But that was not all. After my performance Edward Johnson asked me to sign a contract with the Metropolitan, and one of my fondest dreams had come true.

It was 1945, another year of special dates in my career. After I had signed contracts with the San Francisco Opera, the Metropolitan, and the foremost management of that time in the concert business, my career took off like a rocket. The day I signed with Freddie Schang, he went to work for me. He guided me and supervised every move I made. Concert programs were carefully reviewed, and I was taught how to balance a program. He introduced me to one of the finest accompanists, Lester Hodges, who had accompanied Moore, Swarthout, Tibbett, Björling and many other great recitalists. Hodges taught me most of the repertoire I have used over the years and also personally helped me select the beautiful Steinway piano which I have had for more than thirty years.

Freddie Schang opened the door to many outstanding radio programs on which I appeared regularly and exposed me to an enormous American public with whom my name became a household word in a relatively short time. There were significant engagements with all the leading symphony orchestras and conductors throughout the country. Freddie's reputation was such that everyone had the greatest confidence in him. If he recommended an artist, that was enough.

He used to call me his "number nine," for I was the ninth prima donna he had successfully guided to fame. When he retired from Columbia, and Humphry Doulens, my other dear friend who traveled everywhere with me, passed away, it was the end of what I called "the old-fashioned way of management." I regret so much that the young artists of today do not have the guidance and attention I experienced at the beginning of my career.

Love and Marriages

The loves in my life have been few but enough to experience every emotion from delirious happiness to utter despair. What I thought was my first real love was a beautiful encounter in Italy with a handsome young Sicilian tenor while I was there to study. This was an awakening well timed in my life, for I was at last about to find my way of expression after all the pent-up emotions and ambitions of my youth. Being in love was a great inducement to sing with one's heart, and what better way to express one's feelings than singing? It was a new world full of exciting adventure. Capri was enchanting and I had never felt this kind of attraction for a man before.

As a young girl, until I met Ugo de Caro, romance hadn't been very important in my life. I had dates, of course, and lots of boyfriends but none of them serious. This was different, and when the war forced me to return to America, the thought of leaving Ugo was almost intolerable. How one can get so caught up in the web of a love so unquestionably impossible to manage is more than I can explain. By the time he was able to arrange a visa and follow me to New York, my naïveté was quite obvious in my reaction upon meeting him again. With time to think, I had come to my senses and realized the difficulties which would arise if we were ever to consider marriage seriously.

Despite his admirable and touching attempt to fit as rapidly as possible into the totally different American way of life, Ugo's Sicilian background was too deeply imbued in him to allow his adaptation. Once back in my own environment, and away from the romantic atmosphere of beautiful Capri, I realized that my feelings for him had changed. I was still tremendously fond of him and deeply touched by the gigantic effort he had made to come over, but now my career had begun to grow rapidly. When I realized once again his possessive nature and extreme jealousy, which he could not control, I found it increasingly difficult to handle. We went through some emotionally difficult weeks for I felt responsible for hurting a sincere and proud man. However, I knew there could be no real solid future ahead for us together.

I was more and more disturbed by this situation because Ugo was totally unable to accept a separation. I was determined that our relationship had to come to an end. In reflecting upon that unhappy time, I believe that this distressful encounter drove me back to an old friend.

Edward Oates had been on the staff at radio station WINS in New York at the beginning of my radio career. He was the engineer on my show and taught me a great deal about singing into a microphone. We had occasional dates but nothing more serious at that time. I had never lost contact with Ed, but when I left to study in Italy, he joined the Army. When I returned, I began singing in camps all over the country. Hearing of this, he asked if I would make an appearance at Fort Dix, New Jersey, where he was stationed. We began seeing each other again, and Edward lost no time in asking me to marry him.

When he was on leave in New York we often went out to dine together and when he proposed marriage one evening, I realized I had become very fond of him. Before I knew it, in January 1943, I found myself walking down the aisle of the Little Church Around The Corner in Manhattan, with all my family present. Edward looked handsome in his uniform and I really talked myself into thinking I had fallen in love with him.

Needless to say, Ugo was utterly crushed and I have never blamed him for feeling that I had let him down. I did not see him for a long time and then, after one of my performances at the Metropolitan, he turned up in my dressing room to congratulate me. Nothing was said about the past but his wonderfully expressive eyes were still burning. How and why he did not make a career for himself with his superb voice is still a mystery to me. He eventually married and became a successful coach. Among his pupils was Renata Tebaldi after she had undergone some vocal troubles.

Not long after my marriage to Ed, I discovered it was by no means the ideal partnership. It had all happened too fast and my troubles began all over again. I was extremely busy with radio shows on the West Coast and between concerts and opera it was like living on a merry-go-round, never stopping to think and putting off the inevitable as long as possible. It was becoming more and more difficult to go home, and I was avoiding New York instead of facing the problem, which was not like me.

When I did return, it became quite evident that Ed and I were incompatible and a decision had to be made. He was a kind man, interested in my professional activities, but other than that we had little in common. Coping with this situation became difficult for us both, but the only solution seemed to be divorce. I had to be free in order to concentrate on my young career. He did not want to cooperate, still thinking we could work things out. I knew this was impossible and finally got my way. The divorce was finalized and little did I know that emotionally I had ahead of me the most difficult and troubled years of my life.

The San Antonio Opera Company was flourishing under the direction of Max Reiter and I began to sing with them regularly. In February 1949, my return was to be in the role of Mimi in *La Bohème*. It was a great pleasure to work with this company, and I had many friends there.

The opera lovers of San Antonio always had a lovely party after the performance and this time was no exception. My personal representative, Humphry Doulens, had been called back to New York, leaving me without my regular escort. The hostess informed me that she would ask Dr. Eugene Chapman, a close friend and prominent obstetrician, to accompany me. I soon learned that although the doctor was married, he was often invited as an extra man, as his wife seemed to be out of town frequently. He was the most handsome man I had ever met and delightful company as well. We were immediately attracted to each other, and before the evening was over we knew we would meet again. This was later to develop into a very serious affair.

While Ugo had been a young man my own age, Eugene was a bit older and had been married several years. I was quite captivated by him. Soon I found myself asking my management to book me in cities that were not too distant from San Antonio, affording us the opportunity to meet more often. Gene also began to visit me whenever his practice would permit, and our telephone bills expanded considerably. In the meantime, since many of my radio shows originated from the West Coast, I rented a house in Hollywood where I settled with my secretary, Vicki, who had come into my life a few years earlier and became invaluable to me.

Life became another merry-go-round, but this time Gene and I both felt we had won the golden ring. My glow must have been quite apparent, for my friends and colleagues were curious about the new man in my life. Soon it became a family affair and I was introduced to his sisters and his daughter. Susan and I were good friends for a while, and I was thrilled with the thought of having a beautiful stepchild. Gene's sisters assured me of his loneliness, and I have never felt guilty about our affair. But alas, the life of a celebrity in the company of a married man, no matter what his problems may be, is fodder for the cannons of the press. The newspapers really "gave it to us," and the publicity that followed stunned us both and shocked our families and friends.

How different it would have been today! However, knowing the doctor would suffer most, being a highly respected physician, we tried in vain to quiet things down. When the situation became unbearable I decided I must get to San Antonio to be with him. By this time my every move was being watched by the press, so there was no use in trying to hide my plans.

I remember how difficult it was to make plane connections in Dallas, but I was confident that when I was that close to San Antonio, I could, if necessary, hire a small plane to get me there. Sure enough, I missed all connections. While explaining to the agent behind the counter that it was vitally important that I get there today, and not tomorrow, I heard a voice next to me say, "I'll get you there, little lady. I got nuthin' to do for a few hours."

Without hesitation, the man I was speaking to said, "You're lucky, lady. He's an excellent pilot and he's got a great little plane out there." I knew this was crazy, but I phoned Gene, and not letting on how I was coming, just told him I'd be at the airport in two hours. Where I got the nerve to do this I do not know, for I am a terribly nervous flier.

I climbed aboard the little Bonanza and away we flew. We were not up long before he put a map in my hands and said, "You just have to be my navigator, little lady, and watch for those ground clues along the way!" In the early fifties the Bonanza had a habit of swaying in the back, and that little plane wagged its tail all the way across Texas to San Antonio. As we darted between the clouds, I watched for railroad tracks and the other landmarks he called out. I had no time to be frightened, nor was I conscious of the chance I was taking.

I thought Gene was going to have a heart attack when I jumped out of the tiny plane. I cannot remember the pilot's name but when I tried to reimburse him, he simply said, "Let's chalk it up as my good deed for the day, little lady." He had no idea who his passenger was, but if he should read this book and remember that day, I wish to thank him again for being such a gentleman to a lady in distress.

I had only a few days between performances, but it took no time before the newspapers tracked me down, and the telephone never stopped ringing. In the meantime, Gene was having one complication after the other getting a divorce from his wife, who was demanding a large settlement. As so often happens, while she previously had paid scant attention to her husband, the realization that he had fallen in love with another woman dealt a blow to her self-esteem. By this time all the gossip writers had become aware of the story and played it for all it was worth, making our lives absolutely miserable. We tried to avoid them, but it was no use. Even Walter Winchell and Earl Wilson had to get into the act.

I was particularly distressed for my family, which had never been touched by any kind of scandal. This was the only time in my life that my name was involved in such unpleasant notoriety, and I hated every minute of it. I was made to realize then that there exists no privacy or respect for someone who is in the public eye, and how difficult it is to counteract that. The fact that San Antonio was not a huge metropolis did not help matters either, as the Chapmans were prominent there and their name made news in the local papers. I kept telephoning my parents, assuring them that everything would turn out all right in the end and to have faith in me, but knowing all along how very hard it was on them.

The impasse for Gene was a most delicate one. His daughter, whom he deeply loved, was at college, and he knew of the reverberations and embarrassment she was going through on campus because of all this. During this trying period the doctor's sisters, who were aware of his dilemma, became close to me and did everything in their power to assist us in solving our problems.

After what seemed like an interminable period and struggle he obtained the divorce, but the price he had to pay for it was a very high one. We were finally married in May 1951 and settled in San Antonio where we built a lovely French Provincial home, my dream house, with a delightful garden in its midst. The scandal subsided as we tried to recover from all the unpleasantness. I joined Eugene's church and became an Episcopalian.

Before we married, Gene had told me that while he was stationed in the South Pacific as a full colonel in the Army, he had contracted some form of malaria and a uremic disease. When I learned the fact that his life span was limited, I was more determined than ever to give him all the happiness I could for the rest of his life.

I felt there was no other man in the world for me. My Vicki, however, living so close to me, had been through the frantic phone calls and knew all about the sleepless nights and sad hours of trying to explain my work to him. Even though many friends and my family had urged me not to marry after my former attempt at finding happiness had failed, nothing was going to deter me.

Never did it occur to me that Gene might not understand the sacrifices necessary in making a career such as mine and our marriage compatible. In the beginning he seemed so proud of my work. I was rushing back to San Antonio at every opportunity, often refusing important engagements that would not allow me enough time at home with him. After a while he could no longer hide his possessiveness, and I suddenly realized it was my fate to have attracted another jealous man.

I recall during the time with Ugo how everyone would say, "Well, Dorothy, after all he is a Sicilian. What else can you expect?" But Gene was American all the way, and there had been no previous sign of this side of his nature before we were married. He did not seem to realize that my being so completely in love with him precluded my even looking at another man, even though I had given him every proof of this. But jealousy, which John Dryden, the English poet, so aptly described as "the jaundice of the soul," is illogical. During my tours, when I needed a good long night's sleep before a performance, he would telephone me long distance at various times, like an obsessed human being, to check whether I was really where I had told him I would be. Would not one time have sufficed?

There were moments when I understood, only too well, the wisdom of Lucrezia Bori who had never married. "My career is my husband and one is enough." Eugene's lack of confidence in me had not only a negative effect upon my career but depressed me intensely. But I was still very much in love with him and determined to make this marriage work.

Gene's practice had suffered considerably after his divorce, and we soon realized it was never going to recover in San Antonio after so many unhappy memories. We were both sad to leave our beautiful house, which we had lived in for such a short time, and the faithful friends who had supported us all the way. However, we decided to find somewhere else to live.

I had some close medical friends in Los Angeles and on my next trip to the West Coast a plan was developed whereby Gene would be offered an excellent position as Assistant Dean of the Medical School at the University of California at Los Angeles. He was delighted and we left our lovely home in the hands of my capable secretary Vicki to sell, while we took off for California.

In the beautiful area of Bel Air I found a magnificent house which at one time had been Jean Harlow's home, and I was looking forward to getting settled there. But it was not to be a happy home for us for long. Quite the contrary.

Eugene had been in his office at the university for only two weeks when he became very ill. The tests they made revealed that the uremic poisoning had reappeared in an alarming way. He was immediately hospitalized and my life became hell. I was forever running to his bedside from my rehearsals and performances, which I went through with a very heavy heart. From the beginning of his illness some sort of premonition told me that there was little hope of recovery. I have never seen anyone change so rapidly in the space of a few weeks.

He remained in the hospital for three long months until I was finally able to bring him home to spend Thanksgiving. Distressingly, his condition continued to deteriorate, and I had nurses assisting him around the clock. There is nothing more desperate than to be unable to help those we love and watch their disintegration without being able to do something positive. I stubbornly clung to the hope that somehow he could be saved, but the following January he died. I was in a state of total despair, shock, and exhaustion. I also began to ask myself whether the change in his character, which had come over him after our wedding, had not been prompted by the disease which was quietly resurging within him.

Until then, being a professional, I had honored almost all my engagements, including quick flights for my appearances with the San Francisco Opera, returning to Los Angeles the same night after the performance. But now I certainly was in no condition to continue and canceled all my engagements for the next six months.

Despite the efforts of so many friends to distract me, I was in a state of utter prostration and in no mood to go out and see people. This state of despondency went on and on. I was no longer interested in anything, even in my profession, which had always been my *raison d'être*. We had been married only two and a half years, and I went into deep mourning, feeling the Lord had forsaken me.

Betty Miller, a great friend of mine from San Francisco, decided to take matters in hand, realizing the state I was in. Since her husband, Robert Watt Miller, was then chairman of the board of the San Francisco Opera and also a dear friend, pressure was put upon me to come back the following fall in a new role, Massenet's *Manon*. They tried to convince me that the study of a new score would be the best possible medicine for my depression. I knew deep inside that this was the right thing for me to do. My salvation could only come through my work. I returned to my old teacher, Ludwig Fabri, at his country home in New York to work on my voice and renew my confidence.

After a few weeks it was once again a joy to sing. Everything was there and I was eager to get back to work. The bitterness I felt for having lost what I thought was the only real love of my life was leaving me, and I blessed my teacher, friends and family who had urged me to return to my career.

My work had been my salvation, but each time I returned to my home in California the whole picture was once again before me and I would crawl back into my shell, having to force myself to see my good friends. I was dreading the thought of being alone for the holidays and accepted an invitation for New Year's Day to go to the Tournament of Roses Parade, followed by the football game in the Rose Bowl. I had always been a sports fan.

Dr. Charlie Carpenter, the dear friend who had set up the outing, called me the day before to ask if I would mind if he brought a doctor friend of his. Of course I did mind, and believing my friends were pushing a bit, I tried to back out. My first impulse was to say no, but he was very persuasive and I gave in. Immediately after the call I was sorry and begged Vicki to call him back. Her answer to me was an interesting one and shocked me a bit. "Don't you think your good friends who have been so patient with you are getting a bit fed up with sharing their husbands with a good-looking blonde?" Believe it or not, this thought had never occurred to me. Being criticized by my most faithful friend made me realize how silly I had been.

Since the parade begins very early on New Year's Day, they came to pick me up at 6:30 A.M. With them was the man I had not met, and I was introduced to Jack French. I'm afraid I wasn't too charming that morning, but my friends were most anxious for me to know all about him. Jack at that time was head of neurological surgery at the Veterans Administration Hospital in Long Beach, California. I was told he had been an avid fan of mine, had seen me many times onstage and owned most of my recordings. That seemed to make a difference. What my friends had not told me was that he was a handsome, young, attractive man who had been needling his colleague, Dr. Carpenter, to introduce us ever since he heard I had become a widow.

The stranger appeared to be gentle, tactful and very attentive. My friends informed me later that evening that he was a bachelor and a distinguished neurosurgeon. Jack eventually became the first director of the Brain Research Institute at UCLA and remained in that position for twenty years.

The day turned out to be very different from what we had anticipated. After the parade we started our picnic lunch. Suddenly the heavens opened and sheets of rain began to fall, despite the radio announcer telling the nationwide audience that there was only a slight drizzle in California. Since I always had to be careful not to catch cold, and remembering I was to leave soon for my Metropolitan Opera season, I suggested we skip the game, go to my home, and watch it comfortably on television. Everyone agreed enthusiastically.

It had been a delightful day despite the rain and before the evening ended, Dr. French asked if he could call me. The next day he did, and we made a date to dine together. Since I had only three days before leaving for New York, the following ones were extremely busy. I had to make arrangements with my help to take care of things, pack the costumes I would need, set up housekeeping for New York and all the other things I needed to do for my stay in the East. There was not much time to think of my brief encounter with Jack French. However, the morning I was to leave a large box of white orchids arrived, which made me feel things were moving a bit too fast.

My secretary, on first meeting Jack, liked him very much and was enjoying this whole sequence of events. He had been charming at dinner, we had a lovely evening, I found him to be good company and it was quite evident that we had a lot in common. But I was not ready to entertain any thoughts of serious interest in him.

The year 1955 was an incredibly busy one for me and one which was providential, for I was obliged to get back into action, leaving little time for mulling over all the painful and difficult times I had been through. Jack showed in every way how concerned he was about me by telephoning almost every day, and I began to be increasingly touched by his quiet thoughtfulness and persuasive attention. Unlike the others, this man whom I had really met only twice came on in a decisive yet ever so unobtrusive manner. He was most considerate, excited about and interested in my career. I felt that his concern for me was genuine and began to look forward to hearing from him.

Because of my horrendous calendar and his professional six-week trip to South America, our chances to meet again were much delayed, bringing to mind the old saying, "Absence makes the heart grow fonder." This seemed to be working for us. Looking back, I am convinced that this slow courtship which developed eventually into deep affection and love was the solid base on which our relationship grew by degrees, giving me the opportunity to evaluate and appreciate him.

After my return to California we had the chance to cement our relationship by seeing each other almost every day. His knowledge of music and love for it was a further bond between us, and he always expressed disappointment when his work kept him from hearing me. I could hardly believe that I would have another chance at love, but that summer Jack proposed marriage and we started our life together as Dr. and Mrs. John Douglas French on July 18, 1955. Obviously, this time my instinct guided me well for we recently celebrated our twenty-sixth anniversary.

During our quarter of a century together, we have had our moments of disagreement, but never have they seriously affected our relationship nor our love for each other. I have found true happiness with Jack, which has inspired me to sing better than ever and my voice to mature beyond every expectation. This I know is due to the complete trust which has existed between us from the beginning, and the wonderful feeling of serenity which he has given me. Peace of mind is vital in order to sing and perform well. How many colleagues of mine over the years have enjoyed this blessing?

I am reminded of a lovely formal reception that was given for us by one of our doctor friends shortly after we were married. As we were standing in the receiving line, a wife of one of the doctors was heard to say, "I wonder how long those two prima donnas will last?" If the lady who made that remark remembers, I wonder what she thinks of us now?

My private life has totally changed, for I am frequently in the company of the world's most distinguished scientists, which makes it imperative that I have some knowledge of Jack's work. We have often entertained many of them, which I have found very stimulating, and one day I hope to accept the many invitations we have received to visit our friends all over the world.

I was soon to recognize another important part of Jack's life. He had been a fine golfer and champion of two important golf clubs before we met. His handicap was a four at that time, and I knew it was essential for our companionship that I learn how to play golf well. With my tremendously busy career this was not an easy assignment. Since I am very determined, it wasn't long before a new piece of luggage was following me on tour, and everyone knew I wanted to get in a game of golf wherever I could.

When I was asked to sing a concert in Augusta, Georgia, considered by some to have the most famous golf course in the country, my management was astonished to find that there was only one condition: that I could play at the famous, exclusive Augusta golf course. My dear friend and personal representative Humphry Doulens was delighted with the idea and all arrangements were made.

The day after my concert I was invited to the club for lunch by the woman professional, and I joined a foursome of their finest golfers. It was fall and very cold in Augusta. The course had been closed for the season, but they opened the first nine for me. My handicap was rather high at that time, but I knew Humphry had told them I was a good golfer and I decided to bluff my way through. After all, how much could they expect of a "prima donna" with my reputation in the world of song? When asked about my handicap, I kidded them by saying, "Asking a lady that kind of question is like asking her age."

They soon discovered that I sang far better than I played golf, but it certainly was a day to remember in my sporting life, and one important person I told my story to got a great kick out of it. Just before President Eisenhower became ill, Jack and I were invited to visit with him in Palm Springs. We were told that he was low in spirits, and I was searching for something to make him smile. He was delighted to hear that my caddy (who was called Cimatery) that happy day at Augusta was the same wonderful old gentleman who had always caddied for him.

Jack and I built a lovely Spanish home several years ago in Pauma Valley in Southern California. The house sits on a hill overlooking our beautiful golf course, surrounded by all kinds of citrus groves. It is delightfully quiet and peaceful there and a nice escape from big-city life. For at least a month each year we also enjoy our apartment on the island of Maui where I have a studio for my painting and we golf just about every other day. To have all this and love too is much to be grateful for.

Jack and I had hoped to have a family, but this was not to be. Because I firmly believe in God's will, I finally resigned myself to the inevitable.

Since we have reached our twenty-sixth anniversary, Jack has been anxious for me to slow down my career and spend more time at home, but there is no easy way to do this. Recently, I celebrated forty years on the operatic stage, which is much more than half of my lifetime. At this writing I am trying hard to keep my promise to him, but there are times when it is too long between performances and I feel I will burst with the desire to give forth with the great music which has been my life for all these years.

Although I am happy while I am painting, and it's great to be a fairly good golfer, nothing can ever take the place of standing on that stage, feeling the emotion of a great role, being able to sing with your heart and soul and then hear a resounding response from the audience. This is unforgettable, and I thank God for the privilege every night of my life.

Learning and Performing

I hope that I can succeed in convincing aspiring young singers that a beautiful voice is only one essential component of a great career in opera. The concert singer must learn how to walk onstage with dignity and grace as well as to perform with good deportment, but the opera singer requires a good deal more.

I learned how to handle myself onstage through the study of aesthetic dancing, which teaches body movement. Learning how to be graceful, how to walk, gesture and use one's hands is important. I worked with some fine acting teachers as well. During that time I also studied Italian and French, and I take great pride in the fact that my diction in whatever language I sing is always highly complimented.

A career in opera takes years of study, discipline, and dedication, but when there is a great foundation upon which to rely, there is no greater reward.

When I am offered a new role, I want first to know about the character I'll be playing. It is important that I understand her well and for that reason I read all the background material I can find. I also study the characters around her and I do not work on the music until the story is firmly in my mind.

My next step is to find the best available recording of the opera, preferably with the same conductor who will be directing the orchestra for my performance. In this way I have an opportunity to study his interpretation. I listen carefully, following with my score in hand, and trying to eliminate the singers from my mind as much as possible, so I can get a totally objective insight and familiarize myself with the themes and moods of the composer.

Then I underline in red every word I sing in the score so that when I work with my accompanist, I don't have to waste time searching for my lines. When I feel I know the music and the cues pretty well, I sit at the typewriter and copy every word of my role on six-by-nine-inch notepaper, making little signs to myself as I proceed on "coronas," "portamentos," and all kinds of musical signals, leaving spaces where others sing. These notes of every opera I sing are in my special library and always travel with me, which makes it possible for me to study my role while sitting in an airplane without having to carry my heavy score. They are also useful at rehearsals when I need a bit of prompting with the words now that the music is engraved in my mind.

Singing opera can be physically as well as emotionally exhausting. For this reason I have always had a strict rule that the night before a performance I never accept any type of engagement. I have a light dinner, go to bed early, reading my score from beginning to end, and usually turn out the light by eleven o'clock. If it has been a restful night, I begin to stir about eight-thirty, read something distracting or do a crossword puzzle until my breakfast is served in bed. This usually consists of dry crisp bacon, two poached eggs, toast, a little jam and decaffeinated coffee. Afterward, I slowly rise and do my daily exercises, stretching my body and loosening up in general. When the weather is clear, I like to take a short, brisk walk and, if the air is good, do some of my deep-breathing exercises while walking.

I then relax again with my score, going over each detail of the stage business in my mind and recalling the new action I have planned to do. In restudying the score, I have often been able to discover new things for my roles. I enjoy the comments from fans who have seen me do a part several times and notice my new bits of action.

I always make notes of things to remember as I go through my score, such as one for the director to remind him that I want to check my own props before curtain. For instance, I find it very helpful in *Tosca*'s second act, when using candles which have to be lit, to light them for a few moments before curtain. They are then more receptive to the flame, and I don't have to struggle to find the wick. Any mishap can easily disturb an audience and may even elicit a snicker, which surely would destroy such a dramatic scene.

Never do I rely completely on others when there are props that are important to my action. I carefully place the knife with which I kill Scarpia where I need to find it, since the timing of this moment must be perfect musically. I often make notes to remind my colleagues of certain action we planned in rehearsal that, if forgotten, could spoil an effect. I also learned this early in my career and it has paid off.

After I feel satisfied with my review of the score, I vocalize a bit. When my voice feels free and easy I stop singing. Too often singers "leave their voices in the dressing room," or overwork, having tired themselves vocalizing too much before a performance.

I never speak on the telephone that day, except in the case of an emergency. My secretary screens all messages, and when I must communicate, I either whisper or send notes.

My dinner the day I sing is always served four hours before the performance begins. I have chopped lean sirloin steak, fresh spinach when I can get it, a baked potato and something sweet to give me energy. I suffer from a nervous stomach before singing, but a glass of light beer with my food helps my digestion. I always lose four or five pounds during a performance and become dehydrated rapidly. The only fluid that I find satisfying is warm tea with sugar and a touch of lemon.

People often ask me if I am nervous before a performance. I certainly am. My food tastes like sawdust and frequently remains in my chest as a lump which is difficult to digest. The day seems endless and I cannot wait to get to the theatre, but by the time I am in costume and ready to go onstage my indisposition mysteriously disappears and I am raring to go. While I stand in the wings waiting to make my entrance, my heart pumps so hard I believe I can hear it.

I'm sure many of my colleagues are extremely uptight the day they perform, but when that special moment arrives, all the problems of the day must be forgotten. With a few deep breaths and my little prayer, I am ready and eager to lose myself in my role.

The sense of responsibility I feel and whatever nervousness I suffer seem little enough to pay for the privilege of baring one's soul to the public all these years.

Not being a diva who enjoys going to a big party or a restaurant with lots of people after the opera, I prefer to return to my apartment with a small group of friends, put my feet up, and slowly unwind. I have never been able to eat a lot of food immediately after my performance while I am still keyed up. Later, when my "motor" slows down, I really enjoy something light and it's usually a chicken or roast beef sandwich with lots of mayonnaise and a glass of beer.

Another question people have asked me is why I have not been more adventurous with my repertoire and instead remained with my Italian and French roles, mainly in the *verismo* field. The reason is simple; I became strongly attached to some of these parts, particularly those that have given me ample possibility to act, and I felt that I could go on always developing and perfecting my interpretation of them. Never have I done a role twice the same way. I did make several excursions into other operas, but never found that they gave me the same inner satisfaction of those which became so closely identified with me.

Unfortunately, one of the prices we pay for fame is contracts for some years in advance. Being much in demand not only for opera and concerts, but also radio and television, I found myself tied up when the opportunities came to sing in certain operas, which I would have liked to have done. But in all the repertoire for my voice, there are only a few roles I regret missing: Desdemona, Thaïs, Adriana. Furthermore, I believe that it is better to have fewer roles, which are right for one's vocal abilities, more suitable for one's physical appearance, and more thoroughly studied for interpretation, rather than a large repertoire that is seldom sung and often completely unsuited to the singer. I know that opera singers often feel they have to accept roles that they should not, but I'm still singing because I learned to say "no."

Everything I wear onstage has always been my own. I have only made an exception when I was offered a new production with a major opera company and my costumes did not fit their design. On two occasions I remember protesting a costume I was asked to wear in a major new production. One was a gown designed for the second act of *Manon Lescaut*, which was all bows down the front. I hated it. Don Loper had already designed my costumes for the French *Manon*, which were magnificent. The lovely pink damask gown appearing on the cover of this book, I wore in the Saint-Sulpice scene, and it fit the new production perfectly. Being of the same color and period, it gave me an excellent excuse to insist. After the management saw it, they relented and let me have my way.

The other time I contested was in a new production of *Faust*. The entrance costume was so unattractive that I simply could not wear it. My costume designers have always been the best: Valentina, Edith Head, and Don Loper. My French costumes for *Louise* were made in Paris, and I have always felt they were highly respected for their authenticity.

When I work for the smaller companies, it is greatly appreciated that I have my own wardrobe and wigs. I am always happiest when wearing them, and even though they have cost a substantial part of my earnings over the years, I feel it has been money well spent.

During the first few years of my career at the Metropolitan Opera I had the great pleasure of meeting with the legendary diva Mary Garden. While discussing some of the roles I was preparing she emphasized the importance of one's first entrance onstage and gave me a tip which I have never forgotten. "Dorothy," she said, "that first impression is very important. Exude confidence and let your bosoms lead you."

Singing My Way

*D*uring the course of many interviews I have often been asked to describe how I began and why I survived my long and gratifying career. There is no doubt some people think all we singers need do is open our mouths and sing. Wrong! No matter how gifted one is with a beautiful sound to begin with, it takes years of study to develop a voice of operatic caliber; one which is capable of withstanding the rigors of singing steadily for three hours or so, have a short night's rest, then rise and shine for a rehearsal call in the morning to work on another opera for several more hours. But singing is the expression of the soul, in my view, and studying voice can be a most exciting experience.

Unlike the precious violin which an artist can carry under his arm to a concert, play divinely, then retire to a shelf, the voice is part of us. This treasure that we who sing carry in our throats is the most delicate of all instruments, a gift from God which should be revered. To be blessed with a voice is a very special privilege, and I have always felt a great responsibility to develop it to the best of my ability.

I have studied with three vocal teachers in my career. The first was almost a total loss of time, but I am grateful that no harm was done to my young voice. The second was my teacher in Italy, Astolfo Pescia. He developed my instrument quickly and discovered that there was an operatic voice there, even though it was spread and uncontrolled. My third and last teacher was Ludwig Fabri, a former heldentenor who taught me the fundamentals, put me on the right track and from whom I learned what it means to sing on an even scale. This was my most intensive study. The maestro would constantly preach that a good forte tone is developed out of the properly placed pianissimo one. Therefore, one must learn first to sing softly a round, free tone, with the right depth and support. This must be done before endangering the tone by forcing or pushing to make a big sound which may seem large to the singer but actually has little carrying power.

I started working with Maestro Fabri in 1941. He was a strict disciplinarian. For one year I sang nothing but scales. How many teachers today are able to persuade a student to go that slowly? Because I had already made my debut in opera, this was quite an order of restraint. I studied no arias until my voice reached a certain flexibility, then I was permitted to begin with Mozart. This discipline developed the foundation for my vocal technique and also gave me the coloratura capability I enjoyed in my early career.

Spending this considerable amount of time on basics took patience, but I shall always be grateful to Fabri, who gave me the technique which has stood by me all these years. All students love to make the big sound, but they have to learn that when that sound is unfocused it does not project and is no help in building a lasting foundation. Much like a camera, if the voice is not properly focused, the tone can be fuzzy, distorted, and unclear.

As I worked with Maestro Fabri I became more and more devoted to his word and convinced that he was a great teacher. I studied with him every chance I could, until he died in his midnineties. He often told me that if I would work with the technique he had given me, I would always have my voice and could sing forever. To this day he has been right. Vocally, I have never felt more secure and have been singing his way for forty years. I shall be eternally grateful to my wonderful teacher and dear friend Ludwig Fabri.

Physical fitness and a strong body necessary to support the voice of an aspiring opera or concert singer is essential. I have seen few great singers who smoke, but it would certainly be a deterrent to the two healthy lungs one needs. Breath control should be one of the first and most important studies in learning how to sing professionally. There is no "special way" of breathing, but one must learn how to control the flow, or so-called stream of breath, at the beginning of voice training. After learning proper breath control and studying thoroughly the correct, deep support of the tone, one is eventually able to sing without thinking about the mechanics. It then becomes a habit to prepare correctly for the tone before producing it.

I used to do most of my breathing exercises while walking and still do. First I inhale in short sips with pursed lips, taking in as much air as possible until the lungs feel as though they will burst. Then, as slowly as possible, I exhale in the same way. This method strengthens and develops the lung capacity. I also count my steps while doing this exercise, trying each time to lengthen the exhaling distance. The slowness teaches control and that is what is needed to spin out those lovely long phrases without gasping for breath. When I first learned this exercise in Fabri's studio, he had me stand with my back flat against a wall, in front of a mirror. The idea was to keep the shoulders relaxed and not raise them while inhaling but instead feel the lungs expand and fill to their depth.

The face of a singer while singing is a mirror of his or her method. When it is strained or distorted in any way, that person has problems in vocal production. I have heard many beautiful voices come and go very quickly at the Met and in San Francisco. Most of the time the reason is lack of proper support for the voice and poor focusing. Young singers of today are in such a hurry that the fundamentals are too often skimmed over and not really digested.

The method by which I sing is called "the even scale." I was taught that to have a great voice one must learn to eliminate the so-called registers and even out the scale. The ideal was to learn to pass from one register to the next without any detectable change. In other words, learn to pass over the entire range of the voice without concentrating on head, middle, or chest voice. Forcing the voice down into the chest and pressing is dangerous because the breach between registers only widens more and more until one has to push harder and harder. When the voice is improperly focused and the singer continues to force, the vocal cords become stretched and that is when a wobble begins. During my early career most of us were striving to sing by this even scale method and singers who abused it were often severely criticized.

All great singers are emotional; some more than others. The ability to push out of one's mind everything else and concentrate on our work is something each performer has to learn. Everyone has personal problems and at times it takes great discipline to relax the muscles and sing beautifully.

Looking back over the years of decision, I am quite satisfied that the one most important reason why I have retained my vocal powers all this time is that I progressed slowly. I waited to sing *Tosca* and *La Fanciulla del West* (*The Girl of the Golden West*), those heavy roles which demand the full powers of my voice.

I was blessed with an extremely sensitive ear and will always be proud of the fact that I have never been criticized for singing off pitch. Though I missed an opportunity to sing with the great Toscanini, he paid me a fine compliment after hearing a broadcast of mine from the Metropolitan. He stated that my pitch was truer than that of a pitch pipe.

Several years ago I was asked to write an article for a sports column. This occurred after I had been heard on a radio show talking about the similarities of disciplines in golf and singing. I remember saying that as we learn the fundamentals in golf and strive to "groove" our swing so it is always there, the same rule applies to the voice. If we learn to sing properly in the beginning, it also is "grooved" and will always be there. In singing, the muscles must be relaxed; so too in golf. The closest similarity, however, is that they both demand complete concentration. Just as a great golf professional can have a bad day, so can the greatest singer have an off night.

Other Passions

*P*ainting and golf become more and more important each year now as I slow down my singing and traveling. As I have said many times, nothing can ever replace my career, but these two enjoyable "distractions" make it easier. The art form of painting in oils is a new and wonderful way of expressing myself; and golf, besides giving me a great deal of pleasure, keeps me fit and healthy.

Since I was born and raised in the country, I have always been an outdoor girl. My golf clubs would often accompany me on the Metropolitan Opera spring tour, and the moment I had a break between performances I looked eagerly for a game with friends. The exercise, the closeness of nature, and the beauty of surroundings had a most restful, calming effect upon me. The minute I started swinging a club the world was beautiful, the anxieties of a busy career vanished, and the game became a joyous escape.

However, if I felt a bit uptight standing on the tee, before hitting the ball I would make some kind of remark to amuse my friends, such as, "This one is for that clumsy tenor who stepped on my train last night." It always got a laugh and relaxed me too.

When I married Jack he had a handicap of four, but after three years it had become an eleven. Golfers will agree that there could not be a more rewarding compliment for a new wife. Golf has been a great bond in companionship with Jack, and we play together often. A rule to which we faithfully adhere is to take a month off every year and relax in the Hawaiian Islands where we play some of the best courses in the world.

As for my own game, the best I can muster, because of all my other professional activities, is a nineteen. However, of late, I have slipped to a little higher handicap and hope to change that soon.

For the last ten years I have been invited to play in the Colgate-Dinah Shore Pro-Am Tournament in California. The Eisenhower Medical Center in Palm Springs benefits a great deal from this tournament as do other fine charities, and I am very proud to be a part of it each year.

My biggest thrill in golf occurred the second year I played. Our team consisted of three amateurs and one professional. We won that year with the great pro Jo Ann Prentice. I personally contributed six birdies and an eagle! I was so thrilled that I called my friend Schuyler Chapin, then the Metropolitan Opera's general director, and told him he would have to give me "leave" for my new profession.

Dinah Shore has been a friend for a long time, and as the years passed I have made many new close acquaintances with the Colgate Company personnel. Many celebrities play at this tournament: former President Ford, Robert Stack, Ray Bolger, Lawrence Welk, Frank Sinatra, Bob Hope, Jack Lemmon, and others. Hundreds of people, golfers in their own right, follow their favorite celebrity, and the comedians always put on a show while they play. The greatest enjoyment for the galleries seems to be when a big name makes a big shot. I get a great kick out of their applause; after all we are still onstage, aren't we?

I consider it a privilege to play with the greatest women golf pros in the world. My first was Amy Amazitch who was such fun and remains a good friend. Jo Ann Prentice couldn't have been more helpful and coached me into my best game. Judy Rankin was a dear while I struggled to play well with a fever of 103°. The next day when I was partnered with the sensational new star Nancy Lopez, I resented having to be tucked in bed nursing a severe case of flu.

I have often been asked whether other celebrities miss a shot on purpose to get a laugh. I doubt that, because most of them are serious golfers, but I believe those who make funny remarks do so only to cover their embarrassments. I do too!

On a panel show a few years ago I was asked why I had given an interview stating there were similarities between the art of singing and the game of golf. I explained that in order to play a good game we must develop a great power of concentration and keep the body relaxed. The same applies to singing.

If golf is my hobby, painting has become much more than that; it is turning into a second career. Several years ago, being a very active person, I began to wonder what I would do with myself when I started slowing down in my singing career. My husband began talking about my spending more time at home with him and would say, "For heaven's sake, Dorothy, you have had all the great satisfactions anyone in your domain could ask for. Why not start taking it easy?"

I began to see his point. It was never easy for me to get on an airplane, and my schedule made it necessary for me to fly a great deal. The long and very often delayed air trips were becoming disenchanting. New York, where I had always loved to be, was not the same; there were no walks in Central Park for exercise anymore.

I had been complaining about all this one day while lunching in Los Angeles with my good friend Mrs. Charles (Harriet) Luckman. I told her about my plans to search for a new way to express my artistic nature and slow down a bit. I wondered if she had been talking to Jack because she suddenly appeared to have an inspiration. "Dorothy," she said, "it seems to me that painting should give you satisfaction similar to that of singing. Why don't you try it?"

When luncheon was over, she asked me if I was free that afternoon. As I had no engagements, I jumped into the car with her and she took me directly to an art supply store. At that time Harriet had been doing some fine painting herself. She selected canvases, brushes, paints, and all the essentials to get started, then said, "Now why don't you go down to your lovely home in Pauma Valley as soon as you can, set up your easel, and go to it!" I will always be grateful to Harriet. That little push really got me started.

I was amazed at how quickly she had convinced me, for her suggestion made a lot of sense. Every time I returned to California I looked forward to getting back to my easel. I soon began to study with a local teacher, and the challenge of this difficult métier became more and more vital to me. While on tour I spent every available moment going to the museums and galleries to observe the technique of the great painters and take copious notes. After a concert in Texas, I was introduced to the famous Spanish painter José Vives-Atsara, and went to his studio the next day. It was the first time I had close contact with an artist of his stature, and this meeting did a lot for my determination to succeed.

Fate has always played a major part in my life. Some years ago, when Jack and I were spending our usual Hawaiian vacation in our house in Maui, I met someone who was to be a major inspiration in my endeavor to study the art of painting seriously.

At that particular time I had been concerned about my husband, who was under continuous pressure in his work and considered this break essential for him too. Although he had promised nothing would interrupt our month's holiday, however, after a few days he announced that he would have to go back to Los Angeles. As the director of the Brain Research Institute of UCLA he was to receive a large gift from a generous donor, making his presence necessary. Of course I understood, but was most disappointed and could not help pouting a bit. In order to appease me Jack suggested we go to play at Wailea, my favorite golf club on Maui. On the way back we were stopped by a policeman for a traffic violation and given a ticket. We returned to the house and decided to get this nuisance over with as soon as possible.

Having no idea where to go to settle the fine, we went to the Municipal Building. We were directed to the old jail in Lahaina where traffic tickets had to be paid. In this part of the town there is an enormous banyan tree where a huge art exhibit and demonstration was being held. On the first floor of the building there was a splendid exhibit of paintings, and my attention was drawn to a lovely seascape. I turned to Jack and said how much I would like to paint like that. A lady who was standing next to me turned and said, "If you would like to meet the artist, you will find her outside under the banyan tree."

The crowding and confusion was considerable, but thanks to a special type of "radar" that has often guided me in my existence, I knew immediately that the back of a woman who was painting and answering questions to a crowd of onlookers belonged to the artist I was looking for. Another of her completed paintings was standing nearby and I read again the signature, "Joyce Clark."

I listened for a bit and then began asking her many questions. As I had missed the beginning of the demonstration, I wanted to know more about the procedure. Curious to see who the person was who appeared so interested, she turned to look at me and immediately asked, "Aren't you Dorothy Kirsten?" When I replied, "Yes," she then inquired why I was so interested. "Don't tell me that you paint too," she said. I told her that I was very serious about it and would like to acquire one of her oils. She then invited us to come to her studio later.

My attraction to Joyce was similar to that which I felt when I first met Grace Moore. We liked each other immediately. When later Jack and I went to call on her I asked timidly whether she ever gave private lessons. "I never do," she answered, "but if you are really serious about it I will make an exception, because I have always admired you." I was thrilled and thanked her. From then on I have arranged to be in Maui as much as possible and have since come to love painting almost as much as singing.

In the spring of 1979 I decided to have the first one-woman show of my paintings. They were all oils; still lifes, portraits, seascapes, and landscapes. An exhibit was organized in Palm Springs by Kay Obergfel, who represented me there. It was held in the Farrell House, named after the famous silent screen actor Charles Farrell. To my amazement and delight, within forty-eight hours almost every painting was sold, and I came home with five commissions.

The kind of satisfaction I feel from knowing I have succeeded in doing a good painting, and the complimentary remarks from people who appreciate my work, are tremendously gratifying but quite different from that which I experience when singing before a cheering audience. Painting is an entirely different form of self-fulfillment. It has given me a spiritual lift and afforded me a different type of creative expression.

It was not long after I met Jack that I learned of his interest in birds. When I was young I loved to roam through the woods looking for spring flowers and enjoying the sound of the birds. At that point in my life it never occurred to me to stop and look at them. That all changed when Jack presented me with a beautiful pair of binoculars and showed me how to use them. I developed a whole new interest, and if you have never seen a beautiful bird through a good pair of glasses, I recommend it highly.

At our home in a beautiful citrus valley of Southern California, I feed the hummingbirds and struggle to keep two quart containers supplied with food for them. At one time I counted fourteen birds of three different kinds at one feeder, their tiny wings in perpetual motion, waiting in line for a chance to get at the food. When the feeders are empty, my little friends are quick to let me know. They fly close to the window, making their sort of wheezing call. Before I can hang up a newly filled feeder, they whiz around my head as though they are dive-bombing me, and sometimes even light on my hand as if to say thank you. These are remarkable little birds, some of which are less than two inches in length.

Jack and I had a friend, Don Bleitz, who was a member of the Audubon Society and a licensed birdbander. Knowing I was especially interested in hummingbirds, Don took us to a sanctuary where I assisted him by holding the little creatures while he photographed them and put the tiny band on their legs. The birds are then free to fly where they wish. Later, other bird fanciers net them and send the band to the Audubon Society. In this way information is obtained about their flight patterns.

Jack has his pets too, and the many coveys of quail who make their home on our property and raise their chicks there each year keep him busy filling the grain feeders all year round. Our feathered friends receive our first attention when we arrive at our home in the valley and it's fun to see them gather to welcome us. I guess I'm still a country girl!

Prima Donnas and
First Ladies

Prima donna" in Italian means "first lady." These ladies were the leading stars of a specific opera company. They belonged to one opera house years ago and though at times were permitted to travel, they made only guest appearances with the other leading companies. After coming to the Metropolitan, Sembrich, Eames, Farrar, Bori, and Ponselle, to name a few, belonged to that company, just as Rosa Raisa, Muzio, and Mary Garden symbolized the Chicago Opera for many years; Melba's home was Covent Garden, and so it was all over the world.

That system, however, no longer exists, and today's leading ladies rush across the world from one opera house to the other, singing one week in Rome, the next in San Francisco.

With the number of good companies increasing each year, the demand for great singers is far beyond their availability. The field of top names seems to be shrinking, and those who are busiest in our profession are wearing themselves out trying to sing everywhere. Is it any wonder that careers are shorter and shorter?

Rudolf Bing tried valiantly to have a repertory company when he first came to the Metropolitan, but neither the public nor the stars would put up with it and he finally succumbed to the new trend just as all the others did. The star system is here to stay, but if the pace does not slow down, I wonder what the future era will bring.

It is not only our segment of the performing arts that we need to be concerned about. Though the motion-picture star cannot be compared to the opera star who has dedicated his or her life to study and has worked for years before achieving stardom, this branch of the theatre too seems to be suffering from a similar malady. The number of great personalities has lessened remarkably in recent years. Names like Katharine Hepburn, Bette Davis, Joan Fontaine, Irene Dunne have no challengers. And what about Broadway? Where are the Katharine Cornells, Helen Hayeses, and the great matinee idols? Is it just the times we live in? We can only hope that perfectionism will return and that the trend toward mediocrity will disappear in the theatre.

Maybe it is partly our own fault. The glamorous prima donna is not always glamorous today. I never believed our public wanted to see us looking like the girl next door. The tasteless clothes and careless appearance of some singers I have seen in and out of the opera house are an embarrassment to our profession. If you are a prima donna, or only aspiring to be one, I believe it is your responsibility to live up to the title all the way. I always tried to. If I was called to a rehearsal that required me to spend a good deal of time on the floor, such as *Madama Butterfly*, I brought "working clothes," but when I walked out of that session, I was always a prima donna.

It wasn't easy for me to keep up to my ideals in those early days for we were not making the fees of today. Outside of my cost for coaches and living expenses in New York, I was putting every cent on my back for costumes and clothes I thought appropriate for my future.

I came on the opera scene in an era that was coming to a close. Divas (Webster's definition of the word is goddesses) lived luxuriously, had beautiful jewels, fancy cars, and villas abroad. Though this period was lingering on, there were already ominous signs that times were changing. The enormous increase in taxes began, which no longer allowed them to live the way in which they were accustomed.

Grace Moore, Gladys Swarthout, and Lily Pons, to name those who were best known to me, all had the valuable exposure of motion pictures, which undoubtedly added intangible dimension to making their names famous, even to people who had little interest in opera. Others, like Flagstad and Giannini, who seemed to have neither flair for clothes nor a life-style of great elegance, relied instead on their vocal supremacy and strong personalities.

One of the most respected and reliable singers at the Met when I began there was Licia Albanese. Her contribution to the lyric theatre will always be remembered for her superb, clear Italian diction and the warm, velvety sound of her voice. Of all Licia's roles I most admired her Butterfly. Her beautiful voice was perfect as Cio Cio San, and she enjoyed great success in this opera for well over two decades. I remember her thoughtfulness one night when I first started singing this opera at the Met. She appeared in my dressing room and presented me with a pair of long white stockings, saying, "I always wear these for when I fall after the harakiri. In case my kimono should accidentally open, my legs are not in evidence." It was a clever detail she had worked out. I was deeply touched and have followed her suggestion ever since.

Licia was always friendly, and despite the fact we later sang many of the same parts, proved herself an admirable colleague. After she had left the Met and was doing less singing, she turned up one day as director of a *Butterfly* I was to sing in Trenton, New Jersey. I became apprehensive, because by this time our interpretations differed considerably, and she knew that I had firmly established my own *Butterfly*. Fearfully, I thought it would be an awkward situation and I did not want to hurt Licia. However, she got the message at our first rehearsal that I would be doing my own show and never attempted to direct me.

The mezzo was her pupil, and everything went fairly well until the night before my performance, when at nearly midnight we were still working on Suzuki's scenes. It was then that the entire company heard my resounding "*Basta*" (Enough). Despite my great respect and admiration for Licia, I was going to retire for the evening though we were only halfway through the second act and hadn't touched the third. Such experiences do happen with smaller companies, but Licia, having sung this role for so many years, knew the great demands of the opera and I was surprised and hurt by her lack of consideration for me that night.

Strange how some of those performances stick in my mind. I had a few nightmares about that one. The mezzo was so insecure as Suzuki that she made it extremely difficult. But performers do go through unpleasant experiences; and fortunately the public seldom knows anything about them. We did survive that difficult performance, and Licia and I are once again good friends.

When I first heard Maria Callas, she was singing in Mexico City. She was as yet unknown to the American public, but the news was spreading rapidly that there was a sensational new voice on the horizon. It certainly was a magnificent sound, but she was extremely fat and had an unattractive figure onstage. I heard Maria again a few years later when she weighed about 125 pounds and had transformed herself into a lovely, slim woman. How she performed this miracle is a mystery. Though the great technique was still there, with all the weight loss the beautiful, pure velvet sound was gone.

Callas had a fantastic career. She too was a household name in her time, a consummate artist musically, with an electric personality, and was adored the world around. She had an extraordinary talent for obtaining publicity at any cost, often on an inartistic level.

I remember as a young artist being told by a newspaperman that getting my name in the papers was the only way to build a career; no matter the contents of the story, just make sure they spell the name right. That particular piece of advice didn't seem to fit my character.

Maria initiated a trend that proved disastrous—to sing everything from mezzo to coloratura roles. Though she survived it for a number of years, many others who tried it soon fell by the wayside.

The last time she came back to the Met to sing *Tosca*, I was asked by my dear friend Francis Robinson if I would accompany him to the performance. Francis had been a great admirer of Maria's, and though he knew that Tosca was a part very close to me and that I never go to hear another singer in my own roles, he teased me about it so much that I accepted. I tried hard to analyze her great magnetism that night and Francis was crushed when I told him that she had disappointed me.

I shall never forget Elisabeth Schwarzkopf's superb Marschallin in *Rosenkavalier*, though I have never heard her in any other role. Hers is a uniquely beautiful sound, quite effortless and secure. She is one of the great ladies of the theatre in our era and an artist who never failed to make a magnificent appearance onstage.

The voice of Leontyne Price, for me, is one of the finest of my generation. How well I remember the night of her debut when we were doing the *Carmelites* in San Francisco and she exploded on the scene with that pure velvet voice. In opera I feel the Verdi and Mozart heroines are her best. Her *Aïda*, *Ballo* and *Forza* are absolutely magnificent, while the *verismo* repertoire has never been quite right for her.

But my good friend Leontyne also went a bit too fast into the kind of opera that can take its toll if a singer is not careful. Her venture into *La Fanciulla del West* was disastrous and cost her several months of vocal rest. It takes a big person to stop singing and really rest the voice. But that she did, only to return triumphantly, for which everyone is grateful. Her concerts and recitals have little competition, and her voice is more beautiful than ever.

The mezzo-soprano of my time who has thrilled me most with the beauty of her voice is Giulietta Simionato. Her regal bearing, fire, and total immersion in her roles are extraordinary.

Marilyn Horne, another singer who started her career as a lyric soprano, sang an excellent Musetta with me in San Francisco in 1962. I think I knew then that Marilyn was really going places. She was spirited, intelligent, eager, and great fun to work with. It is amazing how her voice has developed into a great mezzo, with tremendous flexibility and range. My hope is that she will come back to the even scale again. Marilyn is a longtime friend, and it worries me to hear her press on the bottom so much.

Speaking of friends I have made along the opera way, I would be remiss not to include Claramae Turner. We sang together so many times, but the two operas I remember best are *Faust* and *Louise*. Her

Martha in *Faust* was wonderful, but for me her interpretation of the mother in Charpentier's *Louise* when we sang it together was superb. She had found the true character as she was described to me by Charpentier, and with the great Ezio Pinza as my father, there was never a happier Louise. Claramae's fine mezzo has served her well, and she too has had a long, successful career, still singing as well as ever.

A soprano who must also be mentioned is Eleanor Steber. Her beautiful voice and fine technique will long be remembered, especially for the Mozart operas in which she excelled.

Renata Tebaldi made her grand entrance into the American opera world in the early 1950s. Her glorious voice had little competition while she was singing so often at the Metropolitan and with the San Francisco Opera. When she first came on the scene her voice sounded young, vibrant, and more toward the lyric, rather than heavier *spinto* sound; I often wondered if her career was shortened because she pushed it too fast.

Puccini's opera *La Fanciulla del West*, as I have mentioned before, has been a voice breaker for several sopranos. As it is one of my favorite roles, and I have sung it many times, I have written about it and tried to explain the problems elsewhere in my book. Renata and I were both singing this opera in the same period when I was asked to "cover" for her. It was then that I noticed the strain in her voice. Not long after that her struggle became quite evident, and the voice began to lose its warmth and luster. Tebaldi was much too young to be through, and I have been hoping to hear one day that she has found her way once again.

While discussing American singers I cannot resist mentioning a lovely young lady who was one day advertising automobiles on television and, the next thing we knew, was engaged to sing with the San Francisco Opera Company. I refer, of course, to my friend Mary Costa who had a great success singing lyric-soprano roles with the company.

Mary was an exceptionally fine Musetta, and we sang *Bohème* together many times. Among the most memorable were our performances together in Japan with the Metropolitan Opera in 1975, where Mary's flamboyant Musetta was a big hit with the Japanese. She has that special kind of personality that lights up the stage. Kurt Adler, who was responsible for her big chance in San Francisco, seemed to be managing her vocal capabilities wisely and carefully.

Opera impresarios are not always considerate of their singer's voices, and, unfortunately, there are too many who know nothing about vocal technique. When the Met was planning to revive Barber's opera *Vanessa*, I rejected the part on the grounds that it was unsuitable for my voice. When Mary told me that she had been asked to do this role, I was worried about it. As it turned out, she did have problems following that experience. We all have to learn our capabilities. Mary survived that episode beautifully to continue her great career, and I congratulate her. I know she won't mind my using her story if others can learn from our mistakes. During my career I have watched many young artists who deserved to succeed ruin their chances by allowing themselves to be cast in too demanding an assignment. Many times there was no second chance.

There is another diva who most certainly should be represented here, for as an American prima donna, she has topped us all in making a great name in opera. I met Beverly Sills many years ago and have admired her tremendously. Her artistry as a singer and an actress belonged at the Metropolitan long before she came to us. The unknown operas that she brought to the public were a tour de force few sopranos could endure and the number of roles she accomplished is even more astounding.

Beverly's ambitions for the New York City Opera Company, since she became its director, sound promising for our young American singers. I congratulate her.

A story about Lily Pons still mystifies me. Having known Lily's formidable instinct and shrewdness, it is beyond me that she thought she could handle *La Traviata* with her delicate coloratura instrument. She neither had the range, except for the first act, nor the capacity for the emotional impact this Verdi opera requires. Wisely, however, before singing it in the wide-open spaces of the Metropolitan, she decided to try it first with the San Francisco Opera in 1951. The result was such that she never touched it again.

The following year Lily appeared for the last time in the Golden Gate City in *The Daughter of the Regiment*. It was one of her most enchanting accomplishments, ending her long association with that opera house. I understood that the reason was purely financial. As the San Francisco Opera had put a lid on the highest salaries at that time, she refused to accept this new policy and that was that. Lily was a sharp businesswoman; she was able to put aside enough money to finish her life in luxury.

The last time I saw the adorable Lily was at a beautiful party given for me in 1973 at the Hearst mansion after my performance of *Madama Butterfly* in Palm Springs. She was involved with the opera group there and very happy in her lovely home on the hill. When we had a chance for a few words in private, I was amused by her remark in that exceedingly high-pitched voice, always marked by a strong French accent. "Doorooteee, wheeen weel you queeet?" Imitating her accent, I replied, "Neeveer, Leelee."

Clockwise from top left: Newspaper drawing of my aunt, the famous soprano Catherine Hayes; San Francisco, 1852. Grace Moore at my debut in *La Traviata*, New York City Center. My dear friend Grace Moore. First year at the Met—making the cover of *Life* magazine.

Clockwise from top left: As Fiora, *L'Amore dei Tre Re.* (Credit: John Engstead) As Louise. *Tosca.* As Minnie, Girl of the Golden West. (Credit: John Engstead) As Manon, Massenet. (Credit: John Engstead)

Clockwise from top left: *Madama Butterfly*. (Photo courtesy Metropolitan Opera) Marguerite, *Faust*. Violetta, *La Traviata*. (Credit: George Platt Lynes, courtesy *Mademoiselle* magazine, Copyright 1944 by Street & Smith Publications, Inc., Copyright 1972 (renewed) by The Condé Nast Publications, Inc.) Rosalinde, *Fledermaus*. (Photo courtesy Metropolitan Opera) Mimi, *La Bohème*—my debut role both in San Francisco and at the Met. (Photo courtesy Metropolitan Opera)

Above: Manon Lescaut, the role that led me to the Met. Below left to right: As Cressida. (Credit: R. Lackenback, courtesy San Francisco Opera) With Richard Lewis in *Troilus and Cressida*. (Credit: R. Lackenback, courtesy San Francisco Opera)

Tenors and Tenors

$\mathcal{I}$ was fortunate to have started singing at a time when I had the opportunity to appear with some of the greatest tenors of the preceding generation, and then with the top stars of this one, several of whom happened to make their United States debuts with me. Starting my operatic career in Chicago, I was engaged to sing several minor parts my first year, which enabled me to observe the great singers at close range.

The first star who made a tremendous impression on me was Tito Schipa. He was singing Alfredo in *La Traviata* with Jarmila Novotna as Violetta, the same night I was making my debut in that opera as Flora. Schipa was a legendary figure and had already been singing for thirty years. He was considered the number one exponent of *bel canto*. Though his voice was somewhat small and not really beautiful in quality, his vocal technique was extraordinary and his style so impeccable that one forgot the limitations of his instrument.

Although the role in *La Traviata* was considered a bit too heavy for him, in the famous scene during the third act where he chastises Violetta and the singing becomes quite dramatic, the manner in which he used his light voice to show his anger was a fine lesson. He never forced, but obtained with his beautiful phrasing all the necessary dramatic effects. His lightest pianissimo sound, so perfectly projected, reached into the farthest corner of the opera house and was the envy of all tenors. I, a beginner, was learning a great deal from these giants of the opera world.

The famous Giovanni Martinelli, who already had been singing for some time before I was born, had become by the time we were teamed together such a beloved figure with the public that the beginning of his vocal decline mattered little. It was a thrilling experience to appear as Nedda in *I Pagliacci* with him on several occasions.

He was a whirlwind on the stage. So outstanding was his personality and acting ability that the first time I sang with him I realized I had to plan every move carefully to keep my own identity. In the last act of our first performance, when he opened the enormous switchblade knife with which he was to kill me, I became terrified and wanted to run off the stage. To such an extent had he immerged himself in the role of Canio, reliving the part in the most realistic manner. My real fear projected itself to the public, which was undoubtedly what he had planned, for in rehearsal there was no sign of such an instrument.

Offstage he was a charming, delightful man, a giant white-haired teddy bear. At the time Martinelli was still singing his celebrated Otello at the Metropolitan, he began to urge me to learn Desdemona. The great tenor had several engagements of this opera in other cities and, insisting it would be a great role for me, offered me the chance to break it in with him at a smaller theatre. I came to realize several years later what an exceptional opportunity that was, but it was much too early for my young soprano and I knew it even then.

Another veteran who came my way was Armand Tokatyan, a member of the Metropolitan since 1922. My first performance with him was as Micaela in *Carmen* in Hartford, Connecticut. Later we did *Bohème* in Detroit, and then he was Alfredo for my debut in *La Traviata* at the Metropolitan. I recall how grateful I was to have him as a partner for my first performance of this opera at the Met because there had been no orchestra rehearsal. Tokatyan afforded me a sense of security, having sung Alfredo innumerable times in that theatre. His authority onstage and his ingratiating manner made me very comfortable. He seemed to be just right for the role. As Alfredo his noble appearance helped me create the illusion that I was desperately in love with him.

Alas, on many occasions in recent years it took a lot of fantasy and imagination to convince myself that I was ready to sacrifice my all for the Alfredo imposed upon me by the directors of opera companies. From the beginning the "picture" we made onstage and the appearance of my leading men were very important to me. In order to create credibility and be convincing, a pair of lovers cannot succeed if all they have in common is two beautiful voices; unless, perhaps, you close your eyes.

Another tenor who often sang with me in the early days was Nino Martini. He had an enormous following because of the many motion pictures he appeared in. Nino had already sung for a decade at the Metropolitan Opera and when I first joined the Met we sang several *Traviatas* together. His lyrical voice was less than sensational but he was musical and secure. The Hollywood adulation had by no means gone to his head, and I remember him as a charming, cooperative colleague. Nino was an ardent Alfredo; handsome and a fine actor. I knew we looked well together, and it was a joy each time we met.

A much beloved American tenor in the thirties and early forties was Richard Crooks. He was often called "the sweet-voiced tenor." I appeared with him in *Faust* in Montreal early in my career and recall hearing his magnificent Des Grieux in Massenet's *Manon* at the Met. He was considered one of the greatest in this part.

One of the most temperamental and colorful tenors I met a little later was Jan Kiepura, who made a big name for himself in Europe with many films and also in Viennese operetta. Jan often had clashes with his colleagues and a famous one with Grace Moore. Once in a performance of *La Bohème* at the Met when Jan had deliberately moved a chair in which she had to sit far from its proper position, she was forced to have a friendly stagehand nail it to the floor.

A performance in particular that comes to mind was another *Bohème* in Hartford, Connecticut, when Jan was again singing with Grace and I was repeating my Musetta. It was not long after the incident at the Met and the feud was still very much on. The great tenor had arranged to have flowers presented to me over the footlights and filled my room with floral tributes. He was obviously trying to annoy Grace, but she and I had a good laugh over it. Jan got away with these tantrums because he had a truly magnificent voice and was always good box office, though he seemed to care little about being a good colleague.

After my first few years in opera, a new group of sensational tenors became my partners, some of whom held the spotlight for a number of years. The gentleman from Sweden, Jussi Björling, was, in my opinion, the greatest tenor of my generation. His was the most perfect technique and the most glorious sound I have ever known. Never did I hear him sing a note that was not absolutely on pitch and well produced.

After the war, in 1945, Jussi returned to the United States, and I was engaged to tour with him in joint concerts. On the innumerable occasions I sang with him in opera or concerts, his total security, on which I could always depend, made me sing better than ever. I have sung with well over sixty tenors, some of whom were truly spectacular, but with many there could be an insecure moment. Would he make it, or not? Colleagues would say, "Dorothy, why do you worry so about your partners?" This is not easy to explain, but I suffer when I see a singer struggle and expect I always will.

Jussi's voice was truly a magnificent one, but this was not his only gift. He gave the feeling that every phrase was expressed with his heart. He possessed a pathos in his sound that reminded many of Caruso, but there was never the exaggeration that often was heard in the great Neapolitan's voice. Björling's vocal magic in opera was such that, although his acting ability was limited, and his figure too full at times, it did not matter. I remember so well the last performance of *Manon Lescaut* we ever sang together at the Metropolitan (he died in

1960 at the age of fifty-three). After our meeting in the first act when
he sang, "Donna non vidi mai" (Never have I seen such a woman), I
could not hold back my tears. Seldom has the house "come down" like
it did after this aria by Jussi Björling.

Offstage Jussi was pixie all the way, with a round, cherubic, youthful face and a twinkle in his eye. On tour his lovely wife Analisa traveled with us, and I have many happy memories of our trips together.
How fortunate I was to have begun my concert career with this great
tenor. When he died so unexpectedly I knew I had lost a very dear
colleague, but what was more tragic, the world had been deprived of
the greatest tenor voice of our time.

Richard Tucker's technique was the closest to Jussi Björling's. His
relaxed and beautifully focused voice was undoubtedly developed during a long and valuable experience as a cantor. The many scales and
agility necessary to sing this kind of music are akin to doing vocal exercises every time one performs. They also keep the vocal cords flexible and strong. Having known Richard Tucker and Jan Peerce, who
is also a cantor, for many years, I believe that this training was the secret of their vocal security. In fact, Richard went directly to the Metropolitan Opera without any operatic experience. In 1945, the year of
my debut, he had a smashing success as Enzo in *La Gioconda*. Like
Björling, his was not a prepossessing stage personality, but again, he
could write his own ticket with the treasure he held in his throat.

Richard and I sang many performances together at the Metropolitan: *Manon Lescaut*, which he used to tell me was his favorite, *La
Bohème*, *Tosca*, *Fanciulla*, and others. He too loved the operas of
Puccini. My favorite recording with him is the great duet from the
third act of Massenet's *Manon*. He was secure, always considerate, and
a joy to work with.

We also did many joint concerts. There was a fun-loving side of
Richard that I never saw until one evening at the conclusion of a particularly rewarding concert with the New Orleans Symphony. After
the performance a group of friends invited us to see the town with
them. I was familiar with American jazz and always enjoyed it, but I
wondered about Richard. That night we heard some of the greats, and
before I knew it, our tenor was the life of the party, applauding
like mad and stomping his foot to the rhythm just as we all were.

Richard Tucker was a wonderful colleague; a sensitive, disciplined
artist who was greatly respected and loved. He was a fine musician
and completely reliable. I thoroughly enjoyed our work together, be
it concerts, recordings or opera. He, too, is sorely missed.

A sensational entrance to the Metropolitan was made by Giuseppe di Stefano who joined us in 1948. This handsome, sexy-looking Sicilian had a glorious voice. He was tall, with an elegant figure, had a natural stage presence, and always made a fine appearance. We sang together often while he was at the Met, but I remember him best for his appearances in Gounod's *Faust*. His voice was very lyric at that time and perfect for the opera. One of the broadcasts I did with him of *Faust* was pirated and suddenly, in 1978, it exploded on the recording market. His French was far from perfect, but how melting and sensuous his sound was!

I believe it was in *La Bohème* that I sang with him first, and what a delight it was. He was a most attractive and personable Rodolfo with the charming habit of singing to his Mimi as if he forgot that there was a conductor or an audience. How seldom singers sing to each other instead of to a prompter's box or the audience. Nothing has annoyed me more through the years than the tenor who is so egocentric or insecure that he ignores his leading lady standing there several feet from him while he pleads for her love.

Giuseppe di Stefano disappeared from the scene much too soon. Unfortunately, he was lured to the more dramatic roles too early in his career and that beautiful lyric sound was soon no more.

Just a little before Di Stefano, another tenor, Ferruccio Tagliavini, made his debut with me in *La Bohème* at Chicago and then joined the Metropolitan where we often appeared together. He had a beautiful voice though a little short on top; what the Italians call *una voce corta* (a short voice). In stature he was also a bit small, and when singing with him I remember getting myself down to the lowest-heeled shoes I could wear. As I have said before, it is important to me to make a beautiful picture onstage, and I am grateful that, at five feet five, I seldom have had to adjust to my partners. But Ferruccio could sing! In fact, he is still singing. With his light lyric tenor and an exceptional technique much like Schipa's, never forcing, he was able to project his voice over a very large orchestra.

I loved to sing *La Bohème* with him, and no one could top the memories I have of his Rodolfo. In the duets he would always try to blend his voice with mine. When the score asked for a pianissimo, I knew he was going to sing it that way. There was never a competition to see who could sing the loudest. Ferruccio respected the composer and also the partner with whom he was singing.

When he sang his aria to me in the first act, it was a quiet, almost pianissimo, beginning, which is clearly indicated in the score. This makes the words "Che gelida manina" (What a cold little hand) have so much more meaning. His sobbing at the end of the opera following

Mimi's death was so restrained that it achieved far more despair than usual.

Mario del Monaco made his debut with me at the Metropolitan in Puccini's *Manon Lescaut* on November 27, 1950. We had sung this opera together with the San Francisco company only a few weeks before, which was our first meeting, and I knew then that he was on his way to becoming a superstar of opera in this country.

I remember how stunned I was when I first heard his voice. His stature was slight, but the sound that came forth from that smallish man was astonishing. The voice was gorgeous and the tone a luscious sound. He was dark, handsome and vital. Our voices blended beautifully and our personalities were quite compatible. Mario is one of my favorite tenors.

The respect and the feeling, I believe, was mutual. Though I loved Jussi Björling and his magnificent sound in the same role, Mario del Monaco brought an entirely different dimension to the part. His voice, a lusty, more demanding type, and his appearance onstage were decidedly romantic. I was singing the role with both tenors at this time, but with Mario it seemed easy to give the illusion of a smoldering sense of passion between us.

In the third act, when Manon is dragged away with the prostitutes to the ship that will take her to Louisiana into exile, his impassioned cry and anguish were so real that to the cast and the audience it was tremendously moving.

We were also ideally suited in *Tosca*, which we sang together often, both at San Francisco and the Metropolitan. Mario was clever about his appearance on the stage and always managed to look taller than I, although we were about the same height.

Toward the end of his career in this country he took on the role of Otello. The public adored him, but the critics were accustomed to a more dominating figure in this opera and never gave him the credit due him, though few tenors had sung the role as well.

Nicolai Gedda, a tall, well-built, good-looking gentleman of Russian-Swedish heritage, is another tenor I admire greatly. He is an excellent linguist with an enormous repertoire of roles in many languages. Several years ago, when we first sang together, I remember him as a lyric tenor, wide in range and beautifully secure. One of the roles he sang most at the Met was *Faust*, and he was superb in Gounod's opera. His French diction was excellent and at that time there were few tenors singing well in that language. He was a handsome Pelleas; and Lensky in *Eugene Onegin* was a natural in his native Russian. I regret we never had the opportunity to sing Charpentier's *Louise* together. Recently Gedda has taken on heavier and more dramatic roles, but if any singer can handle this transition, with his physique and discipline he can.

I have spoken in these pages of favorite tenors, and Franco Corelli certainly belongs in that category. In my opinion he had more to give than any tenor I have sung with. His voice, good looks, height, and slim figure, with the charisma he created onstage, made him the ideal romantic leading man. In my long career at the Metropolitan Opera few tenors have succeeded in making as great an impact as the one made by Franco Corelli. His voice was an exciting *lirico spinto*. He came to the Met in 1961, and we were cast to sing together soon thereafter. There are always partners in our profession who are more compatible than others, but Franco and I quickly discovered that we enjoyed singing together.

The early part of his career at the Metropolitan was exciting and extremely successful. Franco seemed to have all the confidence in the world in himself and showed it. But as time went on there came a period of uncertainty on his part about his voice, and he became unsure of his vocal production. He was never satisfied with his work and, though the public never knew of his insecurity, he would have his wife Loretta in the wings tape every note he sang so he could check himself between acts. As a singer and friend I understood what he was going through and my heart went out to him.

Franco was a great Cavaradossi in *Tosca*, and I loved singing this exciting opera with him. He was as anxious as I to make the Sardou drama really come to life. When my fans began to tease me about being especially realistic in my love scenes with him, I knew we had succeeded.

Working together as much as we did, and having become good friends with Franco and his wife, I tried to relax his tension when we sang together. Knowing of his anxiety about the first-act aria in *Tosca*, "Recondita armonia," which he sings just before I appear, the first chance I had after entering I would whisper "Bravo" to him. I really meant it, for he always sang it well.

When Corelli and I were cast to sing *Fanciulla* together, I was delighted, for there was no other tenor at the Met who fit the qualifications more perfectly. The play calls for a dark, Latin-type, handsome, dashing singer able to "belt out" some of Puccini's most dramatic music. I know we both enjoyed *Fanciulla*, and Franco accomplished some of his finest acting in the role of Dick Johnson. I tried hard to talk him into doing *Manon Lescaut* with me because that part too was ideally suited to him, but I was unsuccessful.

Though Franco's career had brought him many triumphs, apparently he was unable to regain the confidence needed to continue, and, sadly, at the top of his success he simply stopped. He is still young, for our profession, and I pray that one day he will return. The opera world has missed him.

I greatly admire the Canadian tenor Jon Vickers, for his special contribution to opera as a singing actor. He began his career in opera relatively late and started singing at the Metropolitan in 1960. His interpretation of Canio in *I Pagliacci* during a recent national telecast was the finest portrayal of this role I have ever witnessed.

I respected him enormously when he gave up the role of Tannhäuser at London's Covent Garden after all the fanfare about his debut in this part. When he realized that it was not right for him, he had the courage to admit it and made it official.

We sang together very little and I regret we had so few opportunities. I have always enjoyed working with artists like him who feel as I do, that the drama is as important as the singing in opera.

I have sung several times with more recent tenor idols, Luciano Pavarotti and Placido Domingo, who are now in great demand all over the world. Unfortunately, both of these superlatively fine singers came onto the scene at a time when distances no longer counted. The number of big-name singers is shrinking, and the demands on both of these great stars continue to be overwhelming. It is very tempting to take on too much and overwork when every major opera company is vying for your attention and offering unbelievable fees. I understand only too well, but I cannot believe that even the strongest can survive untouched and stay in good vocal condition with the pace of today.

When I first sang with Placido Domingo on my twenty-fifth anniversary with the San Francisco Opera, his voice impressed me tremendously for its beautiful, warm, velvet quality. He is a compelling figure on the stage and a dear friend. I pray that he will take care of his great gift, not only for all the leading ladies who will follow me, but for his many fans who adore him. There are not many who can sing, act, and look like Placido.

Pavarotti came to the San Francisco Opera in 1969 and I sang many Mimis in *La Bohème* to his Rodolfo. In those days he was slim and a most sympathetic partner with an enchanting lyrical voice. He was young, attractive, eager. Even then it was evident that he had, aside from his magnificent sound, a delicious sense of humor. It has been interesting to see how his confidence has grown by leaps and bounds and his technique matured so beautifully since then.

When the Metropolitan Opera went on its first-ever official visit to Japan in 1974, Luciano Pavarotti and I sang *La Bohème* together again. It was amazing to observe the forward strides he had made. His friends became concerned about the many pounds he had put on, which did interfere considerably with our love scenes, but the beauty of his singing was such that one had to be content with just listening.

On the occasion of one of our *La Bohème* performances together in San Francisco, I was singing my third-act aria, "Addio, senza rancor" (Good-bye, without regrets), when suddenly the stage began to rock. I noticed that the enormous chandelier over the orchestra and central part of the house was swinging. The people occupying balcony seats were first to see this disquieting phenomenon and quickly moved out of the theatre.

Pavarotti, who did not speak a word of English, then whispered, "*Ma cosa sta succendo?*" (But what is happening?). Pressing his hand, the first chance I had I said under my breath, "*Continuamo*" (Let's continue). Fortunately, the conductor, who had his back to the audience, and the prompter were unaware of the commotion in the theatre. Since we kept on with the singing, they too proceeded. We never missed a note, finished the act, and Pavarotti, unaccustomed to the California earthquakes, showed amazing control.

When the tremors calmed down we were able to finish the opera for those brave enough to stay. Being nervous about what might follow, and having experienced various other quakes in California, I told my secretary to make arrangements for us to leave on the first plane out. The next day the newspapers carried the headlines: "KIRSTEN FLIES AWAY LIKE CARUSO IN 1906," referring to the great quake of that time that half destroyed the city.

Jan Peerce has been my friend and colleague for many years. I was lucky to have him as my partner on the night of my debut at the Metropolitan Opera. He was my Rock of Gibraltar that night with his beautiful, relaxed technique; an inspiration, supporting my efforts with affection and true interest in my success. Thank you, Jan, I'll always remember.

The last two tenors on my list of special people are Barry Morell and John Alexander. These two gentlemen have been my close friends and colleagues for many years of my career. Barry and John are two of the most unspoiled and highly respected tenors on the roster of the Metropolitan Opera. I have never seen a display of temperament on the part of either of them. Because both have beautiful voices and attractive stage personalities, they have been a considerable asset to the Metropolitan and many other major opera companies around the world. Their qualities are rare and much appreciated by those of us who have enjoyed so many performances with these two great American tenors.

Opinions and Disillusionment

Webster's Dictionary defines the word opera as a drama set to music, and I believe that the dramatization of a role is equally as important as the singing of it. In my opinion a valuable portion of one's study in preparing a part should be given to getting "into" the character; studying it thoroughly even before working on the music. This preparation has always been a great advantage. Knowing the character before reading the text gives one an even better understanding of the subject. It has been a fascination for me to seek complete identification with the inner personality of the character I was playing. With this method I was ready to be Mimi, Tosca, Minnie, and Manon when it came my time to play them.

This serious desire of mine to be a good actress, and the time I spent early in my career working toward that goal, really paid off and set me at ease to play any type of role, from the angelic to the cunning. What a pity so few young artists study the fundamentals of acting while they are learning to sing, for there is no one to give that kind of instruction when they reach the big leagues.

Another good reason for being thoroughly prepared is the general lack of sufficient rehearsal time prevailing in most opera houses today. Usually I was fortunate to work with colleagues who were as anxious as I to rehearse, and we would often put in more time than the company called for.

I have always been free to plan my own action for the roles in which I specialized. Most of the time my decisions were respectfully accepted by the director in charge. Their job is a difficult one, as some singers need to be led in every step they take. Then there are those who do very little acting. Believing the singing to be enough, they concentrate on the "pearly" tones, forgetting there is anyone else on-stage to whom they should be singing, and face the audience for most of the opera. I have had that experience with certain colleagues and nothing can be more frustrating.

During the last ten years I have been asked to give master classes at several different universities. When the Department of Theatre Arts at UCLA approached me in 1973, the timing was right. The campus was close to my home and I accepted. I was not interested in teaching voice during this short period of two weeks, but selected the subject of "Interpretive Techniques for the Musical Theatre," a topic which I believe is still being sadly neglected.

The sessions were four hours each school day for two weeks. After auditioning the class I chose a small group of singers to help me in my demonstrations. The first session was spent entirely on teaching the class how to make an entrance onstage for a concert, how to bow properly, acknowledge the accompanist, time their solos, manage their hands and feet, and the appropriate posture. There was a lesson on how to stand at the piano and all the many small details which are so important in presenting one's self before an audience.

The students who were aspiring to be opera singers were asked to prepare an aria and have it translated into English so they would know what they were saying. Then they sang for me, concentrating on the words and showing me they knew what they were trying to portray by their expressions. Later I brought various costumes from my wardrobe for the girls. One gown in particular had a long train which I tried to teach them how to control when sitting, walking, and turning. Is it not one of the most embarrassing moments, shattering all illusions, when a prima donna trips over her own costume? A train is not easy to manage, and we all have to learn by practice.

I remember a hysterically funny event that happened in a performance of *Tosca* years ago. An overexuberant baritone reached across the supper table while trying to grasp Tosca and upset a basket of fruit. The contents landed squarely on her train and when she turned to escape him, the fruit rode all the way across the stage before the poor girl was able to rid herself of it. My heart went out to her, for with the uproarious laughter coming from the audience, it no doubt took great control and concentration to continue.

Our next subject was the management of a large hoopskirt, probably the most difficult costume to wear. To learn how to maneuver this cumbersome skirt is another challenging study. My students had to practice sitting gracefully, manipulating the hoop so that when they rose the train would fall freely in its place, and controlling it against swinging while they walked. I stressed the importance of thinking about one's next move, so as not to get cornered by furniture and be forced to make an unattractive turn. A love scene while one is wearing a large costume such as this should be well rehearsed, for it can be beautiful if worked out carefully, and ridiculous if it is not. I continued to demonstrate many of my tricks of the trade and do hope some of them helped, but there is so much to learn that these admonitions were only illustrative.

This teaching experience convinced me more than ever that once a young aspiring vocal student decides opera is the career he or she wants, the conservatory is the place to study voice. A college education is not necessary for a singing career, and the study for a career in voice should never be considered just another subject in the curriculum of a university. A master class here and there is not enough help. More concentrated work on music is needed. A further point to be considered is that there are too few good vocal teachers in our universities and if a student is not lucky enough to work with one who knows what he is doing, a tender young voice can easily be ruined. I firmly believe anyone who has not been a professional vocalist should not teach voice. I do know, however, that the background of a few years of piano was extremely helpful to me. I would also strongly recommend a smattering of orchestration, harmony, reading music, and, by all means, languages, depending on one's personal interests whether in opera or concerts. But in the long run I do not believe that a serious career in music can be accomplished at the same time one is working for a college degree.

One day, long after I had attained my own goal, I was discussing the subject of auditions with Schuyler Chapin, then director of the Met. We agreed there was a lack of good prospects sent to the finals as "the best available" for consideration. I suggested that for the regional final contests, from which the winners are sent to New York, the judge who has the final say should be an experienced opera singer. I immediately realized I had put my foot squarely in my mouth. Schuyler lost no time in agreeing and asked if I would accept this assignment myself. Not knowing what I was getting into, I agreed to judge in my own city of Los Angeles.

Most of the singers brought before me and the other judges were poor prospects for the Metropolitan, with voices which were either pushed out of focus or already wobbling because of singing too long with poor technique. The only auditioner with a beautifully placed voice had little else to offer but a large ego. He could "belt out" an aria with free and lovely high notes, but had no experience and did not read music. I was appalled when I was pressured by the other judges to let him be their number one choice. It was grossly unfair to him and embarrassing to me. When will politics cease in auditions and teachers stop pushing their own unprepared pupils? Judges must look for more than just the ability to sing well one or two arias. I understand now why most of my colleagues duck the assignment.

I had just finished writing these last few words when the telephone rang. Much to my surprise it was my good friend and colleague Risë Stevens. How ironic it was that she would be calling at this time to say she had just accepted the responsibility of the auditions for the Met and was asking me to be a judge. I had to regret her offer, but was delighted to learn that a new Young Artists Development Program was being organized. Perhaps with that and a new set of standards for the competitions, those young singers who reach the finals and have the necessary qualifications will have a real chance to succeed. I am hoping for our aspiring youngsters and Risë that their dreams will all come true.

In the early 1960s the exciting news that Los Angeles would have a large civic center for the performing arts was received with great joy. The announcement that the facility would include a beautiful symphony hall, which would also accommodate opera, was the most exciting news to those of us whose major interest was in that field. However there were some discrepancies in the new Music Center's plans where opera was concerned. The orchestra pit was too small to handle the instruments necessary for the repertoire of a major opera company, and the dressing rooms were so small that one could hardly turn around in a good-sized hoopskirt. Many have wondered how that happened.

During this time I was being urged by local music lovers to help organize an opera company. There was more potential talent in this city hoping for a chance to find a career in their hometown than anywhere, except perhaps in New York. Large amounts of money were donated to this cause, including some of mine. I was sure that these contributions would be the incentive for the city of Los Angeles to get behind someone and support their own opera company. But in the end many people joined me in being disappointed. I was one of those who tried and failed, but at least I had lots of company. There must have been ten others who gave their valued time and concentrated efforts only to be disillusioned, finally retreating. Unfortunately, we never received the support of those influential people who should have given it.

James Doolittle had produced some excellent performances of opera at the Hollywood Bowl and the Greek Theatre for several years. In 1963 when he asked me if I would be interested in collaborating with him, I accepted. The conditions were that I would direct and cast my own performances. Alice Taylor, a highly respected musicologist and another soul dedicated to promoting opera in Los Angeles, frequently worked with Jim Doolittle and was a great asset.

Because the performances were to take place at the open-air Greek

Theatre during the summer, the off-season time of the Metropolitan, I was determined to surround myself with as many of my top colleagues as possible. Our first opera was *Madama Butterfly*, the appealing story which everyone knows and is so lovely in an outdoor atmosphere. Jim was well acquainted with the importance of having prominent names, and everyone we engaged for leading roles was currently singing at the Met. We also invited Fausto Cleva, the leading Italian conductor of the Metropolitan. I persuaded each of our artists to perform for half their fee on the premise that we were planning to get a Los Angeles opera company started. We played to sold-out houses and thought we were on our way.

In 1964 we put on three performances of *Tosca*. Again we had a great cast of Metropolitan Opera artists, and this time the great basso-buffo Salvatore Baccaloni was with us. Jim persuaded me to sing every performance, which I did, even though it presented quite a challenge indeed. I insisted on plenty of rehearsal time, worked out a schedule for each day and had a young aspiring singer stand in for my part while I was directing. We used as many local people as possible for the smaller parts. A number of singers from the Roger Wagner Chorale worked with us and several of them had promising talent. Jim Doolittle could not have been more cooperative.

My schedule was so demanding for the following five years that I had to forgo our project, but in 1970 we were able to pick up where we had left off. Once again we dusted off the lovely *Butterfly* sets, refurbishing them a bit, and added some new ideas to the production. For this performance of *Madama Butterfly* I engaged two adorable young ladies, Fujima Kansumi and Kyoko Hayakawa, both from Mme. Kansumi's dancing school, to do a charming dance during Butterfly's wedding celebration. We had the fine artist Kuniaka Hata as the Bonzo, who had also been in my first production of *Butterfly*. Being Japanese, Hata was extremely helpful in assisting me with teaching the men in the chorus how to wear their kimonos and showing them the typical oriental attitudes and mannerisms.

There was no way I could sing these performances and run the show as well, so I owed a great deal of thanks to my good friend and colleague Patrick Tavernia, a stage director at the Metropolitan for many years. Pat came out to assist me and took over while I sang. He was with me for every opera from then on and became a regular with the company. The last season we were at the Greek Theatre, Pat directed a fine production of *The Barber of Seville* with great success.

We assembled a number of famous artists who joined us, hoping that a fine company was in the making. Jim had engaged William Tury, an excellent set designer and able artist who was a great asset to the company and always eager to help. With the opportunity now to carry out my own ideas, I drew floor plans to scale for a production of *Madama Butterfly*, planning exactly the space in which I would work and furnishing my little house for the opera. From my plans Bill Tury designed the beautiful sets. We collaborated the same way for *Tosca*. I was sacrificing some high-paying summer dates but believed I was accomplishing something important. By giving our local singers an opportunity to learn from the pros, and seeing my own ideas come to life, I was alleviating many frustrations and enjoying the work. It was evident that the San Francisco Opera was not planning to return to Los Angeles, and with the excellent houses we were playing to we were all quite confident that a local opera company had a chance here.

That same year (1970), while I was celebrating my twenty-fifth anniversary in San Francisco, James Levine, music director-to-be of the Metropolitan Opera, was making his debut conducting my performance of *Tosca*. I was so impressed by this young man that I asked him if he would like to be introduced to Los Angeles by conducting my *Tosca* at the Greek Theatre the following summer. He was delighted, and with Anselmo Colzani and Barry Morell from the Met we had an exciting performance. The opera lovers turned out in droves to hear us, and Jimmy Levine returned several times after that as a guest conductor with the Los Angeles Symphony.

The sets were magnificent, traditional of course, but with some new ideas which made them more adaptable to the action I had planned. One thing in particular was added. The last act had always been a bit unbelievable to me. When the mob of soldiers enters at the end of the act to arrest Tosca after discovering she had murdered Scarpia, it was never made clear why they were unable to capture her. Our scene was designed from a picture of Castel Sant'Angelo where Mario's execution was to take place, and we added a large iron gate through which the soldiers had to enter. When Tosca hears them coming she wedges a table against the gate. The soldiers jam against it, trying to get in, but are delayed, giving Tosca time to escape. As Spoletta, Scarpia's aide, cries, *"Ah! Tosca, pagherai ben cara la sua vita!"* (Ah, Tosca, you will pay dearly for Scarpia's murder!), she decides to jump to her death. Saying *"Colla mia"* (With mine), she runs to the top of the parapet and cries, *"O Scarpia, avanti a Dio"* (O Scarpia, before God). The soldiers stop, shocked by her action, and she jumps into the river.

I requested that Bill Tury, the designer, make sure I would be seen in flight as long as possible in the jump before landing on a special mattress of cut foam rubber which was placed twelve feet below. Unlike most productions where Tosca's jump is short, this one was designed to show most of the long leap of twelve feet in profile and in full vision of the audience.

My jump was the most sensational stage event I have ever attempted in my quest for realism. Each day while the cast was on their coffee break I worked from a tall ladder, gradually jumping farther until I made it from the twelve-foot height. Everyone had been sworn to secrecy because I knew if my husband learned what I was planning, I would be grounded and in trouble.

The sensation of jumping that distance was frightening. The floor seemed to rush up to grab and then hold onto me. From that height the mattress looked like a postage stamp. The audience audibly gasped and my poor husband rushed backstage to see if I was all right. Even though it was daring and dangerous, it was also realistic and exciting.

After the inspiring reaction to this performance, Jim Doolittle tried hard to work out something with the Music Center, hoping we could take the company there for some performances. Much to our dismay Jim was always given excuses and we got nowhere.

A performance of *Madama Butterfly* in 1975 was the last time I worked with the Greek Theatre. In this performance I introduced a beautiful new ceremonial kimono which had been in the making in Japan for nearly two years. While singing in the Orient with the Metropolitan Opera, I selected and shipped back new costumes for the entire cast including a few key props. We went all out that year with beautiful new additions to the scenery, and I also added many new touches to the action. Jim Doolittle gave me everything I asked for, and it was one of the most beautiful productions of this opera I have ever appeared in.

Weeks earlier I had auditioned nearly a hundred singers for the chorus, selecting the best voices available. The majority were from the Roger Wagner Chorale. I was anxious to have the best blend of voices possible, and Robert Herr, who was our chorus master, did a superb job.

As an artist who has traveled to every state in the Union, it is incredible to me that our city, one of the largest and richest in the country, does not have a resident opera company. The state of Florida, half our size, has companies in Miami, Tampa, Orlando, Palm Beach, and Sarasota, all doing well and engaging good artists. Our neighboring city San Diego has a splendid company. Many great singers who have lived in Los Angeles have tried to help get opera established here, but they too finally gave up. What is the matter with our city? I have a few good guesses.

I enjoyed collaborating with Jim Doolittle and respected his knowledge in all kinds of theatre. I considered our performances first class. Too bad we could never muster the support we needed and have a chance to perform at the Music Center where we belonged. My colleagues say, "Relax, Dorothy, opera is doing well everywhere else. You've done your best and it's off your chest."

We Can't Win 'Em All

cannot believe there is anyone who has always made the right career decisions, no matter how great he or she is. We all have made mistakes and have had some regrets too. I do not mean to imply for one second that I hold the smallest amount of bitterness for my mistakes and misjudgments. I couldn't, because I am far too grateful for all I have accomplished in my career. However, those glaring errors for which I can blame no one but myself are also a part of my story.

I consider my recording business the big faux pas of my career. In 1946, my second year at the Metropolitan Opera, I signed a contract with RCA for five years, and made several successful recordings with this company. One of them, the duet from Massenet's *Thaïs* with Robert Merrill, won the Best Record of the Year award. Others were recordings of operettas, operatic arias, and popular music but there are no complete operas. I was quite unhappy and notwithstanding the entreaties of the company and my many friends there who were urging me to stay, my management was convinced I should make a change.

Columbia Records was making promising overtures to me with the added attraction of a large, lucrative guarantee. Though RCA advised us they were ready to meet this offer, I signed a long contract with Columbia which bound me to them exclusively.

Almost immediately troubles began with the musicians' union, and Columbia, along with all the other recording companies, was forced to make most of its recordings in Europe. The plans for my new company to do more opera were scrapped, therefore promises meant nothing and I lost out. The best that came out of that association were the arias I did with Fausto Cleva plus the operatic duets with Richard Tucker. The Gershwin and Kern albums with Percy Faith were a joy and very successful, but I never recorded a complete opera with the company. In the meantime, to my misfortune, RCA, also forced to operate in Europe, decided to make many complete operatic recordings abroad with several of my Metropolitan Opera colleagues. I certainly had missed the boat.

Ironically, it was I who was singing *Manon Lescaut* and *La Fanciulla del West* with sold-out houses at the Metropolitan, while someone else was recording them. This really hurt, and was the only great disappointment of my career, as it also has been for my faithful fans who continue to search out every pirated record of my voice they can find regardless of cost. Though my list of recordings may be shorter than some of my contemporaries, I shall always be proud of what I have recorded.

Who was it who said, "You can't win 'em all"?

Another unfortunate happening occurred in my hometown of Los Angeles, which curtailed my singing in the Hollywood Bowl and also with the Los Angeles Symphony. When I invited James Levine to direct my *Tosca* performances at the Greek Theatre after his big success in San Francisco, Ernest Fleischmann, who had recently become manager of the Los Angeles Symphony, came to the performance. He was obviously impressed, for shortly thereafter Jim was engaged and I too was offered a gala opera night at the Hollywood Bowl. I had been a regular there for years, singing with the symphony, opera, and popular nights with my good friend John Green. When Mr. Fleischmann's offer was presented I was pleased, and wanting to make it a special occasion, I offered to share it with a tenor. Since I desired to do some of the less hackneyed operatic duets in my repertoire, I felt we needed a tenor familiar with them.

I departed for New York almost immediately after this initial offer, leaving the matter in the hands of my capable West Coast manager, Herbert Fox of Columbia Artists. The agreement was that I would have approval of the tenor. Upon my return I was informed by Herbert that the tenor had already been selected without consulting me. This turn of events was considerably disturbing. I knew the singer well, had sung with him, and admired him greatly, but doubted he was right for these particular duets. The second blow came when I asked about the conductor. This person's name was completely unknown to me at that time, and when I questioned whether he was an opera conductor, Mr. Fleischmann's indignant reply was, "How dare you question my judgment." I had had too many experiences over the years with symphony men who had no feel at all for opera, especially those by Puccini, Cilèa, and Charpentier. My answer had to be, "I think I should know better who can sing the operas which have been my career for the last forty-plus years as well as who can conduct them."

I have had a wonderful career in this area and few knew why I was no longer singing in Los Angeles. Obviously I was never forgiven for questioning Mr. Fleischmann's judgment. It was therefore his privilege to decide that I would never again sing with the Los Angeles Symphony. It has been said there were other famous artists in Los Angeles who have experienced similar problems with Mr. Fleischmann.

My long engagements at the two major opera companies in my own country were certainly the most valuable part of my career. But when I count the many exciting invitations I missed to sing abroad more often, I wonder how different my career might have been.

In 1960 I was given the opportunity to go to Rome with Basile to record, which might have been a step in the right direction. And an engagement at the same time to sing at the London Palladium may have mended my poor relations with London. A few years earlier I had been offered a contract to sing thirteen performances of *Madama Butterfly* in English at Covent Garden. During those years everything was sung in English at this great opera house, and they would make no exceptions. Since then, however, they have accepted many operas in their original text and still do today. I was so much in love with the Italian text of *Butterfly* that I could not bring myself to do it in English and turned the offer down. That was the end of Covent Garden for me, and I admit now that I had been foolish.

Another very possible error in judgment was my declining of an invitation from Lazlo Halas, the first director of the City Center Opera and an excellent conductor. Lazlo, with whom I began my career in New York, asked me repeatedly to come to Barcelona to sing *Louise* with him, but again I allowed myself to be so tied up with the Met that I was never able to accept. That engagement I should have done.

There were numerous Broadway shows offered along the way which tempted me, and one in particular. Cole Porter had written a new Broadway musical, and when I met him a few weeks earlier, he told me about his new work, *Kiss Me, Kate*. Soon afterward he asked me to meet with him at his home when he was casting this wonderful show. I was sure he was going to ask me to do Kate, and I was thrilled with the idea even though it would be necessary to sacrifice my opera dates for a period of time. When I discovered that it was Bianca he had in mind for me, I didn't accept and have often wondered if that too was a mistake.

Looking back now, these missed opportunities and things that might have been were not to be. They might have even disrupted my wonderful career. I will never miss the things I didn't do, and I'm so glad I did the things I decided to do.

The Red Carpet in Russia

One of the most unusual experiences of my entire professional life came in the form of an invitation from the Ministry of Culture of the Soviet Union to be the first American opera singer to sing on a tour of four of their leading lyric theatres. Realizing how fascinating this could be, I accepted gladly, particularly as at the same time my husband Jack had completed arrangements with the Soviet Academy of Science to come and lecture at their Institutes of Biology. He had entertained several of Russia's leading medical scientists at his own Brain Research Institute at UCLA.

This gave me the idea that we could go at the same time, and we waited for the opportunity to work out the trip together. However, it became clear after a while how difficult this would be, since the ministries of Culture and Science did not seem to be able to coordinate our travel schedules.

I was fully conscious that there were many people, friends and fans who disapproved of my trip. Even some journalists were shocked that I would consider performing in a Marxist country. But I always felt that as an artist I had no business being involved in politics. Jack eventually was convinced that the way was clear for him, too, so I signed a contract for my appearances.

We had reservations to leave Los Angeles on January 14, 1962, at 12:15 P.M. The day before, a member of the Russian Embassy in Washington telephoned, informing us that we must delay our departure. It would be only a matter of a few days, he declared. I made frantic calls to my secretary, Vicki, who had remained in New York after my Met performance a few days before, and to Peter Gravina, who was going with us to handle the press relations. The plan was for them to meet us in Paris.

In the meantime, there was no word whatsoever about Jack's visa and we canceled our reservations with Pan American. The airline unfortunately gave the newspapers this information, with the result that our telephone never stopped ringing. I tried my best to put off the reporters, not knowing what had caused this counter-order. To calm my nerves I went off with my husband and played eighteen holes of golf.

Tuesday morning at 7 A.M., Leverett Wright, at that time my manager from Columbia Concerts, woke me up out of a sound sleep to say he had received notification from the Soviet Embassy that it had all been a mistake and that I was to depart as soon as possible, since my singing dates had to be respected. "But what about Jack?" I asked. "Don't worry about him," he replied, "he will undoubtedly follow soon. You must leave without him or we will be in trouble with the contract."

"I don't want to leave without him," I answered firmly.

"Don't you realize that a signed agreement must be respected," he pleaded, "or the consequences will not be pleasant."

More calls immediately followed to New York to alert Vicki and Peter. The arrangements were that there would be three first-class fares paid by the Soviet Union, plus all our hotel expenses, with my fees to be paid in American dollars. They also gave me fifty rubles a day for pocket money.

The next morning I flew alone via the polar route to Paris, bringing with me three large suitcases carrying my elaborate costumes, wigs, tiaras, and even several important props in order to make sure that my presentations would be faultless. I was relieved to be met by Vicki and Peter, who had arrived a short time before, and we took off immediately for Moscow. From Los Angeles to the Russian capital I was in the air for twenty-three hours and arrived in a state of utter exhaustion. We landed on January 17, and it was snowing hard. Ice was everywhere, but the air was crisp and dry.

We were met by a large delegation that included Mme. Offitzerova, head of the Ministry of Culture, with whom I had lunched in Los Angeles; two scientists, an interpreter, and several other people. The reception committee could not have been more surprised when Jack was not with me, and it was apparent they were not informed that his visa was delayed. And this was not all. They had met several planes for two consecutive days, expecting us to be on one of them. I began to be somewhat apprehensive for it seemed quite clear that there was no coordination whatsoever. What was in store for me?

But I was so tired I followed them into the airport where I was presented with some lovely flowers. We sailed through customs, all formalities of entry set aside; we were given the VIP treatment. The welcome was very cordial, and it was made clear that we were guests of the State. Conversation was not difficult, since several members of the party spoke English. Finally we left for the long drive to Moscow and the Ukraine Hotel. I simply could not believe the size of the people we saw in the lobby. We were later told that these huge men came from Siberia. They were heavily bearded and wore foot-high fur hats.

We felt like midgets, and weary as I was, I wondered whether I was somewhat delirious!

We met my interpreter, who was introduced as Galina. We later called her Gala, and she informed me that we would be leaving for Tbilisi early the next morning, a long air flight south of Moscow over the Caucasus. The city used to be known as Tiflis, but its name had been changed at the time of the revolution. We slept very little that night, for the hotel was very cold. I was also fighting jet lag. Vicki got me up with difficulty shortly after dawn with some Russian tea and a dry bun (and I do mean dry) and we were off.

Gala, who traveled with us on the whole tour, had never been to Tbilisi. She gave me fifty rubles, then the equivalent of about fifty dollars, to pay for the meals on the plane. It was a jet and our seats were reserved. All the eyes of the passengers were glued on my enormous mink coat. Vicki was taking a picture of the high and rugged snow covered peaks when Gala gently took the camera out of her hand and said pleadingly, "Please, please no pictures!"

We arrived at Tbilisi, one of the Soviet Union's most ancient cities, and the reception we received was very touching. The director and five artists of the opera all stood in line at the foot of the plane's steps and applauded. The women received me with broad smiles and violets (at that time of the year they must have come from Africa). There were welcoming speeches in Georgian, a language Gala barely understood, so the translation was an approximation. Nevertheless I felt their warmth and sincerity. Three cars drove us to the hotel; a relic right out of the distant past with ceilings twenty to twenty-five feet high. All the members of the party escorted us to our rooms. On the table in the large drawing room of the Royal Suite we found fruit, chocolate, cakes, candy, and wine. Everyone drank wine and there were many toasts.

I found the Georgians to be the most warmhearted and charming of all the Russians we met, with an emotional, Latin type of warmth. After they left I had a short rest and then began to get ready, for we were to be the guests of the theatre's director at a ballet performance in a pretty theatre of fourteen hundred seats that reminded me of the beautiful Teatro Fenice in Venice.

A wire from Jack announcing his arrival in Moscow was awaiting me at the hotel. What a great relief that was. There was also an invitation to lunch with Ambassador Thompson at the United States Embassy on my return to Moscow. The following day, Friday, January 19, was to be my first rehearsal, but that night we again suffered agonies from the cold. I wore all I owned to bed—leotards, undershirts, and two flannel nighties.

When breakfast arrived it consisted of shashlik, raw onions, goat cheese, and tea. I had asked for eggs, but they never materialized. There was no point in ringing the bell for it did not work. It was still there from czarist days but only as an ornament. Despite the faded splendor of the living room and the bedroom, the only warmth I could find was in the enormous bathroom. The first thing Vicki, Peter and I did was to make that our headquarters. The hot water was a problem; it ran only a few hours a day or when I specially asked for it.

Upon arriving at the theatre I was ushered into the salon, which was jammed with artists, the chorus, and many visitors. At first it was not easy to sing *La Traviata* in Italian with everyone else singing in Georgian and Russian. But I was delighted to find that the conductor and the principals were all very good, warm, expressive, and eager to please me. The tenor was handsome and had a fine voice.

In the U.S.S.R. most Soviet performers sing in Russian and visitors in other languages. Knowing this opera inside out was a considerable help, for I had to sing all the other parts to myself in Italian in order to get my cues. What caused endless complications was that frequently the Russian words did not fit in time and length with the Italian text, which often happens in a translation, and in this case they interpolated extra notes, which was more confusing.

In the second act when Violetta cries her heart out, *"Amami, Alfredo,"* the tenor sang, I am not sure what, along with me, making it a duet rather than a solo. I stopped the conductor and asked through Gala what this was all about. He answered, "Verdi did not write it, but we like it this way." Again he sang with me when I bade him farewell, and I still have no idea what the words were that had been added. I decided to let them do it their way and not create any problems with this odd version.

As we proceeded with the piano rehearsal I realized that a run-through with orchestra was absolutely necessary. Too many details had been changed. As I was stepping into a role of an opera that had already been much rehearsed by the company, they had not planned an orchestra rehearsal for me. But I insisted on it, and my wish was granted graciously the next day. I realized the importance of a smooth performance for my debut in the Soviet Union because it would be covered by the press.

After the first rehearsal I was given a tremendous banquet in the hotel restaurant, which lasted from three o'clock until seven in the evening. Dishes came and went with many local specialties; all sorts of superb wines were served, and I had to nibble and drink as much as possible so as not to offend their sensibilities. Interestingly, their wines are numbered and each one is ordered numerically. After a long visit from some members of the company, we were finally allowed to go to bed and get some rest. Problems again arose with my colossal breakfast the next morning. The eggs I had asked for seemed impossible to obtain, and as a result of language complications, two entire chickens were brought instead.

The rehearsal began at noon, and to my amazement the orchestra only played the scenes in which I appeared, skipping all the others. The stage was a madhouse, crowded with people who obviously did not belong to the theatre. Gala explained, "They have all come to see the American."

In the four cities in which I sang I discovered that the Russian system never seems to have the same artists who have done the rehearsals for the performance. I always had a different tenor and baritone from those with whom I had done all the preliminary work. I invariably met my performing colleagues at the very last minute; they usually introduced themselves and presented me with a floral tribute just before I went onstage.

Regarding the stage direction, I soon realized that my fluent Italian was inadequate; French was seldom better, and English was impossible. However, I found the artists eager to cooperate with my action and anxious to have me direct them.

That night we again went to the ballet and this time saw one of their "greats," a fifty-three year-old who had danced in the United States thirty years before. He was magnificent, and when we went backstage to congratulate the performers, they presented me with the flowers that had been thrown onstage to them.

Upon my return to the hotel, a distinguished-looking man was waiting. He explained that he was the impresario of the company, "like Hurok," he said. "If you give me a kiss, I shall hand you a very special present." He was so charming, I obliged. He then gave me a telegram from Jack, announcing that he would have to miss my Tbilisi debut. He had been scheduled for a speaking engagement that same evening in Kiev, but he would definitely make my Wednesday performance of *Madama Butterfly*. The telegram had obviously been opened and read, for it was well worn.

On January 21, I made my Russian debut as Violetta. The trying circumstances of Georgian and Russian being sung along with my Italian, and my preoccupation with the sets and props (so modest according to our standards), all vanished after the delirious success that greeted me. The audience chanted my name in unison and yelled, "We love you," as they hung out of the boxes so far I was fearful they would fall. The only incident that marred the performance was the loud hissing directed at the tenor when he stepped on the train of my dressing gown in the last act.

There were flowers in profusion thrown to me. The public simply did not want to leave the theatre; they kept calling me back repeatedly. Peter counted twenty-six curtain calls. Masses of people followed me to the hotel, demanding autographs. In a conversation with someone who spoke English, I discovered that the reason they all knew me was because the film I did with Mario Lanza, *The Great Caruso,* had been showing all through the Soviet Union and was a smash hit. Everyone seemed to have seen it. This also explained why they kept calling me "actress" as I walked on the streets.

The people seemed to know my every move, and the next day many were again waiting in the lobby to follow me and hand me little bouquets as I was leaving for the theatre. I was anxious to get an idea about the scenery for *Madama Butterfly,* my second opera there, and although none of it had come out of storage yet, we began to work musically.

After the rehearsal there was a beautiful banquet given by the entire company, including the Georgian Ballet. The site of the feast was a restaurant atop the Television State Building, fifteen hundred feet above the city, where we found a magnificent table waiting with all kinds of food and specialties of the area. Before each assigned place there were five bottles: two of wine, one each of brandy, vodka, and soda. I never saw anyone touch the soda.

The courses were endless and there were many, many, many toasts. Peter and I were kept busy responding, and as the evening wore on they became more sentimental and even political at times. Their custom of putting the glass upside down upon the head after a toast was to prove they hadn't missed a drop, but for those of us not accustomed to drinking so much, it was a rough experience. We knew we had to be on our toes, and I am very proud of that evening. One toast I recall most vividly was delivered by the director and touched me deeply. "Dorothy Kirsten, you are the strongest link in our chain of friendship between the United States and the Soviet Union." That one made the papers back home.

They then asked me how they could entertain us, and I told them that, having enjoyed the Georgian dancers when they were on tour in the United States, I would love to see them again. The dancers seemed pleased with my request, jumped to their feet and before I knew it were forming that familiar circle, shuffling their quick steps along the way and giving us a great show. My host, a huge man, lifted me off my feet and I joined them, trying the best way I could to imitate what they were doing. I thought Peter and Vicki would burst with laughter. Singers and dancers singing together the old sentimental Georgian folk songs made it a gay and happy occasion.

Despite the censorship and lack of communication, the Russians all knew about the Twist, which was then the current rage in America, and asked me to show them how to do it. Peter came to my rescue and we put on the best performance we could, disregarding the fact that the man banging on the piano did not play Twist music, nor did he have the slightest idea what the rhythm should be. Of all things, this made headlines in the New York *Times*.

At the stage rehearsal scheduled for the next day, the baritone never turned up. I was given to understand that he was ill. The second act depends so much on the byplay between Cio Cio San and Sharpless, and with so little rehearsal I became quite concerned.

Suzuki, sung by an excellent mezzo, and the little girl who played Trouble, my child, disconcerted me by weeping all the time. "They are so profoundly touched by your interpretation," Gala offered. In the third act while I was singing, the child kept patting me affectionately. It was very nice, but all this worried me. Dealing with such highly emotional people, I knew that my performance would be deeply affected. *Butterfly* is so moving in itself and my own tears are drain enough on my emotions.

Peter had taken off in the morning to do some sightseeing and it became a source of preoccupation back at the hotel when he did not return. He finally turned up in considerable distress and told us of being arrested because he was taking pictures. At the jail he kept saying, "Dorothy Kirsten, *The Great Caruso*," and finally was allowed to go free. There had been considerable publicity about us and the police were at last convinced he was Mario Lanza! Vicki and I laughed and laughed, but not Peter. He did not find the experience at all funny.

Jack's call finally got through from Kiev. He had been trying to reach me for days, and still hoped to arrive in time for my performance.

Suddenly it was that day, and at the theatre chaos reigned backstage. Since there had been no dress rehearsal, props were brought in for my inspection. Next, about five hundred photographs arrived taken at the performance of *La Traviata*. They were some of the best I have ever seen. I was asked to sign the pictures so they could be given to the public outside who were clamoring for them. Cameras were brought into the theatre, for there had been such a rush for tickets that they had decided to televise the performance with my permission. "Why not," I said.

In the midst of all the confusion I was trying to keep my equilibrium in order to prepare for this difficult opera. Having my own costumes gave me a certain feeling of security, but I needed time and concentration to do my make-up. The dressing room was quite nice, but with all the flowers and gifts, when they brought in a large television set there was little room left to move around in.

The set for the first act was pretty, but the stage was dangerous. The flooring was quite uneven and I had to be careful where I put my feet. The bridge on which I had to make my initial entrance was made of wooden slats with large spaces between them. After managing not to fall, I sang the rest of the evening in my *tabis* (little Japanese socks). The stage director had asked me to draw for him a sketch of the screen that I had requested for my death scene. After I explained that it must be a certain height, I kneeled and showed him it had to measure as high as my nose. He and his associates all said, "*Da, da, da,*" in unison. The screen was made of white cloth and bamboo, a bit too high, but I said, "Perfect," and their faces showed great pleasure . . . so did mine. They just couldn't do enough to please me.

My next request had been for the petals with which Suzuki and I decorate the house in the second act. Paper was at a premium in Russia at that time and there was no way of explaining what "crepe" paper was. But we did get our petals. They were too heavy to float, but part of the effect was there, and I was greatly pleased when Peter said it came off beautifully.

To my great surprise Pinkerton appeared wearing a sword with his uniform. It did not inhibit him at all when he lifted me off my feet, as I suggested he do, and carried me into the house after the wedding scene at the end of the first act. The public went wild.

But there were more surprises in store for me. My attention was caught by the supposed photograph of Pinkerton onstage, which looked nothing like the tenor but was that of a heavily mustachioed commissar instead. And when I saw their version of our American flag, I nearly died—twenty stars and nine stripes. At the end of the performance I could not resist asking for the flag, which they graciously gave to me. How strange it was that in this part of the Soviet Union they knew so little about the Japanese, and it was hardly believable that they did not know the American flag.

That particular second act of *Butterfly* was probably the most emotionally upsetting one of my career. The child who played Trouble was a "doll." I learned how to direct her with a few words in Russian. She was fine, except for wanting constantly to hug me. When she saw tears in my eyes, she affectionately patted my face and whispered something I could not understand. Suzuki, a fine actress, wept the whole way through.

The third act went well, but by this time I was becoming concerned about where Jack was. Each time I had a chance I would glance toward the wings, hoping to see him there, but the act ended with no sign of him. The roar of the people and the never ending curtain calls distracted me. I had thought my *Traviata* received an exciting reception, but this was something unbelievable.

The crowd waiting for me was not going to be deprived of a close look or the personal touch of a handshake. They handed me everything from flowers to little charming boxes, Russian recordings, and candies. My interpreter took her silver bracelet off her arm and insisted I take it. We left the theatre at last and my feet never touched the ground. They carried me on their shoulders to my hotel with the whole crowd following us and carrying my flowers behind.

At the hotel the impresario, "Mr. Hurok," rescued me from the crowd and accompanied us to our rooms. By that time I was determined to get some answers about where my husband was—and did.

It seemed Jack was still in Kiev. His trip had been canceled because of a storm over the Caucasus and he would miss coming to Tbilisi. What a disappointment! It seemed strange to me that I had no wire from him to that effect, and I insisted I would not leave Tbilisi until I communicated with him. The confusion that followed was ridiculous —the Bolshoi Theatre in Moscow calling me to come, and the Embassy trying to locate Jack. However, we finally got things straightened out, and I was told Jack would be at the airport in Moscow to meet me.

Leaving Tbilisi was difficult for us, as we had made many friends. There were two talented people, the conductor of the orchestra and the mezzo who sang Suzuki, whom I wanted very much to help. However, there appeared to be no way I could, and for that I was sorry. I received several cards from the mezzo, but there was never a return address.

We had great difficulty in packing all the gifts I received, putting as many as we could in our luggage. When we got to the airport, where again I was deluged with recordings, books, fruit, and a basket with four bottles of my favorite wine, we had to be helped on the plane. As we pulled away from the runway, our Russian friends were all waving and throwing kisses. I'll never forget Tbilisi!

The trip to Moscow was bumpy. I was emotionally drained, but delighted at last to see my husband waiting there. Because of my delayed departure I had missed my reception at the United States Embassy; however, I knew there was ample time in Moscow to see the ambassador and pay my respects.

Several days before I had told Gala that I would refuse to return to the Ukraine Hotel, and it was arranged that we be taken to the

Budapest. It was warm and comfortable, which was a blessing, for I was to make my debut at the Bolshoi Theatre two nights later.

The next day I went to rehearse at this famous theatre and was overcome by its beauty; superb crystal chandeliers, six tiers of boxes, gold leaf everywhere, and red velvet—a fabulous sight! I was intrigued by the hugeness of the stage and the excellent organization used to keep all the sets and costumes. That day the temperature had dropped considerably to 30° below zero. It was quite a change and I had to be exceedingly careful not to catch cold. I was told that every representative of the American papers, radio services, and magazines would be present for my debut in Moscow and I wanted to be at my best.

When I was advised there would be no orchestra rehearsal because this opera had already been rehearsed for the season, I was astonished but not dismayed. I knew my role and was quite confident that with a good piano rehearsal and a workout with the tenor and baritone I would be able to relax.

The company was apologetic and when I asked to see photographs of the production to study my action, they were immediately supplied.

The stage director, a woman, spoke no English, Italian, or French, the languages in which I was prepared to communicate. Through my interpreter she simply said, "Tell Miss Kirsten to do her own action and we will follow." We worked out all my scenes and everyone was overly cooperative. Then came the "bomb." They told me that the Alfredo and Germont with whom I had rehearsed would not be those with whom I would sing the performance! But there were other shocks to follow. When I reached the theatre early that evening among the masses of flowers and gifts awaiting me was the unwelcome news that the conductor with whom I had rehearsed was ill and there was a last-minute substitution in the person of a young, inexperienced replacement. There was no opportunity to meet or speak to the new conductor before the performance began.

The two leading men whom I had not met arrived at my dressing room door to introduce themselves bearing flowers and broad friendly smiles. A bit stunned but determined, I prepared to enter the strangest performance of *Traviata* in my life.

Things went well until it came time for my big aria at the end of the first act. The conductor had not been told that I sing an uncut version of that aria and I was forced to jump several bars to cover this misunderstanding. No one seemed to notice but me. From then on it was smooth sailing, and the reception once more amazing.

The entire production was lovely and I was particularly struck by a detail in the last act. In Violetta's room, when she is dying, there were marks on the wall that subtly indicated the fact that most of her paintings had been sold because she was penniless. Another nice touch was Germont bringing her flowers when he came.

When I was receiving the applause at the end, much to my astonishment two enormous white lilac trees were presented among the other flowers and wheeled in by two hefty stagehands. When the last curtain call was over, I was ushered into a reception hall where it was requested I do separate interviews with the different press media, a long and protracted affair. The American press waited to be last, and it was then that I met the attentive men of our press offices and promised to see that they continued to get the stories of the whole tour. They also received my beautiful white lilacs.

The train trip from Moscow to Riga, capital of what used to be Latvia, followed the next day. We were amazed to hear two days later when Jack made the same trip that he had been very comfortable on that train. Something must have gone wrong with ours, because it had been a totally different experience. Vicki, Peter, Gala, and I spent most of the night in the same compartment. It was like traveling in a refrigerator. The water was frozen everywhere, and the windows had an inch-thick coating of ice.

Those seventeen hours seemed eternal as we huddled up in our fur coats with all the blankets we could gather covering us. There was absolutely no way to reach the diner because of the ice between the cars and when Peter went out to try to get some food, he found the doors completely stuck. The saving grace was the tea, available all night in our car, and the brandy which we fortunately had brought with us. We sat up most of the trip trying to escape pneumonia and learning Russian card games from Gala. When we finally decided to try sleep we simply wore everything to bed, and I kept on my fur hat.

Upon arriving in Riga the next morning we were a bedraggled group, but when Gala informed us that there would probably be a large reception committee to meet us, we spruced up and tried our best to look fit. She was right. At the station stood more than a dozen people, two with a large package covered with newspaper. As I stepped down the packages were quickly unwrapped and a dozen beautiful white calla lilies were presented to me. I was so touched that I held them close to me only to hear them crack. It was 40° below zero. They were frozen stiff and upon reaching the hotel room immediately turned brown.

The Hotel Riga, which we had looked forward to, was almost as cold as the train, but we did manage to get hold of an electric heater that we placed in the bathroom and, as in Tbilisi, that became our headquarters.

Riga is often called the Paris of Russia and it still has a certain worn elegance. Many more people spoke English, though not in the theatre. I was better able to communicate there in French.

Our first evening we were invited to hear a performance of *Eugene Onegin* so I could see the theatre and hear the tenor and baritone who were to sing opposite me in *La Traviata*. That evening I also learned my performances had been switched and that *Tosca* would be my second opera.

The leading tenor told me he had sung *Otello* here with Leonard Warren but I would be the first American woman ever to sing in this opera house, nearly two hundred years old. The conductor seemed very good, and my colleagues too, so I was eagerly looking forward to our work together. Both of my operas had been sold out long in advance and the company was already asking me to delay my departure.

The pace was exhausting, but I never felt better in my life and knew that this would be an experience like none other in my career. Being of partly Nordic origin was no doubt an asset, for I seemed to thrive in the cold, crisp air even though at times I was uncomfortable. My voice was always "there" for me, clear and strong, and I was enjoying every note I sang.

As usual there was little rehearsal, just a run-through, as we call it, of the music. But this time the sounds I heard were more strange than ever. The tenor was singing in Bulgarian, the baritone in Russian, and the chorus in Latvian, all combined with my Italian. It was a riot, and when Germont sang something that sounded like "*Plotshcka, Plotshcka*" (*Piangi, piangi*, weep, weep), I had to keep myself from bursting out in laughter. But the singers were great and no one seemed to care.

Traviata was another unbelievable triumph, with the ever present flowers, the rhythmic applause, and the shouting public. At the stage door I was confronted with a regular mob scene and carried once again to my hotel on the shoulders of two big Latvians, surrounded by some two hundred opera lovers. The people were so warm and friendly that I was never frightened by this unusual custom.

Before leaving the theatre I had been asked to join my colleagues onstage for a touching ceremony. A seventy-year-old musician who had been with the orchestra for fifty years was retiring. He was carried through the opera house in a large gold chair on the shoulders of six of his fellow musicians and serenaded with Latvian folk songs by the chorus and orchestra while we all threw flowers to him. He wept and so did we.

Back at the hotel, we really celebrated. Jack was once again with us and it was a joyous time. Our supper was divine and I remember so well the enormous bowl of the most delicious caviar I have ever tasted. That, with my special Georgian wine, ⚹19, was a feast.

Peter Gravina played an important part on this trip by handling our press relations, and when business called him back before we were through with the tour, I was more than reluctant to see him leave. However, when we had left Moscow the press advised me that they would be calling and hoped I could give them stories directly. I had been keeping a diary most of the time, but now I went to bed every night with pencil in hand. My notes for them and for my book have paid off.

Jack and I had seen little of each other until Riga, and it was such fun to compare notes. He had been lecturing and visiting the Institutes of the Soviet Scientists and their members who had come to see him in Los Angeles. Until this time we had both escaped catching cold, but poor Jack was nursing a beauty, and I was forced to take all precautions.

The rehearsal for *Tosca* was more complicated. This opera has a very dramatic second act, and the action seldom succeeds without careful planning. The baritone was excellent, but the only way we could communicate was for me to play both roles and indicate what I wanted. When he wanted me to do something for him, he did the same. We both exchanged new ideas, and he seemed as pleased as I was. It was from him that I learned the interesting treatment with the dagger that I speak of elsewhere in this book. Their entire conception of this work, particularly in the second act, was so different from ours that the director let me take over and enact all the parts to show them how we do this opera at the Met. They all seemed delighted to see a different interpretation.

After this demanding rehearsal I felt tired and began to feel I too was catching a cold. Some anxious hours followed, but between Jack's tender care and Vicki's good nursing, plus God's will, I got through with flying colors and no one at the theatre knew anything about it.

The director of the company brought greetings from the heads of the Latvian state who were in the audience, and at the end of my performance they came onstage to congratulate me along with the entire company and the orchestra. As before we went through the same treatment with a wonderful mob of smiling faces, and I was proud of my job again that night.

The next morning was a busy one; people arrived to say good-bye to Jack, and newspapers wanted "statements" and my "impressions." As we started to leave the hotel, much to my astonishment, there stood my cast of last night and the director of the company. They all accompanied us to the plane and when we arrived at the airport, they gathered around and I answered questions about all the American singers they knew by their recordings. It was amazing how many they did know. They spoke about my film with Lanza and were eager for any information about us. I told them our purpose in coming was to better relations with the people, and we were happy to be there if it helped. They were cautious about responding to that in front of my interpreter, and I felt more fear in these people than in those below the Caucasus.

The plane trip to Leningrad took less than an hour. The entire company was there to greet us, just as the one in Riga had been at the airport to wave us good-bye. The city is very beautiful, and the Astoria Hotel gave us rooms on the square just across the way from St. Isaac's Cathedral, a fabulous old church which is now a museum.

When I arrived at the theatre for my rehearsal, after meeting the director, I was ushered into the hall where the cast was waiting. The walls were lined with people. There had always been a hundred or so everywhere I rehearsed, but this was incredible and a bit unnerving. It was another challenge and being on my best behavior I decided not to complain.

There were no props to work with, as usual, and as we went along the director indicated a chair here, a sofa there and so on. This was my fourth version of this opera in the U.S.S.R. and a great deal of concentration was needed. The curtain was always at 7 P.M., except at the Bolshoi, where it goes up at 6:30. This meant I was at the theatre at 5 P.M. in order to warm up and prepare myself calmly. My costumes had never been so well cared for, and being as fussy as I am about my appearance onstage, it was a delight to know I looked my best.

They told me ticket prices were doubled for the second performance because of the demand, and people's heads popped up out of every available space; standees crowded the wings; and even the prompter's boxes along the front of the stage held three or four observers. Since he was no help to me, prompting in Russian, it didn't matter.

In the first act, along with the chorus, there were several dancers onstage. As Violetta invites her guests to dance, I couldn't have been more pleased to be swept off my feet by the leading dancer of the ballet in a grand few steps of the waltz. This was something new, a charming bit of business and very fitting for the scene just before Violetta collapses.

It was also in this theatre, in the second act, when we had an unprecedented stop in the performance. After my impassioned cry, *"Amami, Alfredo"* (Love me, Alfredo), and the highly emotional music that followed, the response of the audience was so great the tenor could not continue. The conductor was finally forced to put down his baton and the stage director motioned to the tenor to come off and bring me back. This had never occurred before to me, and I think shouldn't happen, for the sake of continuity.

Unfortunately, the poor tenor was so shaken that he forgot his words, and it must have been very difficult for the baritone who was about to enter for his big aria. I was again embarrassed when, bowing with the other artists whom I knew were among their top people, the audience started yelling, *"Nyet, nyet,"* and they had to leave me alone onstage.

Leningrad had produced the loudest yet of the demonstrations, and I was way up there on cloud nine. The former Russian capital, said to be the most sophisticated city of the Soviet Union, overwhelmed me with the reception of my Violetta, once more the role of my debut, and moved me deeply. At the end every important artist of the company came to my room with flowers and little gifts. I can think of no other place in the world where such respect and warmth is expressed between fellow artists.

There was little time to see the sights or go to the theatre, but we did manage to visit the great Hermitage Museum long enough to know that I would love to see it again. We were also thrilled to see a great performance of *Boris Godounoff* one evening from the Royal Box of the Kirov Theatre where I was performing. Curiously, the Bolshoi and the Kirov are almost identical theatres, except for the velvet, which in Moscow is red and in Leningrad blue.

About a year after our return from the Soviet Union, Jack came home from the office one evening with a story which had us both puzzled for about two weeks. He told me that he had received a telephone call from a representative of the State Department in Washington to ask if he would give an appointment to a principal dancer of the Kirov Ballet troupe, which was touring the United States at the time and was expected in Los Angeles two weeks later. Jack asked the representative what the dancer wanted to see him about, only to be told mysteriously that no further information was available except that the person was a male lead of the company. Out of curiosity Jack agreed to give an appointment as requested, and we waited eagerly for the unfolding of the mystery.

Two weeks later a strikingly handsome young man, probably in his early thirties, two State Department representatives, and a translator arrived at Jack's office. The young man almost blurted out, "I danced with your wife," which did nothing but complicate the mystery. The answer was forthcoming in a slowly unfolding conversation through the interpreter and a letter withheld until the last. It seemed that the young man was the leading male dancer of the Kirov Ballet who had swept me off my feet for the waltz in the first act of *Traviata* at the theatre in Leningrad.

The story that followed was fascinating. I mentioned earlier that in almost every city we visited together we were entertained by all of the principal scientists where Jack lectured. It was our custom to invite our hosts to attend the opera as our guests. In this case Professor Airipetience, head of the Pavlov Laboratory at Koltushi, attended the performance with Jack. It was he who had written the letter. He described the dancer as his promising student in neuroscience at the university. The letter, which was very interesting in itself, revealed a facet of life in the U.S.S.R. quite unusual here.

The dancer (Jack has mislaid the letter and we don't have his name) had entered ballet school as a child and had been performing leading roles with the Kirov for twenty years. Realizing that he was approaching "retirement," he decided to study at the University of Leningrad as the equivalent of a graduate student in biology to prepare for a second career as a teacher and scientist. We have often wondered if he accomplished his goal; he probably did.

We returned to Moscow for my final appearance in Russia, which was to be in Gounod's *Faust*. It was mid-February, snowing and 45° below zero. I loved the crunching snow as we walked late one night in the almost empty square of the Kremlin. It was a thrilling sight. There was a flower kiosk still open, with an old woman bundled up like a bear. When Jack spotted some violets, knowing how I loved them, he put his hand full of coins through the small opening in her window and indicated to her to take what she needed. Gesturing to me to put them under my collar, she quickly shoved them in my hand. They didn't last long, but they were beautiful. Walking in that temperature, my breath created icicles on my coat, but it did not feel really cold, since the air was crisp and very dry.

Having a little time, we did a bit of sightseeing and accepted some interesting invitations. One evening a friend of Jack's, Professor Anokhin, gave a dinner at the Georgian restaurant Aragvie. There was wonderful music on old Russian string instruments, great food, and my favorite Georgian wines. Another friend, Professor Beritashvili, the most famous scientist in the Georgian Republic, sang Georgian songs, and it was another lovely evening.

One of the most interesting and delightful evenings I remember was dinner with Professor Asratyan, whom Jack had entertained in California. He lived in a modest flat, and his wife, a charming woman, cooked us a delicious dinner, serving it herself and helped by their ten-year-old daughter who spoke fluent English. We were then entertained by their two young sons, who played their Beckstein piano like professionals.

The next afternoon I was back to work. Since I had been told that this was a new production of *Faust*, I asked about a stage rehearsal. Again, at first I got blank stares, but when I told them that there had to be a rehearsal or I did not want any part of it, they quickly arranged for one the next day and promptly brought the photos of the sets that I requested. As they had promised, when I arrived at their enormous rehearsal stage, everything was already set up, props and all. The garden scene was beautiful, and the tenor, a nice man, was asked to cue me in on the strange entrances and exits. He signaled me with his eyes when I seemed to be unsure and it worked well. We spoke no English, but between French, Italian, and sign language, I learned the moves and felt comfortable despite the considerable complications in this new version of the Gounod work.

For the performance, the entire Walpurgis Night scene was done with the Bolshoi Ballet and hundreds of people onstage. There was so much time between my scenes that I was invited to sit onstage, just beyond the curtain, where I viewed the action closely. It was spectacular. I had never seen this act in its entirety as it is generally omitted. Without a superb ballet company, it only tends to make the opera too long. Much to my surprise, I discovered that my tenor was a fine dancer who danced a lot in this scene. In fact, I was more impressed by his dancing than his singing.

The last act was also a shocker to me when I discovered that the Russians had completely changed Marguerite's death scene. Of course she could not go to heaven, because they did not believe in that. Instead, as I fell dead after the great trio, the lights were lowered. I ran off the stage and, in what seemed two seconds, transformed myself into the first-act costume, returned as in a trance to center stage where we joined hands while the chorus sang, *"Sauve"* (Saved). Poor Gounod! Although it made no sense, they loved it in Moscow and the evening ended in another wild success.

Everywhere I sang in Russia the tickets were more expensive for my performances. This saddened me, as I realized that many music lovers could not afford them. However, the houses were always sold out and for that I was grateful. Each company asked for extra performances, which I had to refuse, since many engagements were awaiting me back home.

During my Russian stay I received an invitation from J. Graham

Parsons, our ambassador to Sweden, to stop in Stockholm en route
back to the United States for some performances with the opera there.
The previous year I had an enormous success as Tosca when I was
asked to reopen the opera house, which had been closed for some time
for repairs. There had also been television appearances and a concert
with the Stockholm Symphony. The ambassador informed me that Set
Svanholm, the company's director, had asked that his good offices be
used to persuade me to return, an offer I had been obliged already to
turn down because of my crowded schedule. Svanholm, who had been
one of the great Wagnerian tenors of his time, and the best-looking
Siegfried imaginable, had curiously been one of my very first tenors in
Tosca. Alas, again it had to be "no" with much regret.

The Soviet Ministry of Culture and all the dignitaries representing
that country who had visited me backstage during my tour made me
feel I had succeeded in putting on a great show for my country. This
view was also shared by Ambassador Thompson and his wife, as well
as the greatest prima donna of the Soviet Union, Galina Vishnevskaya.
I had accomplished what I went over for.

Despite the discomfort, the cold and lack of rehearsals, I will always
remember this tour of Russia with gratitude for the friendly warmth
of my colleagues, their eagerness to help, and their desire to learn all
they could about American theatre. Because of them, and the overwhelming response of the public, I left the Soviet Union with a warm
feeling. And how shall I ever be able to forget some of the greatest
successes of my career?

Our last twenty-four hours in that country were exhausting but exciting. Many of Jack's friends and colleagues had arranged to come to
my performance of *Faust* and had invited us to a supper party afterward to bid us good-bye. I was exhilarated after my final performance, and Jack felt good about his exchanges with the Soviet scientists.

The supper table was, as usual, crowded with all kinds of liquors
and tasty dishes. Professor Asratyan, the senior scientist, served as
tomeda, a kind of toastmaster, to assure the gaiety of the party by
calling upon guests for toasts, and to make sure they did not become
speeches. It was a rousing, rollicking party that ended reluctantly
about 3 A.M., with Jack, Vicki, and me skipping down a narrow Moscow street singing "California, here we come" at the top of our
voices. The next day we were somewhat more subdued but still talking about the party as we were driven to the airport. Our last activity
was to buy up all the beluga caviar we could carry in our bulging
pockets, with the remaining unspent rubles. It was great while it
lasted.

My Glamour Boys

My radio career was booming by 1948. I was a regular on the "Kraft Music Hall," and appeared often on "The Railroad Hour," "The Voice of Firestone," "The Standard Hour," "The Telephone Hour"; the Bing Crosby, Jack Benny, and Edgar Bergen shows, and many more. I did all of this between my opera dates and concerts, of course, making me a busy girl. Living in California at that time helped because most of the big shows were broadcast live from there.

Realizing my popularity in radio, my clever and imaginative manager Freddie Schang helped put together a most interesting and fun engagement. I had already been at the Metropolitan Opera for four seasons and was well established as an opera star. The combination of Dorothy Kirsten and Frank Sinatra, the "bobby sox" idol, was a preposterous idea according to some, but the Lucky Strike Company thought it was sensational and immediately grabbed it.

A new radio show was planned for us, called "Light Up Time," on the NBC network five days a week. The show began with John Green as guest conductor. Jeff Alexander took over after John and later Skitch Henderson was our regular conductor. Skitch had a fine knowledge of the classics as did the others, as well as the popular songs of the day. The music was certainly varied. I sang everything from Gershwin, Cole Porter, and light classics, all the way to Puccini. Together we did duets like "People Will Say We're in Love" and "Old Fashioned Walk." Frank sang all the songs that he still does so well, and for two years we had a ball.

After hearing all the stories of how his fans would squeal and crowd around just to touch him, I wondered if it would be embarrassing to me. Outside of the studio that was pretty much the way it was, but I was amazed to find that their behavior was quite different for the show. The audience was mixed, teenagers down front where they could gaze up at Frank with dreamy eyes and adoring looks, and farther back people of all ages who were fans of us both. Much to my surprise I was accepted completely by the bobby-soxers and my fan mail was overwhelming.

When Frank had to leave for a short time, I took over alone. That was when we did a semiclassical show and I had my chance to sing a Puccini aria from *Madama Butterfly*. The orchestra was augmented and we invited the great Italian conductor Fausto Cleva from the Met to conduct. Lucky Strike was delighted and the bobby-soxers still yelled and carried on. Some of them even followed me to the Met and remained devoted fans.

I began my career singing show tunes and it never occurred to me that my occasional return to popular music, after I became an opera star, would be resented. Today almost anything goes, but at that time, unfortunately, I was criticized by two classical music shows on which I had been a regular guest and one of them never asked me back. I have always felt their reaction was bigoted and unreasonable, but there were many other compensations. Columbia Records engaged me to make a Gershwin album with Percy Faith, which became a winner. It was one of the top records of that time and is now a collector's item. Some critics were still upset at me for "wasting my time on pop music" and, although one said the album was great and complimented me on my singing of popular songs, he remarked, "It's like pouring beer from a champagne bottle." But all this never touched the success I was having at the Metropolitan Opera.

In our show's first year Lucky Strike decided to put on a festival. It was to be held at the Tobacco Bowl in Richmond, Virginia, during the half-time intermission of the football game. Frank and I were asked to make an appearance. I was to be dressed in the robes of a queen and during the ceremonies Frank would crown me the "Queen of Tobacco." Being particular about how I appear before any public, just as soon as we arrived in town I asked to see the costume I would be wearing. It was fine and elegantly regal but the sponsors were unsuccessful in finding an appropriate tiara. I immediately offered my own beautiful one that I wore in *La Traviata*, but it was stored at the Met in New York. A quick telephone call arranged for my crown to be flown down and it arrived just in time.

The festivities were quite hilarious: a star of the Metropolitan Opera who didn't smoke being crowned the "Queen of Tobacco" by Frank Sinatra before thousands of cheering football fans. The Lucky Strike people had asked me for an endorsement, which was understandable. They knew I did not smoke, but when I offered to say, "*When* I smoke, I smoke Luckies," they graciously accepted. Pictures were taken of me nonchalantly holding a cigarette, and everyone was satisfied. This could never happen now, because there are guidelines that restrict endorsements made by artists unless they actually use the product. But Frank with his sense of humor could not let me get away with that. After the celebration at the stadium there was a reception where we were introduced to the directors of the company and their guests. Waiting until I was surrounded by the top brass of the company, he whipped out his Luckies and offered me one. I faked it pretty well and the laugh was on him.

Working with Frank five times a week I got to know him well. Rarely have I encountered a more generous, thoughtful, and considerate colleague. The show originated in Hollywood, but when I had to be in New York for the Metropolitan Opera season, Frank and the entire crew moved East with me. He loved the opera, regarded highly my position at the Metropolitan, and was always most respectful. In fact, once he asked me whether I thought there was any chance for him to become a classical singer and whether I would introduce him to my teacher. I took him to Maestro Fabri, who listened and was impressed by his sincerity and the pleasing sound of his voice. He explained to Frank that if he seriously wanted to study voice it would be necessary to interrupt his activities in the popular field for at least one year and concentrate entirely on a new vocal technique. With all the fabulous contracts Frank had signed for a long time in advance, this was not feasible and the project was abandoned.

I learned more about how to sing a ballad or a popular song from Frank Sinatra than from anyone. He sings the words and you know he means them. His timing is perfection. No wonder he is still the greatest after all these years. He can still mesmerize millions with a song, and his charisma is something special. I have known that particular sound of his voice for so long that I recognize it immediately. I'm glad he is still "doing it his way."

Over the years Frank has always been a loyal friend. Many times he came to hear me at the opera. One extra-special performance when I was singing *Madama Butterfly* in San Francisco, he flew up with a group of our friends from Los Angeles. I'll always remember the delightful party he gave me after the performance.

It was a delight to work with the great Bing Crosby. His nonchalance and relaxed manner always put me at ease, and the experience was a happy one. Let no one think Bing was not a serious and disciplined professional, for he was anxious to rehearse and eager to cooperate. Between opera and concert commitments we did many shows together while I was commuting between New York and the West Coast for his and other radio engagements. I also enjoyed immensely making my first motion picture, *Mr. Music*, with Bing, for Paramount Pictures. Although the film won no academy awards, I was introduced to the fabulous designer Edith Head who made my gorgeous costumes and has since then designed several of my lovely concert gowns.

It is difficult to find one word to describe my feelings about this great performer's voice: sexy, smooth, suave, and ever so personalized. As with Sinatra, many have tried to emulate his sound, but there was only one Bing Crosby. Bing and I were close friends for quite a while and enjoyed some good times together. He was a warm person with a gay and light personality. At one time we actually became quite serious; however, there were two important careers to consider.

The "Kraft Music Hall" was one of my favorite shows. For several seasons I was a guest on this program with the famous Al Jolson, after which Nelson Eddy and I took over the show for two consecutive years in 1948 and 1949. It was a joy to sing the Romberg, Victor Herbert, and lovely Jerome Kern duets along with Nelson's fine voice. On this program I had many more opportunities to sing my opera and concert repertoire with an excellent orchestra under the direction of the talented Robert Armbruster, who also wrote some beautiful arrangements for me.

Nelson was a serious student of vocal technique and had a magnificent voice. His diction was superb and he loved singing operatic duets. The love scene between Nedda and Silvio from *I Pagliacci* was one of his favorites and I have always thought it a pity he did not sing more opera. I am told that he did sing a performance of Wolfram in *Tannhäuser* with the San Francisco Opera to excellent reviews, but other than that sang very little opera. There was fun and informality on this program but always in a dignified manner. Nelson had his own particular brand of humor and I found him a charming partner. His great career in motion pictures built a name that will be long remembered by his adoring public. His following was tremendous and even now, years after his death, his fan club is still active.

Al Jolson was an enormous surprise to me. The strange sounds he emitted that made him famous seemed to fit his character, but actually, aside from these, he possessed a considerable voice. When he was not clowning, I was aware of a completely different side of this unusual performer. When the Kraft people told me that I was to sing a duet with Al Jolson, I was skeptical, to say the least. However, the result was charming. When we sang some of the straight, simple duets together, he showed a whole new way of singing in a warm, pleasant baritone. Al was a friendly, warm-hearted star who had found his successful niche, and it was fun to work with him.

"The Railroad Hour" was a wonderful program and happily it introduced me to another fine baritone, Gordon MacRae, who was the regular star of the show. I was his co-star many times and this was one of the most enjoyable engagements of them all. We played the characters and sang all of our favorite operettas and later recorded several of them together for Capitol Records. Gordon was an excellent leading man with a romantic flair, just right for the dashing parts he played. He is a fun guy to work with and that baritone with its sexy, velvet tone was a natural for all those bittersweet, melodious operettas. He made several motion pictures including the film version of *Carousel*, and I was delighted to travel with him on so many "Railroad Hours."

Many fine actors from stage and screen, such as Hans Conried, Kurt Kasznar, and others, were engaged to perform with us. Our conductor was the talented Carmen Dragon who was particularly sympathetic to the type of music we performed on "The Railroad Hour." Carmen is also the director of the Glendale Symphony and I have sung with him on many occasions. He can go from the lightest kind of music to an operatic aria with the greatest of ease; a talent few have today.

I did not sing as often with Perry Como, but the shows I did with him were most enjoyable. Like Bing Crosby, he always appeared so relaxed and had a most attractive way of handling his guests. Perry also developed his own individual style, and combined with the effortless way he sings, this will permit him to go on forever. What a pity there was no television in the early days when these good-looking men were young and could have been seen by their admiring public!

One of my greatest surprises in the popular entertainment world was an offer from Liberace to do eight performances with him at the opening of a new theatre in the round, the Carousel, in West Covina, California. I was slightly apprehensive about his flamboyant clothes and flashy showmanship. However, upon meeting him and working out a show, I realized he knew exactly what he was doing and was extremely knowledgeable about show business. He is an excellent pianist and never for a moment was I worried about his accompaniments, whether of light or classical music. Believe it or not, the evening closed with us dancing together the waltz from *The Merry Widow*. Knowing he would be resplendent in jewels, I did my best to keep up with him and had a special gown designed for the occasion.

I had no idea how much exercise I would get traveling back and forth to the stage as fast as I could gracefully manage on what seemed like mile-long ramps in that kind of theatre. My gown was so heavy with rhinestones and beads that the next day I was shocked to find my ankles covered with black-and-blue marks. I swore to myself I would never again appear in a theatre in the round, and I haven't. Liberace is a sensational performer, an unrelenting worker, and a very nice man.

Of all the radio and television shows on which I have appeared, working with my dear friend Edgar Bergen and his little wooden "partner" Charlie was the most enjoyable. For a number of years Edgar wrote all his own material. His sparkling wit was delightful and folksy. He was clever and knew how to put a joke over with subtle showmanship. Never was there anything vulgar, or a word spoken that was in any way offensive. His ventriloquism was completely natural and his timing with Charlie was great.

After several appearances on his show, he planned a television film that was to be the first TV show to be broadcast live coast to coast. It was called *Ghost Town*. I played the part of the nineteenth-century prima donna Jenny Lind, who was stopping off at an inn run by Charlie McCarthy. Our scenes together were hilarious. The late Ray Noble, who was the conductor of Edgar's orchestra on the show, played the part of a honky-tonk piano hack in the bar. He wrote a lovely song for me, entitled "One Red Rose," which I sang in this delightful film. Edgar presented me with a copy of that film, which I treasure.

Working with Charlie was an experience. The first time I met him I found myself easily addressing that little wooden imp as though he were real. Edgar was a magnificent man and artist. I was proud to have worked with him as many times as I did. Frances and Edgar became our good friends, and we miss him.

Jack Benny also invited me to sing on his show several times, and I think of him as one of the funniest men I have ever met. His timing was incredible. You never knew what to expect, aside from the written script, and consequently you had to be on your toes at all times. He kept me laughing so much that it was not easy to deliver a straight line to him. On one show the writers dreamed up a funny "spoof" of the *Rigoletto* quartet. While I did not feel it was in any way disrespectful to Verdi's music, you would not believe the furor it caused among my opera fans. However it did teach me a good lesson, and I never again allowed myself to become involved in that form of satire.

Most of Jack's friends knew how serious he was about his violin. He raised a lot of money for many different charities by appearing as a guest of the great symphony orchestras all over the country. I remember one such concert we did together with the Los Angeles Symphony and Alfred Wallenstein. Jack was pacing the floor backstage, practicing his violin, and his darling wife Mary was as nervous as he was. He was a serious musician and it must have been particularly difficult for him when he had to clown with his instrument.

It was always thoroughly enjoyable to return to Jack Benny's show Don Wilson, that charming teddy bear; Dennis Day and Rochester were such fun to be with, and of course, so was Mary.

Ed Sullivan's show, "Toast of the Town," introduced to the television public many great artists and, fortunately, many great opera singers who until then had only been heard on radio. At that time "The Voice of Firestone" and "The Telephone Hour" were also engaging classical singers; however, Sullivan's show had a wider exposure. Ed always enjoyed a "touch of class" on his program. He did not always pronounce our names right, but I'm sure he knew who we were. In 1960 while I was appearing with the San Francisco Opera, Mr. Sullivan moved his whole crew out to film a scene from *Madama Butterfly* with me in the lovely Japanese gardens there. Every effort was made to find the most authentic atmosphere possible. On different occasions he invited the two famous Italian tenors Franco Corelli and Mario del Monaco, when they were as yet unknown in this country, to sing operatic duets with me. His knowledge of opera was limited but I knew he obviously enjoyed it when he would say, "Dorothy, that was a smasheroo."

A fine show my California manager, Wynn Rocamora, arranged for me was the summer Chevy show that ran for two consecutive years. This afforded me an opportunity to sing opera, lovely duets with the talented John Raitt, many of my favorite show tunes, and fun things with Janet Blair and Edie Adams. We were the regulars on the show but there were guest stars invited almost every week; among them Carol Burnett at the beginning of her career. Soon after we met, Carol began her sensational career as a great comedienne and I'm delighted to see how beautifully she is developing her talent these days as a serious actress.

Nothing was spared when it came to designing the sets for this show. On one occasion it was a beautiful Viennese ballroom scene with lavish costumes. While waltzing with one of the dancers I sang "I'm in Love with Vienna" to an exciting orchestration led by Harry Zimmerman. Another was an ice-skating scene where they brought in a small rink. I had not been on skates since I was a kid and I remember so well learning a routine with John Raitt who was my partner. We had to struggle to remain on our feet while Janet Blair, who was very pregnant at the time, was bundled up in a sleigh pushed by Eddie Foy, making circles around us. It was a hard week of rehearsals, but lots of laughs.

For my *Madama Butterfly* scene they built a lovely Japanese set. I wore my own costumes and even dressed one of the chorus girls who played my Suzuki. The set for *Louise* was charming, and John Raitt sat in as my Julien while I sang Charpentier's beautiful aria "Depuis le jour." When I complimented the designer, he later presented me with a beautifully framed color picture of this scene, which still hangs on my wall.

Every week was another interesting adventure on the Chevy show. Dinah Shore had made this program one of the most highly rated attractions in television, and when she returned in the fall I was invited back several times as her guest. These were delightful programs; it is a shame they disappeared from television.

I also played Jenny Lind early in my television appearances on "Matinee Theater," which was a wonderful show. Albert McCreery was the fine producer, and working with top actors such as Werner Klemperer and host John Conte was what I liked to do best. There was little singing on this show, but lots of acting.

Wynn Rocamora, who handled many top movie stars, decided it was about time I was introduced to Metro-Goldwyn-Mayer. They were doing musicals galore at the time and he wanted me to meet Louis B. Mayer. A screen test was arranged; it was successful, and Mr. Mayer promised he would find a picture for me. I was wined and dined lavishly in the movie-set manner. While I was dining with the great man one evening shortly after my test, we discovered that our birthdays, which were coming up soon, happened to be only two days apart. When he graciously suggested we have a combined party, I was of course delighted but curious about what to expect. Wynn had told me that there was usually entertainment at these parties by the current young stars, and I remember thinking, "Oh, how dull."

The dinner was held at the MGM Studios in a large dining room with a stage at one end. Mr. Mayer confided he had a big surprise. He was anxious to have me hear "the greatest tenor voice I have ever heard. Even greater than Caruso!" he said. Because it was Mayer's birthday party there were many of my favorite big stars present and after introductions a lovely dinner was served, joint birthday cake and all.

When the stage curtains parted after dinner and Mario Lanza made his entrance, I could have gladly disappeared under the table. He had appeared with me in a concert only a week before and was quite familiar to me. I knew about his extraordinary voice, and he sang magnificently at our concert, but I could not forget how this cocky little tenor had kept me waiting one hour to rehearse with him without apology. His peculiar antics onstage that night embarrassed me and I thought him the most irresponsible, uncouth character I had ever worked with. It was extremely difficult to control my reaction, but of course none of my feelings showed. Mr. Mayer knew a good voice when he heard one. Mario's gift was great and the studio had high hopes for him.

Lanza was suddenly one of the top "properties" at MGM, doing one picture after another and thriving on all the adulation that goes with life at the studios. Almost a year later I signed a contract to play the role of Louise, the American prima donna, in the motion picture *The Great Caruso* with Ann Blyth and Mario Lanza. The picture was a smashing success for MGM and is still playing all over the world. It was chosen on an exchange program to play in the Soviet Union and was a fine introduction for my trip to sing in that country early in 1962. Several of my Metropolitan Opera colleagues came out to sing parts in the operatic scenes: Jarmila Novotna, Blanche Thebom, Nicola Moscona, Giuseppe Valdengo, and others.

At this point Mario was being coached by the fine old maestro Giacomo Spadoni, who had been with MGM for years and at one time was with the Metropolitan. The maestro confided in me that his job wasn't easy, for Mario could not read a note of music. Lanza was a handsome young man with devilish eyes and a good deal of charm, but he was totally undisciplined. He ignored completely our first unpleasant meeting and I enjoyed most of my work with him in the film in spite of his bad manners.

Mario could have sung in any opera house in the world. The Metropolitan and San Francisco operas were both open to him at one time and his career could have been sensational, but he could not learn a score. I believe he could have been one of the greatest tenors America ever produced if only someone could have given him the will to study and the discipline it takes to apply one's self. When I think of the eager young singers who have auditioned for me with such meager vocal gifts but the will to sacrifice everything to have careers, it makes me sad to think of Mario, his great gift, and what an incredible loss to the world of opera his passing was.

A most celebrated glamour boy on my list of favorites is Bob Hope. I admire this great comedian tremendously. Bob earned the love and highest regard of not only his colleagues but of his country for his untiring efforts to entertain our armed services and will be remembered always for this great contribution. During the War Bond days of 1944 and 1945 we worked together on several Bond shows here and in Canada. Looking through some of the photographs I have assembled for this book brought back fond memories of those days.

The last time we appeared together was to receive our degrees from the University of Santa Clara, his a doctorate of humanities and mine of fine arts. Because we are both great golf enthusiasts, we meet occasionally for the Colgate-Dinah Shore Pro-Am Golf Tournament in Palm Springs where Bob and his lovely wife, Dolores, are usually part of the celebrity group.

One of the most glamorous leading men with whom I have worked was our former governor of California, and our new fortieth President of the United States, Ronald Reagan.

When I was a popular radio artist and television was beginning to come into its own, I was engaged to appear with Ron on his great show, "General Electric Theater." I remember that experience as an especially enjoyable one. This was one of early television's most successful shows. It lasted for years to the great acclaim of a new audience, and was a large part of what the motion picture companies considered a real threat to their industry. All of these shows were filmed. Ron was host and starred in many of the dramatic plays specially written for the program. His warm and congenial personality, which won him many friends, was also responsible for his success in motion pictures, television, or any kind of show business.

Triumphs and Tribulations at the San Francisco Opera

My long association with the San Francisco Opera Company will always be remembered as among the happiest times of my career. During my first years in San Francisco the season began in mid-September, while the Metropolitan started much later. This made it possible for me to sing some engagements in California before I was expected for my commitments in New York. Though I did a lot of traveling between these two companies, I was a regular with both of them for most of my career.

The War Memorial Opera House of San Francisco is not the most beautiful theatre in the world but it is a wonderful place in which to sing. The seating capacity is 3,252, yet the acoustics are excellent for both the artist and the audience. The San Franciscans have always been ardent opera lovers. They are knowledgeable about music and eagerly support their company. Generally the audience is more elegantly dressed than in most opera houses in the country, but notwithstanding all the finery it is an audience which most enthusiastically proclaims its appreciation when something great happens on the stage.

There was always a grand feeling of welcome upon arriving for the season, and I shall never forget the many loyal friends who entertained me so generously through the years. Mrs. Robert Watt Miller, widow of the president of the San Francisco Opera Association for many years, is still one of my dearest friends to this day. Howard Skinner, manager of the symphony for many years, showered me with constant attention; Whitney Warren engaged the great couturière Valentina to design my magnificent *L'Amore dei Tre Re* costumes and then made a present of them to me. I became very close to Charlie Blyth, the financier who taught me something about investments, and his wife, Kay; and Ken Monteagle, president of the opera company when I joined them and his wife, Lucille. I shall also always remember Dan London, longtime manager of the St. Francis Hotel, and his wife, Claire.

Gaetano Merola was the general director when I joined the San

Francisco Opera Company on November 9, 1945. This wonderful man was respected and loved by every singer who worked for him. Merola stimulated confidence in the artist. He was a perfect gentleman, a warmhearted, considerate man who was knowledgeable about the art of singing and most helpful in guiding my young career.

He started the San Francisco Opera Company in 1923. A native of Naples, Italy, Merola was a conductor for several years with the Hammerstein Opera Company and an assistant conductor at the Metropolitan during his early career. He fell in love with the West, particularly San Francisco, on his first visit. Merola enjoyed reminiscing about his early days there and the tremendous effort it was to get started with his company. His stories of engaging Martinelli, Gigli, Rethberg, and of coaxing all the top stars with the Met to come West demonstrated his determination to have a first-rate company for San Francisco. The city owes a great deal to Gaetano Merola for establishing this fine company, and is fortunate to have had his successor in Kurt Herbert Adler, who has succeeded in maintaining those high standards.

In the fall of 1945 the great Swedish tenor Jussi Björling and I were on our first long concert tour together through the northern and western states, finishing up in Los Angeles. At the same time the San Francisco Company was touring the major cities of the West Coast. I made my debut with the company at the Shrine Auditorium as Mimi in *La Bohème* with Jussi Björling as my Rodolfo.

The following season my commitments with Chicago and other engagements again deprived me of singing with the company at the opera house in San Francisco during the regular season. However, I did join them on tour for performances in Portland and Seattle.

In 1947 Mr. Merola offered me two great new roles to add to my repertoire. I was at last to make my debut in San Francisco! The first opera was Charpentier's *Louise*, which I anticipated with much joy, for I had recently returned from Paris where I studied *Louise* and had the great privilege of reviewing the opera with its composer, Gustave Charpentier. Upon learning that the Met had already engaged me to sing *Louise*, Mr. Merola jumped the gun on New York and asked me to make my debut in this role with San Francisco. The first performance was set for October 3, with a superb cast: Ezio Pinza was my father; Raoul Jobin was Julien, my sweetheart; and Claramae Turner my mother. We were celebrating Merola's twenty-fifth anniversary season with the company and it was an exciting night.

The second role I was to sing was Fiora in Italo Montemezzi's *L'Amore dei Tre Re,* which followed only eleven days later. I had sung a small part in this opera when Grace Moore sang Fiora in Chicago, and was delighted with the opportunity to study this role with the composer. Again I had a sensational cast. Pinza was a thrilling blind King Archibaldo; Robert Weede, the great American baritone, portrayed my husband; Charles Kullmann was my lover, Avito; and the composer Montemezzi was in the pit conducting his magnificent score. I was, indeed, a busy girl that year, concentrating on two such complicated and completely different characters, one in French and the other in Italian.

When Pinza sang the soliloquy "Italia, Italia," in the first act of the opera, he literally shook the scenery. His anguish was so penetrating that while I was waiting in the wings to make my entrance, it put me in exactly the right mood to pity him. I'm sure no one has sung this role more magnificently. With the abundance of great bassos in recent years it is a pity that *L'Amore dei Tre Re* has disappeared from the lyric theatre.

This was my first experience having the composer of an opera in the pit, and regretfully I must agree with some of my colleagues that it is seldom an ideal situation. Charles Kullmann, who had sung the opera with Montemezzi before, warned me to be prepared for slower tempos and stretched-out phrases. I was grateful for that tip, because the vocal line that Montemezzi wanted without an interfering breath was already very long. It was truly a tour de force. I understand that this is generally true of most composers who conduct their own operas. It is assumed they have a deeper feeling for each note and therefore dwell upon it longer. Later, when I sang the opera with other conductors, including Tullio Serafin, it was a much easier task.

Louise and Fiora in *L'Amore dei Tre Re* were definite highlights of my career and became two of my favorite roles outside of my Puccini repertoire. I only wish I could have sung them both many more times at the Met.

During the next three years Merola kept me busy with performances of *Madama Butterfly*, *La Traviata*, and *Manon Lescaut*. One of the most pleasant memories of the 1950 season was my first meeting with Mario del Monaco. He had a sensational debut with the company as Radames in *Aida*, and later when we sang *Manon Lescaut* together I thought he was the most handsome, sexy Des Grieux I ever worked with. He looked the part and sang it magnificently.

It was at this time that Merola began talking to me about *Tosca*. He thought my voice had now developed enough dramatic quality to take on this role. I had been looking forward to singing the great heroine and immediately accepted. The following summer I studied *Tosca* with the fine conductor Nicola Rescigno. Nicola was a wonderful coach, precise and thoroughly familiar with the score, and I very much enjoyed working with him.

On October 12, 1951, I sang my first *Tosca*. The cast, as Mr. Merola promised, was a great one. Jussi Björling, one of my favorite partners, was Mario; and Robert Weede an excellent Scarpia. Fausto Cleva, who so often conducted for me, was in the pit, and over the years he became my favorite conductor of Italian opera.

This night was special and I was very happy. Maestro Merola could not have been more complimentary and I was exhilarated. But throughout the entire day they held back the news that my dear mother had suddenly passed away that morning. Mother had been ill for quite a long time, but it was still a great shock when I was told after the performance. A few dates were canceled while I went back to New Jersey, but my mother would have been proud that I soon returned to continue my work.

There were more operas to do in San Francisco. I returned to finish with *Bohème, Butterfly*, and more *Toscas*. The last performance of *Tosca* for that season was scheduled in Los Angeles, where one of my most embarrassing moments on the stage occurred. I still hear about it from people who were in the audience that night.

There is a fire law in this city prohibiting real flame on the stage. This restriction required us to use an electric candelabra instead of candles that were to be blown out at a crucial point in the final scene of the second act. Tosca must light two smaller candles from a larger fixture which is usually on Scarpia's supper table. After these are placed near the body of Scarpia, whom she has just killed, Tosca turns to make her escape, extinguishing the lights of the candelabra and putting the room in near darkness.

I had carefully rehearsed the timing of each switch with the head electrician. While I was pretending to blow out the light, the man backstage was supposed to control the switches. Everything worked fine when I was lighting the first two smaller candles, but when I came back to extinguish the larger candelabra by blowing, the first light went out but suddenly came on again. As I continued blowing, each bulb popped right back on until the candelabra looked like a Christmas tree. The audience was hysterical. I was so mortified and frustrated with the complete destruction of my final scene that I was reluctant to go before the audience for my curtain call. My hesitation was noticed, and the morning paper's review reported that it was likely I was busy killing the electrician after that fiasco.

In 1952 Mario del Monaco and I opened the San Francisco Opera season with *Tosca.* Robert Weede was Scarpia, and I was always happy when Fausto Cleva was in the pit. During that season I was singing all the wonderful operettas regularly on "The Railroad Hour" from Los Angeles. My schedule was extremely tight in this period with opera, radio, and concerts. In one frantic week I sang a concert, two operas, and three radio shows! Because my commitments at the Met did not begin until November, I was able to sing more engagements on the West Coast.

Maestro Merola had planned a revival of *L'Amore dei Tre Re* for me with a new cast. This time Nicola Rossi-Lemeni came to sing the role of the blind king. This fine artist looked the part, but Pinza was a hard act to follow and Rossi-Lemeni's interpretation was less exciting.

In a later version, when Kurt Adler revived this opera in 1959, Giorgio Tozzi, the American bass, sang the role and had a much bigger success in every way. He was excellent vocally, an imposing figure and dramatically impelling. I had an idea for the strangulation scene that I believed would make it even more exciting. With a big strong bass such as Tozzi I was confident the effect would be sensational.

When Fiora admits her guilt to the old man, the father of her husband, flaunting the truth to his face that she has a lover and is untrue to her husband, his outrage is uncontrollable. In the original version he drags her to a bench on the side of the stage to strangle her, then lifts her and throwing the body over his shoulder he exits. My idea was for the old king to catch Fiora trying to escape at center stage, forcing her to her knees, her back to the audience. As the music clearly strikes certain chords to indicate he is choking her, she finally becomes limp and falls right there. In the performance, he controlled my fall so I would be flat on my back, raised me to a sitting position, and, putting his right knee behind me, lifted my body over his right shoulder so most of me hung down his back, with my long blond hair nearly touching the floor. As he started to exit he faked a slight stumble. The audience audibly gasped. It worked perfectly, but by the time he got me offstage, I had been upside down for so long that the blood had rushed to my head and it was a few minutes before I could stand on my feet to go before the curtain. There were cheers and whistles which are usually uncommon in San Francisco, but it was all worth it.

Though Brian Sullivan had sung Avito's high tessitura in *L'Amore* with ease in the earlier production and was quite successful, my favorite tenor in this role was Giuseppe Zampieri of the Vienna Staatsoper who was Avito in 1959. I have always appreciated tenors who looked at me instead of the conductor while doing a love scene. Giuseppe was a handsome man with a magnificent voice and we were very much attracted to each other. The love scenes were so convincing that rumors started to fly, and I had some explaining to do.

Speaking of partners on the stage and love scenes, I remember a performance of *Tosca* for which I was engaged by the Philadelphia Opera Company in 1960. The scheduled tenor was ill and canceled very late, leaving the company in a dither. In desperation they were forced to engage a singer who had a beautiful voice but was only five feet tall. Never having met the gentleman, I didn't know this, but when I made my entrance onstage and saw him I nearly died. I am not tall for the stage at just under five feet five, but that night I felt like a giant.

The last time *L'Amore dei Tre Re* was revived it was in celebration of my twentieth anniversary with the company. The cast was disappointing. Giuseppe Campora sang the tenor role, but at that time the part was a bit too demanding for his voice. The King was sung by Nicolai Ghiuselev, a fine basso, but surprisingly, considering Adler's usual expert judgment in casting, he was miscast. Since he was of small stature, there was no way to work out the dramatic impact of the strangulation scene, which demands a more commanding figure. The casting of an opera such as *L'Amore dei Tre Re* is extremely vital to its success and it is a pity the public was left with this poor impression.

In the spring of 1953 San Francisco and Merola's many friends were shocked and utterly dismayed by the sudden death of our beloved maestro. While conducting his favorite composer, Puccini, at an outdoor concert near San Francisco, he collapsed with a heart attack. He was a man who had dedicated his life to the opera company and will always be missed by his friends.

Kurt Herbert Adler, who had been his close associate during the last few years, capably picked up the reins and eventually was appointed to succeed Maestro Merola as our general director. During my first years in Chicago, Kurt Adler was also with the company, serving as chorus director. In 1943 Mr. Merola invited him to join the San Francisco Opera in the same position as chorus master for which he was highly regarded. Ten years later Kurt Adler was appointed our new director and since that time he has become the most successful general director of opera in this country. He must be complimented for his generally fine casting ability and his expertise in blending voices. However, I have to admit there were a few times when I was extremely uncomfortable with the partners he chose for me.

My first year with Mr. Adler was a sad one because my former husband, Gene Chapman, was terminally ill and I was forced to cancel most of my engagements to be with him. The following year, 1954, was Kurt's first opportunity to plan his own season. The new role he offered me was Massenet's Manon. That was one time in my life when I needed a strong incentive to work, and this was the answer. Gene had passed away a few months before and my only salvation was to immerse myself in learning something new. I was living in Bel Air at the time and engaged Victor Trucco, an excellent coach at the Metropolitan, to come West and work with me on the role. Having sung Puccini's Manon many times, and being extremely fond of the character, I was more than interested in doing the French version.

Massenet's *Manon* requires at least two more glamorous costumes for scenes that do not exist in Puccini's opera. To design my new gowns I engaged Don Loper, the famous California couturier. Don had made some beautiful clothes for me and was excited about doing my costumes. These turned out to be some of the most magnificent creations I own.

The famous French conductor Pierre Monteux was engaged for this opera and came to Los Angeles to review the score with me. I was thrilled to have the opportunity of working with this great man. He was already seventy-nine years old at the time, but spry with a twinkle in his eye and a fine sense of humor.

I met the maestro with his wife Doris and their fat little poodle and drove them to their hotel. As we were driving through a street in Beverly Hills lined with tall palms, he asked what kind of trees were those with the large pompons. When I told him they were palms, he laughed heartily and said, "They are the silliest trees I have ever seen!"

Maestro Monteux had been the conductor of the San Francisco Symphony for several years, was well known and loved in the Golden Gate City. He told the press there he felt that the conductor of the symphony should not also conduct the opera, but now that he had retired from his old post he was "ready to join up." Having sung this opera many times since our collaboration, I realize how fortunate I was in breaking in this role with Monteux.

In September of 1955 Mr. Adler revived Charpentier's *Louise* for me; it had not been performed since 1947 when I last sang it with the company. This time, though, with a different cast, it did not have the success of the first one. However, Mr. Adler was now beginning to hit his stride in developing the company's repertoire and when he secured the first American rights to Sir William Walton's *Troilus and Cressida*, I was chosen to create the lovely role of Cressida. This was the first opera I sang in English, and it became my favorite role in my own language.

Troilus and Cressida had been introduced to the world at Covent Garden only ten months before our American première, which took place on October 7, 1955. The text, beautifully done by Christopher Hassall, was based on Chaucer's tale. Cressida is an intriguing character to play and a melodic role to sing. The love themes are particularly amorous with a beautiful lyric line.

Troilus was sung by Richard Lewis, the English tenor who had also created the role in London. Robert Weede sang Diomede; Giorgio Tozzi was Calkas; and Ernest McChesney of the New York City Opera was Pandarus. Richard was handsome as Troilus and sang the role as though it were his favorite. Rose Goldstein, who was supplying the opera company with costumes, and I designed some beautiful Grecian gowns for Cressida.

Erich Leinsdorf was our conductor, and before going to San Francisco he came to my home in Los Angeles to review the role with me. Sir William Walton arrived from London in time for most of the rehearsals and remained to witness the first performance of his opera in America.

We performed *Troilus* twice in San Francisco and once in Los Angeles. With the enthusiastic reaction from the audience and the favorable reception by the press, it is inconceivable that, aside from the few performances which followed by the New York City Opera, I have not heard of the opera ever being staged again in this country. I have heard there were many requests for a revival, but evidently it was not to be. This is difficult for me to understand, because the American public has been clamoring for opera in English, and here is a work far superior to many which have appeared and quickly disappeared over the years.

In 1956 I opened both the San Francisco and the Los Angeles seasons with *Manon Lescaut* and closed the season with *Madama Butterfly*. Financially this was one of the most successful seasons of the San Francisco Opera's visits to Los Angeles. We sang to houses of up to six thousand. Again, my great colleague Jussi Björling was with me for the *Manons*. I have always enjoyed performing in the Shrine Auditorium for these engagements. It was a fine place in which to sing and though it lacked the beautiful crystal chandeliers and elegance of the Music Center, it was far more compatible with the voice.

Kurt Adler's next offer was a second interesting opera in English and another grand coup for the San Francisco company. The American première of Francis Poulenc's *Dialogues of the Carmelites* was performed in San Francisco on September 20, 1957, only eight months after the world première at La Scala. I sang the leading role of Blanche de la Force. Erich Leinsdorf conducted the Debussy-Moussorgsky-influenced score expertly, and as usual with great consideration for the singers. The success of the opera was compelling enough to demand a third performance. Though the story is an intensely moving one, the subject is gory: a band of nuns sentenced to the guillotine during the French Revolution. Blanche, an unhappy, confused girl, joins the Carmelites because of her fear of life and decides to end it all by going with her sisters to the guillotine. This was the most emotionally upsetting part I have ever played. Her character touched me so deeply that I could not sleep at night. The long rehearsals in this depressing mood bothered me, the troubled image of this girl constantly on my mind. It had been such a traumatic experience that I would never do the role again.

The San Francisco Opera Guild each season puts on a money-raising affair called Fol-de-Rol. Most of the leading artists contribute their talents to this gala night. The orchestra participates, and some of the performers simply sing arias or duets, but those of us who were regulars with the company often were asked to bring something lighter to the program. One evening it was suggested I sing a Gershwin song I had recorded, so, in nightclub style, wearing a slinky gown, I sat on the piano while doing my "number." Another fun evening occurred when Ray Bolger was our master of ceremonies. We had a ball dancing together a routine he had prepared for the occasion.

There was also a night when I was unable to do the Fol-de-Rol because my performance was scheduled for the next day. However, when one of the stars canceled out at the last moment, the pleading voice of my darling friend Betty Miller, who had been asked to call me, could not be denied. Though I was already snug in my bed, hair up in curlers, concentrating on my role for the next day, I somehow got myself together and rescued the situation.

Once again I opened the San Francisco season in 1960 with the popular opera *Tosca*. The cast was great, with Giuseppe Zampieri as Mario and Tito Gobbi as Scarpia. This was my first opportunity to work with Tito and I was enormously impressed with his interpretation.

This was the year the company planned to bring back Puccini's *La Fanciulla del West*, which had long been absent from the repertoire. I was chosen to sing Minnie, the only woman in the opera except for her maid. Because this was also my sixth Puccini heroine, I was earning the reputation of being a specialist in his music, and I liked that.

The opera had been performed in 1943 but was sung in English. It failed miserably. The audience laughed when they heard the words "whiskey," "Wells Fargo," "Sacramento," and found extremely funny the "ugh" sounds which the Indians made when they greeted each other. The tenor was much shorter than the leading lady as well, and that did not help sell the opera. This time it would be sung in Italian, the language in which Puccini wrote the opera. The words would fit the music and Kurt was going to see that *Fanciulla del West* had a fair chance to succeed with the right cast.

Before the season began, Mr. Adler asked me to join him with a group of the San Francisco Opera Guild members on a trip to the old gold-mining town of Virginia City, Nevada, as a publicity stunt for this Puccini opera. A plane was chartered and the press was flown over with us. I was asked to bring along riding clothes and was told there would be horses available. After we checked into the old hotel, I changed into my boots and culottes and was on my way to meet the horses. The press had already chosen a beautiful animal for me to ride for the picture-taking. I explained to the owner that I had done considerable riding in my youth and had no fear of horses but hoped the horse was not too frisky. Upon her assurance, I mounted with confidence. We were standing still, but when the cameras began to click the animal and I were suddenly off like a shot. The cries of my friends and Mr. Adler only seemed to make matters worse, and it was a hard ride until I finally controlled the beast. My determination to keep my seat must have dawned on the horse at last, for he slowed down and we arrived back on the scene at a much slower pace, to everyone's relief. There was a great party that evening and it was a fun trip, of which much was made in the San Francisco papers.

This revival served to introduce Sándor Kónya, the tall good-looking Hungarian tenor with a robust *spinto* voice, as Dick Johnson. Tito Gobbi sang the baritone role of Jack Rance and was superior as the sheriff. Molinari-Pradelli, a great Italian conductor, was in the pit, and the feeling with which he led his orchestra clearly demonstrated his love for the opera.

When the boys shouted, *"Whiskey per tutti"* (Whiskey for all), there was still a giggle here and there, but this time the audience took the opera seriously. They followed the story and responded with great enthusiasm. The opera had an enormous success and Minnie was one of my own greatest personal triumphs in San Francisco.

In 1962 I opened the season as Mimi in *La Bohème* and did my regular repertoire with the company that year. The part of Lisa in Tchaikovsky's *Pique Dame* (Queen of Spades) was my next new role with San Francisco. The opera is based on Pushkin's story, which, when I read it, I have to admit did not make Lisa too appealing to me. She is another complex, unhappy character, and though I threw myself into the role, I did not like her. The opera was sung in English;

my costumes were beautiful; and it was considered a fine production. Vocally, Lisa has some lovely music to sing and it is quite lyric. Nevertheless, I found her famous aria in the last act a bit too heavy for my voice. The aged countess was magnificently played and sung by my colleague Regina Resnik, and James McCracken sang the difficult and highly emotional role of Herman. In spite of my feelings about Lisa, I had a fine success in San Francisco. However, when I was offered this role again later, I resisted.

That year, 1963, we did three performances of *Pique Dame* in San Francisco and one in San Diego. The performance scheduled for Los Angeles was canceled on short notice when the news was broadcast of President Kennedy's assassination that morning.

Manon Lescaut was again one of my assignments for 1967. This year Mr. Adler introduced the new Hungarian tenor Robert Ilosfalvy. He had a fine voice but was another stiff partner who could not give the illusion of a lover. Most of the conversations during rehearsals were in German, a language I had studied but seldom used. Ilosfalvy spoke no Italian or English, so there was little communication between us.

Lotfi Mansouri, a fine stage director who has since become successful internationally, was with us for this production, and I recall his frustrations in getting the show together. Most of the cast was very "un-Puccinian." Mr. Adler really missed on that one and it was a great disappointment to us.

In my career with the San Francisco Opera I was honored with opening their regular season on five different occasions. My fifth opening was on September 18, 1970, just twenty-five years after I made my debut with the company. The opera was Puccini's *Tosca*. We had planned that a later performance would be closer to the date of my debut; thus November 28 was chosen for the night of my celebration. Standard Oil of California gave me a special tribute with the first live broadcast of a performance from San Francisco. On this same night I was also presented the opera company's first Silver Medal, commemorating my twenty-five years.

When Kurt began to discuss this occasion with me months before the performance, he told me he had engaged a very young, talented new conductor to make his debut with me. I was looking forward to this gala night and the cast with whom I would be singing. Placido Domingo, who had made his debut with San Francisco in 1969, was to be my tenor, and the fine Canadian baritone Louis Quilico would sing Scarpia.

When I walked into my first rehearsal at the opera house and was introduced to the new conductor Kurt had praised so highly, I was startled by his youth. But as we began to work, the authority with which he directed and his knowledge of the score were immediately impressive. He knew exactly what he wanted and I liked the way he got it. At our first break in rehearsal he quietly came to me and asked if I would mind discussing a few points with him privately in his dressing room. I thought it was a rather unusual request but gladly followed him. As he sat at his piano he hesitated slightly and then said, "You don't remember me, do you, Miss Kirsten?" I must have looked puzzled for he continued, "We first met in Cincinnati where you were singing this opera about ten years ago." With that it all began to come back to me. During a break in a rehearsal of *Tosca* a young man about sixteen years old had stopped me and, holding out his score of *Tosca*, had asked me to autograph it for him. I remember having been disturbed by something which had happened onstage and rather impatiently saying to him as I signed it, "Just what are you planning to do with that score, young man?" He readily replied, "Someday, Miss Kirsten, I hope to conduct a performance of *Tosca* for you." Recalling I had seen him sitting behind Fausto Cleva, the conductor, I realized he was serious, but I never gave another thought to the meeting.

Jimmy Levine's dreams were coming true. He was making his debut with a major opera company and fulfilling his greatest ambitions. I was very happy for him. All this happening on my anniversary with the company added something very special to my celebration. Jimmy's talent and love of opera are now well known, and his feeling for Puccini's music in particular is extraordinary. He is what we call a singer's conductor. He breathes with the singer and that makes for a fine collaboration.

Mr. Adler could not have made me happier with the cast and conductor he chose for my gala evening. Placido Domingo is a tenor who knows how to play a love scene and sings his heart out; Louis Quilico, my old friend with whom I have sung so many times, gives his all as Scarpia and is a great one.

I arrived at the theatre early that evening to find my dressing room decorated with colorful ribbons and clever reminders of the past twenty-five years, and overflowing with flowers and gifts. Margaret Norton and the press department were responsible for this touching scene that greeted me.

We were all very charged up that evening and the rewards of such a night are indescribable. It was one of those exciting evenings when everything went right. Jimmy's debut was a huge success. Our *Tosca* was received with great enthusiasm, and the response was tremendous. As I came onstage for my solo bows I was showered with bouquets and was given a standing ovation.

After the performance, when I finally got to my dressing room and had a chance to read my messages, I was especially attracted to a large box that had arrived with a lovely bouquet of red roses. When I opened it I was delighted to find two elegant silver goblets, accompanied by a note that read, "*Tosca, finalmente mia!* [Tosca, finally you are mine!] Love, Jim." To this day I still get a kick out of that.

Another thoughtful gift was a beautifully engraved silver knife from my tenor with an amusing note saying, "I'm very proud to sing with you on this great occasion. I hope that with this knife you will take care of at least 100 more Scarpias. Congratulations, Placido Domingo." The next package I opened, believe it or not, was also an engraved silver knife. This one was from Kurt Adler.

Following this occasion I received a touching letter from Jimmy. He wrote:

> Your encouragement and help, as well as your fabulous vocal and dramatic artistry made the whole experience exciting for me and I never could have imagined that my first Tosca and San Francisco debut could take place under such satisfying circumstances. . . . I hope I will always have your encouragement and your favor. With hopes for many more operas together, much love,
>
> Jim

Perhaps I should have made that memorable night my farewell to San Francisco, for my return in 1972 was a complete letdown in a new Jean-Pierre Ponnelle production of *Tosca*.

After that disappointment I was ready to discuss a last performance with San Francisco. When I mentioned this to Mr. Adler his reply was, "Ridiculous, you should sing with us for a long time yet." I truly appreciated his reaction, but decided that with the Metropolitan, concerts, and other commitments I had already accepted for the next few years, I was busy enough. We began to plan a gala farewell, but when Mr. Adler surprised me by wanting to hold the affair in a large auditorium instead of the opera house, I strongly objected. There was no further communication, and that was the end of a long and warm association between us.

I did go back to San Francisco five years later, after a great deal of pressure from my many friends there, to co-emcee the Silver Anniversary Gala the company gave Kurt. I agreed to sing an aria that night, but I cannot ignore the fact that Kurt Adler deprived me of a farewell performance for my San Francisco audience.

Yes, there were tribulations in San Francisco.

After so many years of service and collaboration with Mr. Adler, what a pity we could not have ended our relationship on a happier note.

Ecstasies and Agonies
at the Met

From the beginning of my operatic career I viewed the Metropolitan Opera as the pinnacle, the top of my aspirations. After serving my apprenticeship in Chicago and singing in many of the other good smaller companies around the country, I began to set my sights on that particular goal.

The "Metropolitan Auditions of the Air" were in full swing, and singers who had been through numerous auditions were clamoring for a chance to try out for the Met. I knew several who had been through the mill, had been given contracts with a small weekly salary, had sang a few *comprimario* roles hoping to become stars, and had come and gone within a season or two. For me that seemed the wrong way though there were a few exceptions. I was going to wait until I could go through the "front door" as a star. Consequently, when Grace Moore suggested I enter this competition and told me that Maestro Wilfred Pelletier, who was in charge of the program, had heard me and thought I had an excellent chance to win, I was dismayed to have to disagree with her for the first time. After I told her of my plan to join the Met as a star, there was no further pressure and later she complimented me and admitted I was right.

Before I was engaged by the Met I had been fortunate to have had considerable experience with the City Center Opera in New York. This company was organized with the full support and blessings of Mayor Fiorello La Guardia, who was frequently in the audience. It was housed in the old Mecca Temple on West Fifty-fifth Street between Sixth and Seventh avenues. Though it was not a glamorous theatre, acoustically it was excellent. Many colleagues of my vintage had sung there, and it became an ideal showplace for the powers that be at the Metropolitan to watch for the youngsters who were showing real talent. I broke in several of my major roles in that old theatre, including the one that won me the coveted contract with the Met when Edward Johnson, the general manager of the company, came to hear me in *Manon Lescaut*.

Eddie Johnson was a charming, delightful, and sympathetic manager. He had enjoyed a great career himself in Europe as well as at the Metropolitan, singing all the romantic leading tenor roles for many years. Johnson was always there to wish us well before a performance and was never afraid after the opera to say, "You sang a great performance." It makes a difference! Serious artists can always receive a compliment and not take advantage of the well-wisher. His familiarity with the characteristic peculiarities of singers and his sympathy for their problems endeared him to us all. This attitude invariably brought out the utmost in his artists.

I remember so well one instance that is a good example. I had arrived early as usual at the opera house with the worst sore throat I can ever remember having. When I awakened that morning, miserable with fear that I would be forced to cancel my performance, my doctor came to the hotel to examine my throat. He found that my vocal cords were not affected and the muscles around them were not inflamed. After treating the sore area he said, "Go sing, Dorothy, I'll be in the theatre if you need me." He was not exactly sympathetic but at least he had convinced me that I would not be doing any damage to my vocal cords. My secretary called the Met to make sure my standby would be there, just in case. This, of course, alarmed Eddie, and he was in my dressing room as I entered the theatre.

By this time I was getting pretty sick to my stomach from all the cough drops I had taken, the honey and lemon mixture, plus the awful stuff the doctor had applied to my throat, and I was feeling quite sorry for myself. Before I had time to complain, a quiet but serious lecture began. "Now, Dorothy, I know how you feel and I suffer with you, but I have a sold-out house waiting for you. They have paid a lot of money to hear you. If anyone can sing over a bad throat you can, and I know you won't disappoint them."

He kissed my cheek and with his familiar *"In bocca al lupo"* (an Italian expression meaning good luck), he left. I began to relax, and by the time the curtain went up and the music for my entrance began, I found myself swept along as usual into my role with my voice responding as well as ever.

How fortunate I was that for those first five years of my career at the Metropolitan I had the support and guidance of a manager such as Edward Johnson.

My debut at the Metropolitan was set for December 1, 1945, in the role of Mimi in *La Bohème*. This was going to be the first time the opera would be performed that season, which meant I would have the opportunity for a full dress rehearsal and a chance to get accustomed to singing in that huge house. The old Met seated approximately 3,800 and terrified many Europeans who came here to make their debuts in that theatre. Opera houses in Europe are seldom anywhere near that size.

The tenor for my debut night was my good friend Jan Peerce, who was singing often at the Met then, and he proved to be a warm and devoted Rodolfo. Martial Singher, the French baritone, was Marcello and the wonderful basso-buffo Salvatore Baccaloni did Benoit and Alcindoro. It was my first introduction to Frances Greer as Musetta and I always thought her exceptional in that role. The conductor was Cesare Sodero.

One year before, on the same night in 1944, Grace Moore had sung *La Bohème* with the same conductor and an almost identical cast. Even more interesting was the fact that in 1928 she also made her debut at the Metropolitan in the role of Mimi! For my debut, Grace and her husband were sitting in Box Number One, close to the stage, where she could watch my every move.

Upon arriving at my dressing room I found myself surrounded by flowers. One beautiful bouquet attracted my attention at once. Next to it was a small box and a message in Grace's impressive handwriting. When I opened it, I was deeply touched to find a small ermine muff. As I put my hand in it I drew out a furry object that appeared to be a rabbit's foot. The note attached read:

My dear Mimi,
    The rabbit's foot will always bring you luck. Use this little muff tonight and think of me.

I used the little muff that night and since then have never sung a Mimi without it. The rabbit's foot has served me well and is always with me wherever I sing.

I will never be able to express the feelings I had when I made my first entrance on the stage of the Metropolitan. I had an excellent following at the City Center Theater and it seemed the entire audience had come over to hear my debut at the Met. The welcome was more than I had hoped for and unnerved me for a moment, but back again flashed the words Dinty Doyle had engraved on my mind, "Don't blow it, kid," and I quickly recovered my composure. It was *my* night and I was off to a great start.

As the performance came to an end and I was sent out for my first solo bow, the audience responded with a roar. I looked up to Box Number One from which a shower of bouquets began to fall. Both Grace and Val were throwing them onto the stage, and when a few landed on the heads of musicians in the orchestra, Grace kept smiling and enjoyed a few bows herself. The audience was delighted with this exhibition and it was a most memorable and thrilling night for me.

The excitement continued backstage and when we were finally ready to leave the theatre, Grace suggested we wait at a nearby restaurant for the morning papers. Gathering together a few of our close friends, we walked a short distance from the old Met to the Artists and Writers Restaurant, then a popular after-theatre spot. There we dined and waited for the notices. They were great! I was launched and there was much celebrating into the wee hours.

The Met lost no time in putting me to work. A few days following my debut I appeared in the second act of *La Traviata* at a benefit concert under Maestro Paul Breisach, and only ten days later made my debut as Juliette in the lovely Gounod opera based on the Shakespearean tragedy. I had never sung the role before and was faced for the first time at the Met with no orchestra rehearsal prior to my performance. Fortunately, Raoul Jobin was my tenor and a most secure partner. The conductor, Emil Cooper, provided little assistance, seemed bored to have to put up with a debutante, and actually was not much interested in the opera as well. At the first piano rehearsal I remember how upset I was because Cooper's English, heavily laden with a thick Russian accent, was incomprehensible to me.

In each of these operas I wore my own costumes, having a young designer, D. Lawrence Roth, create a portion of my first operatic wardrobe. He did lovely things for Juliette and *La Traviata*, my third role at the Met, in which I had had a good deal of experience at the City Center.

Lawrence Tibbett was my partner on one of the Sunday night concerts when I sang the second act of *La Traviata*. This was my first performance with the great baritone, and he asked me that evening if I would consider appearing with him in a production of *Porgy and Bess*. Tibbett was anxious to convince Mr. Johnson to put it on at the Metropolitan. Now many of the major opera houses in Europe have added the Gershwin masterpiece to their repertoire and, since it was an American composition, the Met had seemed a natural place to stage it. Much to our disappointment this never took place.

Grace had made her debut at the Met in February 1928 and sang with the company approximately sixteen years. Charpentier's *Louise* was revived for her in 1939 and became one of her most beloved roles and greatest triumphs. Shortly after my debut at the Metropolitan she presented me with her own score and told me I would be singing that opera some day.

Toward the end of my first season the management asked me to prepare *Louise*, as they were planning a revival of the opera for me. Grace had sung her last performance of this role in 1943, but since she was still available I could not bring myself to accept the offer. I was flattered when the company then suggested *L'Amore dei Tre Re*, which had also been one of her best roles, but I asked to be excused from them both while she was still singing. Edward Johnson was tremendously fond of Grace, and when I resisted he told me he understood my feelings; the operas were temporarily removed from his plans.

On my first Metropolitan Opera tour I sang Micaela to Risë Stevens' Carmen, and I believe this was the last time I undertook the part of Don José's timid fiancée. The following season, after taking on Marguerite in *Faust* for the first time with the Met, I was called in on an emergency to sing *Madama Butterfly* for the ailing Licia Albanese. This was disappointing, because my own debut performance in the role was planned for only a few weeks later. I received but a few hours' notice for this extremely demanding role, and not being familiar with the sets for *Butterfly*, had to do a good deal of improvising. Though there are always anxious moments in such emergencies, they are a tremendous challenge that I find exciting and stimulating. Charles Kullmann, who for so many years had been Grace Moore's leading man, was my Pinkerton, so once again I had a reliable partner.

My second season at the Met was shattered by the news that Grace Moore had been killed in an air crash. On January 26, 1947, as she was taking off in a plane from Copenhagen for a concert in Stockholm, the plane went down taking Grace and everyone on board. I was literally numb and to continue my work took a tremendous effort.

Three thousand persons attended a memorial service for Grace at Riverside Church in New York where she had been a member. Lawrence Tibbett sang "The Lord's Prayer" so touchingly, and I was asked to sing Schubert's "Ave Maria," which proved to be a heartbreaking assignment. Everyone who loved Grace was there, including many of the great names in the entertainment world. I accompanied her husband and the family to her hometown of Chattanooga, Tennessee, where she was buried. The funeral service was made all the more impressive by a twenty-four-man color guard from the American Legion. In June of that same year Eugene Conley and I sang at a memorial concert for Grace in New York at Lewisohn Stadium.

More than ever I wanted to live up to the dreams she had for me, and I have a feeling she is still my guardian angel.

In those early years I was regularly engaged for the spring tour with the Met and remember the excitement of many of those performances. The entire company at that time would travel by two private trains. Atlanta was one of my favorite engagements and the Southern hospitality of that city when the Met arrived was special. Cleveland, Minneapolis, and Boston were all wonderful stops.

The many friends we made on those trips will never be forgotten, and it's a pity things are so changed now. Travel by train was more relaxing than traveling in the jet age of today, where singers fly in the day before a performance, sing, and fly out. The company used to frown on artists who left the tour unless they had more than a few days off, but that's all past. Touring now is not the same, and I think it was far more fun in those days.

On the Met's 1947 spring tour I was engaged to sing Marguerite in *Faust*, with Ezio Pinza as Mephistopheles. This was the first time I would sing with the great bass and I was delighted. Ezio had the reputation of being a Don Juan offstage as well as on. My compartment on the train was next to Mr. Johnson's, where (as he put it) he could keep an eye on me. However, Ezio arranged to move in on the other side and tried his best to keep me "company" while my "guardian" slept through it all.

Pinza was a fantastic Mephisto, and when he left the Met two years later for Broadway to star in *South Pacific*, he was sorely missed.

When I look back at the record and realize the work I was doing in that period, I wonder how I did it all. People have asked why I didn't sing more in Europe, but I had everything I wanted right here in my own back yard: opera, concerts, recitals, and lots of radio all year round. That particular year I was a regular on so many radio shows that it was difficult to find time to study new roles.

The 1947 Met season was over and the spring tour was about to get under way when Mr. Johnson told me he had arranged for me to go to Paris and study *Louise*. In fact, I learned both *Louise* and *L'Amore dei Tre Re* that summer for the following season.

In the meantime Gaetano Merola, director of the San Francisco Opera, had learned about my plans to travel to Paris and engaged me to sing *Louise* with his company in early October while the Met had planned my debut for mid-December 1947. Lawrence Tibbett played my father in this performance; Raoul Jobin was Julien, and Margaret Harshaw my mother. Désiré Defrère directed the action and Louis Fourestier, the Frenchman with whom I worked in Paris, was our conductor.

In those days our two major companies seemed a bit more compatible. Johnson was not only agreeable but delighted that I would have the chance to sing the role first in San Francisco.

L'Amore dei Tre Re was also prepared for an earlier debut in San Francisco; however, my first Fiora at the Met was December 1, 1948, exactly three years after I joined the company. This was my introduction to Virgilio Lazzari, who was spectacular as the old King and considered by most to be the greatest interpreter of this role. Charles Kullmann was an excellent Avito, and Giuseppe Antonicelli conducted.

In late 1950 Sir Rudolf Bing began his career as the general manager of the Metropolitan Opera. Jussi Björling and I were rehearsing *Manon Lescaut* on the day we first met him. This was a dress rehearsal and we were therefore obliged to appear in full costume and make-up. The management had asked us to meet in the Green Room just before the last act.

Manon Lescaut is a glamorous role and I wear some of my most beautiful costumes in this opera. Unfortunately, in the last act Manon trudges through the desert dying, and I was dressed in a drab and torn costume with my hair disheveled and my face dirty. I had been trying to think of something nice to say to welcome our new director, since I couldn't put my best foot forward in my appearance. We were asked to form a receiving line, and being the prima donna, I was first. Jussi stood next to me. As Mr. Bing came forward I said, "I am sorry to have to greet you in such an unglamorous costume." His response was, "I hate glamour." And with that, my dear friend Jussi, grinning all over that cherubic face, said, "Ha, ha, she just returned from Hollywood where she has been making a motion picture."

This seemed a poor way to begin a mutual admiration relationship with our new director and I was stunned by Mr. Bing's remark, but he is a disciplinarian and I soon realized that there was nothing personal intended. We were on fairly good terms from the beginning. He was always direct, but I respected that. There were never promises that were not kept, nor do I remember him ever being that gruff again. However, I do recall hearing him say on "The Dick Cavett Show" that he regarded opera singers as "sick," which was a shocking discovery to most of us.

I had enjoyed a warm camaraderie with Edward Johnson during my first years at the Metropolitan, and I missed his way of making me feel he understood those last-minute jitters. Mr. Bing would generally come to pay his respects, but most of the time he gave me the feeling he was afraid to ask if everything was all right for fear of hearing a complaint.

Though we never became particularly close friends, he did show respect for my judgment, for which I was grateful, when I rejected an offered role I felt I should not sing. I began my career with a promise to myself that I would build it slowly and carefully, choosing the roles I knew were right vocally and the characters that attracted me.

By the time I came to the Metropolitan my voice was secure. I knew its limits and refused to push it. I was determined to manage it with patience and intelligence so that it would eventually grow into the *spinto* dramatic range and allow me to sing the heavier *verismo* roles. I am a perfectionist and it never was my plan to learn many roles and sing them only once or twice and maybe never again.

Helen Hayes expressed my feelings exactly when she wrote in her book *A Gift of Joy:* "I limited myself carefully in order to develop everything that properly belonged to my special individuality, and approach each performance with the hope that I will find something better of myself to give to my role and my audience that night than the time before."

The first role Mr. Bing offered me was the most difficult decision of all to make. It was to be his first opera at the Met and I had been asked to sing Elizabeth in *Don Carlo*. I was flattered by his offer and would have been delighted with a new production and an excitement-filled opening night, but the role was entirely too heavy for my young voice. Who knows how things might have been had I accepted, but I had to learn how to say no at this point no matter how attractive the part and regardless of the consequences.

The second offer of a new role came my way during that same season when I was asked to sing the sparkling role of Rosalinde in *Die Fledermaus* to be presented for the first time by the company. I was not overwhelmed by this part, having sung so much light opera before I came to the Met; however, not wanting to seem ungrateful, I accepted and started learning the role.

About halfway through my study I came down with one of the most severe colds I have ever had. I advised my management that I could not continue my work, and they told the Met I would have to cancel. For some reason the powers that be at the Metropolitan were skeptical of my condition and I was informed that Max Rudolf, second in command, was coming to my hotel to verify my illness. Stunned by their disbelief and shocking intrusion upon my privacy, I played one of my greatest scenes, and the dying Camille on her deathbed could not have put the point across more effectively.

Madame Ljuba Welitch, who was asked to step in for me, didn't appear too happy to do so. When I ran into her at the Met a few weeks later, she had a look to kill and displaying her thick Bulgarian accent as she flew by me, I heard her say, "You bitch."

But Mr. Bing was determined I would sing Rosalinde and in 1962 to show him my good intentions I accepted and sang ten performances between the regular season and the tour. When I sang it in Boston with the company I had a slip of the tongue in the last act while all the clowning was going on that made the house roar. Instead of say-

Above left to right: My debut in Russia, *La Traviata*. Jack meeting me in Moscow with a representative of the Cultural Exchange. Below clockwise from top left: Two views—working with the composer of *Louise*, Gustave Charpentier. Debut as Louise with Ezio Pinza and Claramae Turner, San Francisco. (Photo courtesy San Francisco Opera) Sketch of a third-act costume designed in Paris, approved by Charpentier and graciously signed "Adopté."

Clockwise from top left: With John Tyers in *The Merry Widow*, Dallas. Credit: Squire Haskins) With Bing Crosby on "The Bing Crosby Show." (Photo courtesy ABC) Dancing with His Highness the Duke of Edinburgh after concert given for his favorite charity in London. With Nelson Eddy, "Kraft Music Hall." (Photo courtesy NBC) With Mario Lanza in *The Great Caruso*. (Photo courtesy MGM) Frank Sinatra crowning me "Queen of Tobacco" on "Light Up Time." (Photo courtesy NBC)

Clockwise from top left: With Al Jolson, "Kraft Music Hall." (Photo courtesy NBC) With Jack Benny on "The Jack Benny Program." (Photo courtesy NBC) Artur Rubinstein and Bob Hope on a Bond show. (Photo courtesy CBS) With Gordon Macrae on "The Railroad Hour." (Credit: Herb Ball) With Edgar Bergen and Charlie McCarthy on "The Edgar Bergen Show." (Photo courtesy CBS) With John Raitt on "The Chevy Show." (Photo courtesy NBC)

Above left to right: With Jack, receiving the Handel Award from New York's Mayor John Lindsay. (Photo courtesy Municipal Archives, City of New York) Italian Consul-General Alessandro Cortese de Bosia presenting Italy's highest Cultural Award, the Commendatore. (Credit: Erika Davidson) Below left to right: Receiving from Kurt Adler the first silver medal commemorating twenty-five years with the San Francisco Opera. (Credit: Ms. Norton, courtesy San Francisco Opera) H. Lloyd Hawkins, president of the New Orleans Opera, presenting me with a gold bracelet commemorating the many roles I sang with them.

ing, in a spoken line, "What is champagne for the goose is champagne for the gander," I said, "is shampoo for the gander." The cast was hysterical, and at the next performance of the opera they presented me with bottles and bottles of shampoo.

There were two other operas offered during the Bing regime that I had to refuse. The first was Samuel Barber's *Vanessa*, sung so well by Eleanor Steber. But if I were to take on this part, I knew that I would be jeopardizing some of my lighter roles. I told this to Mr. Bing and offered to sing Erika, the second lead in the opera, which to me was much more lyric and better suited to my voice, but this he rejected.

The last time we discussed a new role he called to say he had a wonderful new part for me. I was eager and hopeful it would be something just right this time. When he presented me with Marie in *Wozzeck*, my heart sank. I knew right then that I could not accept it, for I had witnessed the damaging results to a colleague's voice who had sung the role. However, I promised to review the score in any case before my final decision. The role appealed to me dramatically, and I could have sung it, but the risk was too great and I had to say no. Mr. Bing paid me a compliment which I have not forgotten. He said, "Dorothy, if you had been anyone else and refused that role I would have fired you, but I respect the way you have handled your voice."

Mr. Bing and I did have our differences, however, and one year when he offered me performances of only *Faust* and *Bohème* I told him I was not interested and asked to be released from the season. But when Mr. Bing wanted something and needed me, he certainly knew how to turn on the charm. He had engaged Antonietta Stella to do a new production of *Madama Butterfly*. As the end of the season drew near Miss Stella canceled the entire tour on the grounds of poor health but decided she could still do the upcoming broadcast of the opera.

I was on a concert tour when Mr. Bing called me. He said he was on his knees to me, though of course he couldn't prove that on the telephone. He begged me to rearrange my schedule so I could sing the many performances of *Madama Butterfly* the Met was committed to for the tour. In fairness he also took away the broadcast from the other diva and gave it to me. When later it was learned that Miss Stella was not ill but singing all over Europe, she was promptly fired by Mr. Bing and never returned.

I have never been one to push or demand as others have, and this was probably a drawback in my dealings with Mr. Bing. There were times when he desperately needed me and I was there. I never took advantage of those times by insisting on something new that I wanted to do, and in retrospect that was foolish.

I remember a nice, relaxed conversation around the pool at our hotel in Atlanta on tour one season. There were just a few artists there and we were discussing French opera, which was then so scarce at the Met. I was anxious to sing *Louise* again, and with all the fine basses on the roster at that time, it would have been easy to assemble a great cast. I was shocked to hear Mr. Bing say the opera was boring.

It had been quite some time since I had been heard in a new role at the Met and my fans were pressing for something new. In contrast, the San Francisco Opera Company first engaged me for most of the operas in which I am best known. The Met was soon to follow, but not one of these operas was first offered by Mr. Bing. When I finally decided to ask him if he would give me Desdemona in *Otello*, he said, "Why don't you sing it in San Francisco first?" So that was it! Did he resent the many opportunities and the successes I enjoyed in San Francisco? Never again did I ask him for anything.

It was quite amusing when *Life* magazine came to New Orleans to photograph a performance of my *Tosca* there, before I had sung it at the Met. They headlined their article, "KIRSTEN'S TOSCA GREAT! LOOK WHAT MR. BING MISSED!"

Though I was not one to accuse him of neglecting the American artists, I always felt that I deserved something more in his twenty-one years as general manager. I think it all goes back to the start of our association when I had to refuse the great role he first offered me of Elizabeth in *Don Carlo*.

The mightiest blow he dealt me came with his new production of *La Fanciulla del West* (*The Girl of the Golden West*). I had triumphed in this opera in San Francisco the season before and was looking forward so much to doing my version of Minnie in New York. When the announcement was made that the opera would open the next season with Leontyne Price as Minnie, I could not believe it. I was hurt, disillusioned, and ready to cancel the season. This would have been the ideal opportunity for him to set things right. I decided impulsively that I was never going to sing for him again, but when I calmed down I realized I would be hurting only myself by such a spiteful action. The company needed me. They had to have two strong divas scheduled to do this opera, because the practice was for one to do the opening, with extensive rehearsals, and the first four performances; and the other prima donna would do the last four dates including the live broadcast which was heard throughout the United States and Canada, and taped for most of the world. Being second was not all bad!

It was in this order of appearance that I was offered *La Fanciulla del West*. My other roles of Tosca and Madama Butterfly were also scheduled in the first part of the season; therefore, as I would be walking into a new production without stage rehearsals, it was important for me to attend a performance of the new opera to familiarize myself with the sets. The opening was October 23, 1961. I went to the opera that night but left before the last act because of a dress rehearsal the next morning of my own performance of *Tosca* that was coming up two days later.

All went well with my performance of *Tosca*, and I then settled down to work with the new cast for *Fanciulla*. Leontyne's second performance was scheduled for October 31, Halloween night. We had rehearsed all that day from 10 A.M. to 6 P.M. with the director, Bill Butler, in a studio with only a few props and the floor marked out for entrances and exits. The first and second acts were thoroughly worked out, but we never had time for the third act, the same one I had missed seeing on the opening night.

Exhausted, I went to my hotel and had dinner. Wanting to be sure I would have a good night's sleep, I took a pill and went to bed. About ten o'clock the phone rang and Vicki answered a call from the Met saying that Leontyne was having trouble getting through the second act and would I come to the theatre right away. The ring had awakened me and I responded, "Oh, they're playing a joke on me. It's Halloween; they must be kidding."

When the phone rang again I answered. This time it was Bob Herman, Mr. Bing's assistant. Trying to get my dulled thoughts together I realized they were facing a real crisis. Vicki was already preparing black coffee to wake me up. Bob told me the audience was out for the intermission, waiting for the opera to continue, but Leontyne was definitely unable to go on. I threw on some clothes, gathered my costume and riding boots, which were still at the hotel, jumped into a taxi and "flew" to the Met. As we approached I could see the audience standing out on the street as they did then at the old Met. As I entered through the Thirty-ninth Street door, all the members of the management were standing in line waiting anxiously for me. After what must have been one of the longest intermissions in the history of the Met, I heard Osie Hawkins, the stage manager, announce to the audience that I would complete the opera. When I heard their excited response I almost panicked.

I was told that Leontyne was in tears and I went immediately to her dressing room. I felt very sorry for her. The conductor, Fausto Cleva, was waiting for me in another room and while a make-up man was dabbing whatever powder and rouge he could on my face and the hairdresser was combing my hair, Cleva was banging out cues I must remember on the piano.

By the time I reached the stage, the horse I was to gallop on with had become noticeably restless. As I tried to calm him by stroking his neck, I said, "Don't be nervous, Jordan, I'm in worse shape than you are!" Getting a laugh from the group around me seemed to break the tension, and when I began to sing the call that signals the tenor that I am coming to save him, Jordan was ready. After a kick, the horse took off, and it was an exciting entrance. The audience exploded and greeted me with prolonged and thunderous applause, stopping the performance. It seemed like forever before the maestro picked up his baton and started again. My jitters left immediately, the adrenaline began to flow and I was singing with all my heart.

Shortly after Minnie's entrance she has a lovely sequence to sing, addressing herself to each of her special friends by his own name. I had no idea who was playing which role, having had no rehearsal of this act, and that worried me considerably. My colleagues were wonderful. Each one, as I was about to sing to him, would signal me so I could make no mistake.

This was a role I adored but had only sung a few times in San Francisco the season before. The electricity that went through me seemed transferred to the audience and it turned into one of the most exciting nights of my life in the theatre.

The morning following that sensational experience, I had to rise and shine for a 10 A.M. dress rehearsal of *Madama Butterfly*. Rescuing the *Fanciulla* performance made it necessary for the company to switch operas around for me. I had to give up my second *Tosca* of the season, for it followed too closely, and instead sang *Madama Butterfly* one day later. Because Leontyne had to have complete vocal rest for several months, she was forced to cancel all of her performances of *Fanciulla*, and I found myself doing her dates as well as my own. The billboards out front of the theatre were advertising *Fanciulla*, *Tosca*, and *Madama Butterfly* with Kirsten, all in one week! To say the least I was practically living at the Metropolitan.

La Fanciulla del West was a big success and though the public were slow at first to take it to their hearts, we were soon playing to sold-out houses.

My trip to the Soviet Union followed this exciting but taxing season and was the climax of another busy time. I was not prepared, however, for the enforced rest I had to face on my return. The next two months had been solidly booked for a long concert tour, but I was home only a short time when I learned I had hepatitis and was hospitalized. Most of the tour had to be canceled. It wasn't easy to keep me down. When I was told that I would have to stay in bed for weeks I hit the roof. Poor Jack! Friends and family showered me with reading matter but I was still bored. After a few days my doctors agreed to allow me to go home, providing Jack would arrange for a hospital bed. We were living in our beautiful house in Palos Verdes, one thousand feet above the sea, with a magnificent view. They set up my bed where I could see my garden and the pool that we had built a few months before. Suddenly I was struck by a marvelous idea that could keep me occupied for that miserable time. I set to work immediately drawing up plans for a guest house that I had wanted for some time but had been too busy to think about.

My father had inspired me as a youngster to draw plans and taught me a great deal about draftsmanship. When I wasn't studying on air trips from coast to coast I would be designing houses. The contractor accepted the plans that I had drawn to scale and my little guest house was built right before my eyes. Each workman looked up to greet me as he arrived in the morning. The boss reported to me each day and I amused myself by watching my ideas take form.

Fortunately, I did not have a severe case of hepatitis, and six weeks later I was well enough to join the Met on tour for my scheduled performances of *Fanciulla* and *Madama Butterfly*.

The summer was busy with recordings and my first concert tour in Alaska. After that there was time for a rest in Hawaii with lots of golf, and I was soon ready to return to San Francisco to open the opera season with *La Bohème*. At the Met I celebrated my one hundredth performance of *Madama Butterfly* and continued to commute between the Met and San Francisco for another busy season.

Fanciulla was out of the repertoire for three years and brought back for the 1965–66 season. Again, Fausto Cleva, who especially loved this opera, was in the pit. It was an ideal cast with Franco Corelli, Anselmo Colzani, and the fine *comprimario* tenor Paul Franke repeating his excellent Nick, the bartender. I was given all nine performances that season and the first one was scheduled for December 1, exactly twenty years since the date of my debut with the company. Many of my friends came from the West Coast to help me celebrate the occasion and our wonderful friends Harriet and Charles Luckman of Los Angeles had a beautiful party for us at the "21" Club.

In April 1966 we said farewell to the old Metropolitan Opera building. To those of us who had started our careers in that wonderful old house it was an emotionally upsetting experience. I had sung there for twenty-one years. The old stage held memories for me that would never be forgotten. A grand gala was arranged and all the former great stars of the company were assembled in a semicircle on the stage with the rest of the company in back of them. I was among the artists who were asked to sing that night, and I remember how unnerving it was to walk onstage before that illustrious group: Lotte Lehmann, Elisabeth Rethberg, Lily Pons, Giovanni Martinelli, Bidú Sayão, and many more. I could not put out of my mind that this would be the last time I would perform on that beloved stage. Mr. Bing had asked me to sing "Depuis le jour" (Ever since the day), and being sentimental, those first three words had a truly profound meaning for me.

On September 16, 1966, the new opera house at Lincoln Center opened with Samuel Barber's *Antony and Cleopatra*. The opera was a fiasco, and despite its lavish sets, costumes, months of rehearsal, and colossal expense, it was never given again at the Met after that season.

The new house is magnificent with all its plush velvet and beautiful crystal, lovely dressing rooms and extraordinary facilities, but it will need time to earn its own traditions. Acoustically I found it a wonderful place in which to sing, and to singers that is the greatest blessing. My first performance in the new house was *Madama Butterfly* with my good friend John Alexander.

For several years the Metropolitan in collaboration with the City of New York has made an especially fine contribution to the thousands of music lovers in the city who cannot afford a ticket to the Met. The city sponsors full-length opera performances in concert form at parks such as Central Park and throughout the other boroughs.

An enormous stage was built, which is transported to each concert and assembled to hold the entire company, orchestra, chorus and the cast. Besides the mobile dressing rooms for the artists and management, all the lighting and sound equipment that is necessary makes it quite a project. Many of the top stars appear, and I have participated in several of these performances. People arrive early in the day to stake out their territory as near to the stage as possible. They come with blankets, chairs, picnic baskets, and tape recorders which they hold up in front of us as close as they can manage. There is no prompter, and anyone who makes the smallest mistake may be sure that it is being preserved forever. I remember one of those special evenings in Central Park when the moon was full over the city and the huge sea of uncountable humanity stretched far beyond any crowd I have ever seen.

After twenty-one years as general manager, Mr. Bing relinquished his post at the Metropolitan and a great event was arranged for his farewell at the end of the 1971–72 season. All the stars took part in a never-ending concert. There were duets, quartets, and solos. Again he asked me to sing "Depuis le jour." Apparently he liked the aria, though he didn't like the opera.

Goeran Gentele, of the Stockholm Opera, was to be our new director but was tragically killed in an automobile accident just a few weeks before his first season was to begin. I had been very pleased to meet him that summer during one of my parks concerts. Schuyler Chapin, who was Gentele's assistant, took over and did a fine job. His consideration and understanding of the artists was similar to that of Edward Johnson, and he was totally committed to his job. Schuyler showed his appreciation when I flew in more than once and sang in emergency for an ailing colleague. It was on one of these occasions that we first met. Charlie Reicker, his assistant, telephoned me one day, and when my secretary Vicki told him that I was playing golf, he said, "Oh good, then she's in great shape. We need her for *Tosca!*" Having received telephone calls on the golf course before, I wasn't too surprised, but it was not often necessary to drop my clubs and run as it was this time. I had been engaged to sing *Tosca* later that season and therefore my costumes were ready to go. Vicki, accustomed to quick departures, had arranged everything, and off we went to New York.

At the hotel there were flowers from Schuyler to greet me and the night of the performance I received a beautiful bottle of champagne with this note attached: "I am deeply grateful to you as a great artist for stepping in to save our necks."

After an especially pressing year of commitments, lots of traveling, and a heavy season at the Met, I was ready for our annual rest in Hawaii. Jack and I were enjoying a lovely vacation, when I realized something was wrong. I was not bouncing back as fast as I usually do, but believed it was just due to overwork.

We were invited by our close friend, Charles Luckman, to visit the fabulous new stadium in Honolulu which he designed. Trying to be a good sport I donned the hard hat and climbed to the top with the rest of them to see the lovely view. Struggling to keep up with my friends, I realized my problem was more than fatigue and Jack became alarmed. We immediately arranged to come back to Los Angeles, and within a few days my doctors were planning a hysterectomy. This was a great blow, especially when I was told that after my operation I would not be strong enough to sing for at least three months. The Met was in a tizzy, as my first performance of *Manon Lescaut* was scheduled in just six weeks.

Gradually I began to feel stronger and I was more determined to meet my commitments. My doctors were extremely pleased with my recuperative powers but were still insisting it would be too soon to return to my work. Schuyler was still expecting me. As time drew nearer and a decision had to be made, I called him to explain. He was very understanding but this being a special performance he did not have a comparable cover, and he pleaded with me to come for at least that first performance.

My husband and doctors were extremely upset with me, but I felt I had to take that chance. This was to be my first performance of the season with an unfamiliar cast. My first preoccupation was the weight of my costumes. The second act of *Manon Lescaut* is a tour de force in itself, one of the most physically exhausting acts of all Puccini operas for the prima donna. In this act I wear one of the heaviest gowns I own: jeweled damask with an enormous skirt supported by a huge hoop with two steel bands encircling it. Pulling all this weight around the stage would have been impossible after my surgery, so the costume department at the Met helped me redesign it. The skirt was altered to a lighter and smaller hoop, which helped a great deal.

As rehearsals progressed I found myself running out of gas. My doctor had warned me that this might happen and suggested that oxygen be available if I should need it. Schuyler was considerably concerned and assured me that a doctor would be standing by for the performance.

Only the fact that I had kept myself physically fit and my unyielding determination made it possible for me to get through that night. There was no way of getting any help during the second act because I was on the stage singing continually. But I will never forget gasping for breath as I made my exit and gulping the oxygen which was waiting close by. I was helped to my dressing room and quickly relieved of my costume. They held the curtain until I regained my strength. Fortunately, the act that follows is not too demanding, but I knew right then that I would have to forgo my second performance a few days later.

The following month, when I was fully recovered, I returned to do several more performances of *Manon Lescaut*. I was proud of myself for having survived this enormous test of my strength because this opera is probably my favorite of all the Puccini roles I have sung. My eternal thanks to the immortal Puccini who loved his Manon beyond all his other heroines. I have known her intimately for so many years and I can certainly understand why.

In June of 1975 I was asked by the Met to join them on their first tour to the Orient. This was an experience beyond all expectations. The entire company of more than three hundred were flown to Japan, along with costumes and scenery for three productions: *La Traviata*, *La Bohème*, and *Carmen*. I was engaged to sing four performances of Mimi; two with Luciano Pavarotti in Tokyo and the other two with Franco Corelli in Osaka.

The company was greeted with a lovely reception given by Ambassador and Mrs. Hodgson at the American Embassy in Tokyo. Among the guests were many important Japanese representatives of cultural affairs, the American and Japanese press and officials of the recording companies. As luck would have it, one of the first gentlemen I met at this party was an attractive Japanese, Mr. Tokygen Yamamoto, a representative of RCA. He needed no introduction, having known me through my early recordings for Victor. He ever so politely asked if he could be of any service to me while I was in Japan. Delighted with the opportunity, I responded, "You certainly may. I am a golfer and I would love to play while I'm here." My golfing pals back home had told me of the magnificent courses in Japan, and though I knew women were seldom welcomed, I was determined to try to get a game and had brought my clubs with me. Mr. Yamamoto was a member of the Tokyo Yomiuri, one of the finest golf clubs in Tokyo, and immediately offered to arrange a game. When my colleague Bill Walker, the baritone who was singing with me in *La Bohème*, heard of our plans, he begged to join us. A foursome was quickly set up including Bill and William Bender of *Time* magazine, and we were off early the next morning.

I never laughed so hard or had more fun playing golf anywhere before. Mr. Yamamoto was such a good sport. When he stepped up to the first tee to hit the ball, we heard an astounding samurai yell which took us completely by surprise. Upon seeing our shocked expressions, he quickly explained that this was part of his game and joined us in a big laugh. He repeated this outburst every time he hit the ball and kept us in hysterics the entire game. The course was indeed magnificent and we had a marvelous day which I will long remember.

Before going to Japan with the Met, Jimmy Doolittle and I were busy planning our own production of *Madama Butterfly* for the Greek Theatre in Los Angeles. This trip enabled me to select and buy all of the costumes and some of the props for the production. It gave me a chance to choose for the chorus authentic kimonos in beautiful hues complementary to my own costumes. I also outfitted the men in the opera and bought all the parasols, fans, and footwear for the entire company.

I had inquired of some of my Japanese friends about a shop that might have a good selection of the things I needed. The proprietor of the shop spoke fairly good English and was interested to learn that I was buying these things for a production of *Madama Butterfly* in Los Angeles. This lady could not have been more helpful. She told me that as the Japanese customs had changed considerably, many families were selling their fine old ceremonial robes, and showed us some of the most magnificent kimonos I have ever seen.

Jack's friends in Japan (several medical scientists whom we had entertained in Los Angeles) were anxious to reciprocate our hospitality and did their best in the limited amount of time I had to show me the major attractions of the area. I was invited to their lovely homes with magnificent gardens, one of which had a prize-winning collection of carp.

After my performances in Tokyo, we took a side trip to Kyoto where I could not resist the fascinating shops and the beautiful silks. In Osaka I had to rehearse with my other tenor, Franco Corelli, and between our two performances I managed to get in one more game of golf. Afterward my host invited me to a private tea ceremony in his beautiful home.

The Met put its best foot forward when it took to Japan this galaxy of great stars; I was delighted to be included. Joan Sutherland opened the season with a superb *Traviata*. Corelli and Pavarotti were in top form in our *Bohèmes*. We all sang our hearts out and the Japanese responded most enthusiastically.

For me 1975 was an especially significant year at the Met. My contract called for several performances of both *Tosca* and *Manon Lescaut*. When Montserrat Caballé canceled because of illness, I was asked to take on her *Manon Lescaut* performances too, which made it a very long season. I was also on the road a great deal that year for other commitments between my performances in New York. Realizing that the constant traveling was becoming too much for me, I decided to slow down my career and say farewell to New York.

This book began with the story of that exciting night of *Tosca* when I was celebrating my thirtieth anniversary at the Met. That New Year's Eve was certainly a night to remember. My dressing room could not hold all the flowers sent to me. There were telegrams and messages from friends and very important people including one from President Ford.

When the news was released that it was also my farewell, members of my fan clubs from all over the country showered Vicki with letters begging her to arrange for tickets. Even though it was a special performance and not a subscription night, her task was not easy because my own guest list was considerable.

Before the performance began I was told that after the second act there would be a presentation and the audience would be asked to remain seated. When the act ended, the cast and the entire company returned to the stage where I was proud to be presented with a beautiful, inscribed gold bracelet, commemorating my thirty years with the company. This established a precedent at the Met because I was the first to receive this honor. Flattering speeches followed which built me up to such an emotional state that I wondered if I could utter a word when it came my turn to speak.

After the final curtain calls I had a champagne party in the Green Room, a reception area for such occasions at the Met. This was especially for the fans and standees who were my loyal followers for so many years. After that emotional gathering, the "21" Club arranged a beautiful supper party for my guests who had traveled cross-country to be with me. It was a grand finale to a great night, one which went on well into the New Year.

Allen Hughes of the New York *Times* responded with an excellent review and this quote thereof:

. . . she sang and acted the part of Tosca with the vocal control and dramatic acuity of a prima donna in mid-career.

"I will sing as long as I sing well," Miss Kirsten said during the intermission ceremony honoring her anniversary and farewell. Judging from her singing on this occasion, she will be at it for a long time to come.

Though the title of this chapter is "Ecstasies and Agonies at the Met," the emphasis is definitely on the ecstasies. How many prima donnas have had the privilege of performing with this great company for more than thirty years? Remembering the many thrilling nights of my career at the Met makes me very grateful.

Perhaps my farewell came a bit too soon. I realize now how important a part of my life my career has always been. To pretend I don't miss the Met would be foolish.

Those moments of agony I can easily forget, but the ecstasies will always be with me!

April in Paris

I was Gustave Charpentier's last Louise, coached by him to sing his opera. Every time I sang this masterpiece I loved it more and more. I shall always remember with great affection my first Julien, the real one: Charpentier, the composer himself.

The first performance of *Louise* at the Met was given in the 1920–21 season with Geraldine Farrar in the title role. The opera was revived in 1929 for Lucrezia Bori and sung by Grace Moore ten years later in 1939. Grace too had been coached in the role by the composer and received her greatest acclaim as Louise. Mary Garden was well known in Europe for the role and Charpentier spoke highly of her interpretation. The Metropolitan revived the opera for me in 1947 and my debut was on December 12.

Louise will always mean Paris to me, and Paris always reminds me of *Louise*. I shall never forget the summer of 1947 when I went there to study my new role. I am especially grateful to my sister Eleanor, whom I had invited to accompany me, because this story would not have been nearly so complete without her detailed diary and notes carefully kept on our every move.

We planned to sail on the *Queen Elizabeth* on July 2 and had been anticipating this departure for weeks. At the pier the press was busy taking pictures of the young Met diva who was sailing off to Europe in a blaze of glory to study her new role. Family, my manager Freddie Schang, friends, and fans were there to see me off in style. As the hour drew near for our departure, with everyone's luggage but ours disappearing aboard ship, I became concerned. Just about this time Freddie also gathered that something was wrong and hurried off to find out what. Much to my consternation, there had been an error in accommodations. Another party had been assigned to the same stateroom and while we were entertaining the press and saying our good-byes they moved in. What an embarrassment that was!

As annoyed as we all were, there was nothing we could do about it. The available space offered was unsuitable and the wire service pictures went coast to coast along with the story of a sad prima donna titled, "Dorothy Kirsten Left Waiting at the Dock While the Queen Sails Without Her." Of course we were crushed, but with my fatalistic beliefs holding strong, and the fact that we were promised a new sailing date in a week on the *Mauretania*, I began to relax about our disappointment. As we stood there wondering what to do next, our spirits were lifted considerably by an invitation to spend our waiting period with Fred and Em Schang at their lovely home in Connecticut. Our hosts were marvelous. We played golf, were wined, dined and so beautifully entertained that the time flew and before we knew it we were once again starting our trip to Paris.

Our arrival at Cherbourg revealed a sad sight. The destruction left by the war two years before was incredible, and the train trip to Paris when we viewed all the bombed-out buildings was truly heartbreaking. It was a relief to arrive in Paris and realize how fortunate this great city was to have been spared.

I had chosen to live at the Royal Monceau, which was highly recommended as small and quiet and where I could work and escape the tourist traffic. This particular hotel had been completely taken over by the German Air Force during the war. After we were there for a while, the waiters in the dining room entertained us with stories of how they had hidden their best wines in a secret cellar under the hotel when the Germans came. Their hiding place was never discovered and we were served some of the greatest Alsatian wines I have ever tasted.

Because I had arrived a week late for my studies, I had to get to work as soon as possible. Before I left home I had looked at the score for *Louise* and started my preliminary work on it. Now I was eager to meet my teachers. I wanted to brush up on my French as well, and that would have to be worked into my schedule.

The man with whom I would first study the role was Maestro Maurice Faurè. He was the assistant to Louis Fourestier, the French conductor who was coming to New York to conduct the opera at the Met. After I was secure in the role I would review the part with my conductor, learning his interpretation of the music, and finally I would study the role with the composer himself.

While I worked with these gentlemen, they invited some of the top artists of the French opera to sing the other parts. The great basso Pernet was most helpful and shared with me much of his own staging, for he had sung the father part in *Louise* many times. Charles Fronval, a well-known tenor of the Opéra Comique, came to sing Julien with me. I shall always be grateful for the assistance these artists gave me.

My studies were progressing very well, when one day the maestro asked if Eleanor and I would like to come out to his country home for dinner. Fourestier and his wife would also be there and offered to drive us in their little car. What we could see of the rural country was magnificent, but without a doubt this was the most harrowing automobile ride I have ever experienced. Sitting in the back seat with our knees under our chins, we held on for dear life while we were swung around sharp corners, barely scraping buildings in the narrow streets. Everything scattered before us, chickens, children, and anything in our way while we clung to our seats and pretended to be amused. I began to wonder if the French were even faster drivers than the Italians. But our visit was charming; the delicious home-cooked food and the wine were delectable, and our fearful ride was soon forgotten.

Before we left home, Humphry Doulens, one of my representatives at Columbia Artists, alerted two of his good friends, Frank McCarthy and Rupert Allan, that I was coming over to study. They were both in Paris on business for motion-picture companies and could not have been more charming and attentive. We spent much of our free time with Frank and Rupert, seeing Paris, dining at their favorite restaurants, and taking trips to surrounding points of interest.

Our trip to Reims was a delight. We saw a great deal of rural France that day. We drove through the Marne River Valley, a battleground in both world wars, and passed through Château-Thierry, which had been occupied by the Germans and heavily bombed by our own forces. These areas provided us with a grim reminder of how fortunate we Americans were to have had an ocean between us and Europe.

We dined that day at a charming French café. Beginning with Reims champagne, it was a delicious dinner of many courses and captivating atmosphere. I remember well that gay party. Anticipating the long trip back to Paris, Eleanor and I excused ourselves and started for the restrooms. Frank and Rupert had the same idea and followed, only to discover to our amazement that we had all ended up in the same room! A large mirror reflecting the waist-high partitioned stalls left nothing to the imagination. We laughed so hard I'm sure the woman attendant outside the door thought, "Those crazy Americans!"

Montmartre was the place I was most anxious to visit. The happy little village is perched high on a hill overlooking Paris. This is the setting for the opera Louise and the home of its composer, Gustave Charpentier. It is often called the soul of Paris.

The beautiful Gothic-style basilica of the Sacré-Coeur (Sacred Heart), which stands at the highest point of this little community, towers in all its majesty over the city below. It makes a striking picture and has long been a perfect model for all kinds of artists and painters. The little cobblestone streets and narrow sidewalks crowded with artists displaying their wares and the sound of music coming from everywhere provided the perfect atmosphere to inspire me.

I studied the fascinating character of Louise in a similar house close by to where my heroine had lived. The more I learned about her, the more anxious I was to meet Julien, her lover, who had been Charpentier himself. The opera was performed for the first time in 1900, when Charpentier was forty years old. Not until his seventy-first birthday did he admit to a friend that this musical romance was the story of his own heartaches. He was Julien, and it was he who loved Louise so passionately. He had written not only the music of this autobiographical story but the text as well.

My ambition was to have completed the study of the score before meeting Charpentier, then learn all I could from the composer in order to make my interpretation a completely authentic one and as close to the intentions of its creator as possible. Every day from early morning until late afternoon I worked with my coach, Maurice Fauré, whose studio was near Montmartre. Our hotel packed a lunch for us and each morning we would go in a little bus to the maestro's studio. The room in which we rehearsed was enchanting. It had all the plush of the old French style, a small balcony with a fabulous view of Paris and Sacré-Coeur, the atmosphere of Montmartre surrounding us. There could not have been a more stimulating spot in which to work on this opera. Each noon after a three-hour session, Eleanor and I gathered our lunch and sat in a nearby park, enjoying our bohemian repast of French bread, cheese, and wine.

My agents in New York had asked me to send back pictures for the anticipated press releases about my forthcoming debut. After roaming through Montmartre I knew this was where the photographs had to be taken. My new friends Rupert and Frank knew of an excellent photographer, Carl Stefan Perutz, whom I promptly engaged. I had seen some charming balconies where we could take in a lovely background and some of the view of Paris as well. Because a balcony is the scene of Louise and Julien's first love, I thought this would be quite appropriate. Carl was just as enthusiastic about the idea, and we trotted all over Montmartre until we found the right place where a woman was leaning over a rail six stories up. Projecting our pleas for the entire block to hear, she finally agreed to let us use her balcony, and we made our way up a dark stairway. We were successful and the resulting picture was well worth our effort when it appeared on the cover of *Opera News*.

My costumes for *Louise* were being created in Paris by the well-known fashion designer Marcelle Dormoy. I was introduced to her by Valentin Parera, husband of the late Grace Moore. It was a pleasant coincidence that he was in Paris at the same time. The designs were exquisite, and when the costumes were complete Val came to see them. Before leaving the next day he took me completely by surprise when he told me that he wanted me to have the costumes as a gift in remembrance of Grace. It was a touching gesture and I was deeply moved.

Maestro Fauré knew I was eager to finish my study of the score with him so I would have ample time to work with Charpentier. I was ready now, and much effort had been made to locate the composer but with no success. The more we searched, the more vague seemed his whereabouts. Everyone seemed to know that he lived somewhere in Montmartre, but where? The opera company was no help and my heart sank deeper every day as our time for departure neared. I was determined not to leave, and just as we were about to change our reservations Rupert Allan called to tell us he had the address.

It was late in the afternoon when we found the right house. After a good deal of persuasion and a little *d'argent* (money), a man standing near the entrance gave us the number of the Charpentiers' apartment. With my heart pumping like mad in anticipation, we climbed what seemed like a hundred steps with barely enough light to find our way. I gently tapped on the door. It was a long time before a woman answered and then the door only opened a few inches. Somehow I knew it was Madame Charpentier. Speaking as calmly as I could, I told her I was the new Louise of the Metropolitan Opera in New York and most anxious to meet her husband before I had to return to America. That seemed to open the door a little more so at least now I was facing the lady when she told me that Le Maître (the Master) was resting in their country retreat, Les Sables, a small resort area on the Atlantic coast.

I immediately gathered that she was hoping I would not try to find him, and perhaps was sorry that she had told me where he was. Not wanting to disturb her further, I thanked her, left a message just in case we did not locate him and left. With every moment I was becoming more excited and knew I must try to go to him.

Hurrying back to our friends, I told them of our adventure. They were jubilant and offered to help in any way with plans for us to leave for Les Sables as soon as possible. In the meantime, my good friends Frank and Rupert had introduced me to Maxime de Beix, the European representative for *Variety Weekly*. He was a wonderful man who became intrigued by our mission. He spoke impeccable French and insisted he would chaperone my trip in case I needed help. Since I felt afraid of becoming tongue-tied before the great Charpentier, I was delighted.

Eleanor and I were having dinner that evening with Sara and Richard Tucker, my colleague from the Metropolitan Opera, at Au Père Jean when a call came from Rupert saying he had communicated with Charpentier. The Tuckers were swept up in the excitement of this unfolding drama, and with their blessings and good wishes, we left to meet with our friends who were working on the plans.

My friends had simply sent a telegram addressed to Gustave Charpentier, Les Sables, hoping it would somehow reach him. The message told him that I was his new Louise from the Metropolitan Opera and was anxious to see him. The telegram was promptly answered by Charpentier, saying that he was anticipating my arrival.

It was decided we would leave for Les Sables the next morning at 6 A.M. Eleanor and I rushed back to our hotel and hurriedly packed a few things, not knowing how long we would be there. I wanted to remain with the composer as long as he would have me.

Six o'clock came early that morning. Our friends had arranged for a limousine and on the dot a French chauffeur arrived to pick us up, along with Maxime de Beix and Carl Perutz who was also delighted to join us.

The trip across France over bumpy, hot, and dusty roads was about 325 miles. Stopping only for food or something to wash the dust from our throats, we bounced along as the chauffeur, a typical French driver, took curves at top speed—and heaven help anything that was in our way!

Upon entering the area of Les Sables we were directed to Charpentier's little villa near the famous beaches of Vendée. Word must have reached him that we had arrived, for as we drove up we were astonished to see the great composer standing at the entrance to his villa. He was a picture to behold, anxiously waiting for us. I shall never forget his greeting, and I knew then that this would be one of the most memorable experiences of my career. A small man dressed in a freshly starched white jacket and flowing artist's bow, white-haired and bearded, with dancing light-blue eyes, greeted me warmly and instantly stole my heart. Not knowing how he would react to a camera, I asked Carl to allow me the precaution of introducing him as a friend and suggested he leave his equipment in the car until we viewed the situation.

As we entered Charpentier's little villa, we were ushered into a small dining room, where he had arranged a party for us. A lovely table was set with assorted cakes and champagne. As we refreshed ourselves, entranced by this charming old gentleman, he spoke freely of his opera. With deep reverence he begged me to help him keep alive his *Louise* as he intended it to be; not as the opera was being performed then "in a cut, distorted version," as he put it. When he described Louise's character, her life, and even how he wished her to be dressed, I could sense the deep devotion he felt for her. My apprehension about being able to converse in French with him was quickly forgotten, and our conversation seemed so free and natural that I could barely believe it was I who was speaking.

Hoping to have his approval on my costumes, I had brought along the sketches created for me in Paris by Marcelle Dormoy. As Charpentier admired each one he wrote *adopté* beneath the sketch. For the last act, however, he expressed a reservation. Louise should then be in gray to express her *tristesse* (sadness). He had admired the dress worn by Mary Garden at the Opéra Comique and was pleased when I promised to follow his wishes.

After we talked for a while we were invited to join him in his studio. Already seated at the piano was a middle-aged woman who was introduced to us as his assistant. "Sing 'Depuis le jour' for me," he said, and signaled the accompanist to play the introduction. Without a chance to think or warm up a bit, as though hypnotized, I began to sing. My voice seemed apart from me as it poured out Louise's beautiful aria.

He sat by the piano and after a few notes he began to conduct with electric energy. I could tell by his sparkling eyes and broadly smiling face that he knew I was putting my heart into it. When we finished, one look at my sister, who had dissolved into tears—as had the others—together with the expression on Charpentier's face, said it all. It was truly a most highly emotional moment for everyone.

The maestro then wanted us to see his garden. As we stepped out of his quaint little house, on the wall surrounding his yard sat the entire neighborhood who had come to hear me sing. It was obvious that Charpentier approved when they vigorously greeted me with applause.

This was the time to have our pictures taken, and Carl brought in the equipment. We were cautiously anticipating that this great man might be shy of the camera, but instead he was delighted and obviously got a great kick out of it. He beamed when I straightened his artist's bow and could not have been more cooperative.

For two thrilling days I worked with Gustave Charpentier, going over every line of the part. I worried over his miraculous energy, fearing that it might be too much of a strain on his heart, but the old man seemed to thrive on the revival of those memories from the days when his Louise had first met the footlights nearly fifty years before.

Charpentier taught me many things about his opera. He begged me to urge the directors for whom I was to sing not to place Julien on the stage at the beginning of the third act. "Louise," he said, "should sing 'Depuis le jour' as a soliloquy." He had reluctantly inserted one direction into the score for her lover to be onstage at the première, and actually added the word "Louise" for Julien to sing only to satisfy a stage director at the Opéra Comique. This direction was never removed from the original score and therefore, against his wishes, it was adopted by others.

When I returned to sing *Louise* at the Met and in San Francisco that season, I explained the composer's wishes regarding Louise's famous aria, but because the action was never changed in the score, it was staged as usual. I was too young in my career to force new ideas and although I agreed to comply with the old direction, I understood Charpentier's reasoning and have always felt that he was right.

There was one other criticism about which the master felt very strongly. Louise's mother, he said, was too often played as a shrew, a characteristic too disagreeable. Even as she imitates Julien's wooing of Louise, it should be interpreted as teasing. In a gentle way she is trying to talk her daughter out of a romance of which she disapproves.

I had savored every moment this wonderful man gave me and after learning so much about his Louise, I knew I could interpret her as he knew her. She was now a part of me and I eagerly anticipated playing this charming girl who became one of my most beloved characters. These had been two of the most wonderful days of my life, but now it was time to leave, and with a marvelous feeling of accomplishment and satisfaction we started our long trip back to Paris.

It was an all-night ride, each of us taking turns talking to the chauffeur to keep him alert. Eleanor's attempt was a disaster, for neither of them understood one word the other was saying, but she did manage to keep him awake. We reached our hotel at five in the morning, breakfasted at five-thirty, finished packing and were ready to leave for New York by seven. No one had been to bed.

Shortly after I arrived back home I received an affectionate message from Charpentier wishing me great success. I was thrilled to know that I had pleased the master. A few weeks later his personal orchestral score of my favorite third act with its many interesting annotations arrived. This was a gift to his most recent Louise from the great man who was responsible for her creation.

Louise— Gustave Charpentier

For those of you who have experienced and loved the atmosphere of Montmartre and Paris during the first half of this century, the opera *Louise* will take you back with sweet nostalgia.

The story begins in a typical French apartment of a working-class tenement where Louise lives with her parents. A long window that opens onto a balcony faces another small balcony in front of a modest artist's studio. Here the love scenes take place between Julien, the artist; and Louise, his love. The first theme heard when he greets her is often repeated throughout the opera. It is a melodic arrangement of notes that immediately establishes the atmosphere of Paris and all its familiar sounds.

Louise has been in love with Julien for some time and has begged her parents to consent to their marriage. Her father smothers her with his overpossessive love and they sing a charming duet while he tries desperately to persuade her to forget Julien. Reasoning with her, he makes up his own excuses. *"Qui dit amoureux, toujours dit aveugle"* (Whoever says he's in love admits he is blind). Louise adores him and once again he succeeds in delaying her escape.

It is rather easy to see why, as Charpentier says, the mother is usually played too gruff and disagreeable in nature. Some of the dialogue she has while taunting Louise about Julien seems mean and hard. Charpentier wanted her to reprimand the lovesick girl but still show affection for her daughter. The text also seems to imply that the mother was envious of the great affection between the father and his only child.

In San Francisco, where I first sang this opera, my debut tenor was Raoul Jobin who was the most popular French tenor of that time. We sang many performances of *Louise, Roméo et Juliette* and *Faust* together with different companies. Jobin was a great colleague. Because he was always so secure and had beautiful French diction, he never failed to bring out the best of my linguistic efforts when I sang in his native language.

Ezio Pinza was my first father, and for me the greatest of those I have ever worked with. He was a fine actor and working with Ezio one could always count on the action being well thought out.

Claramae Turner was an excellent mother and played the part much more closely to the way Charpentier told me he wanted it played than any of the others.

Louise works as a seamstress. Her parents are so afraid that one day she will run away from home to be with Julien that her mother insists on escorting her to and from work. In desperation Julien hides one day near the entrance of the factory, waiting for them to arrive. They appear, and Louise coldly accepts a farewell kiss on her cheek from her mother. As her mother leaves, she begins to enter the building. Julien follows and, pulling her back into the street, implores her to come away with him. Though she vows she will soon be his, and begs him to be patient, she tenderly frees herself of his embrace and, with the excuse that she will be late, joins her friends at work.

The tableau that follows is called the sewing-machine scene. In the orchestra one clearly hears the happy sound of many machines at work, and the girls laughing gaily while exchanging gossip of the town. At this point the composer interjects the love music of Louise to suggest her thoughts are only for Julien. He serenades her from the street until she can resist him no longer. Dissolved into tears by his pleading song, she tells the girls that she is ill and must go home, but actually she has at last decided to run away with Julien.

Though the opera calls for only four major roles, it requires an enormous cast of characters. There are sixteen *comprimario* parts for women and seventeen for men, including nine voices heard offstage, and a large number of extras used as vendors, peddlers, and others.

Some of the finest *comprimario* singers of our time have sung roles in this opera: Thelma Votipka, Alessio de Paolis, George Cehanovsky, and Osie Hawkins, to name a few. All of them have sung with the Met and San Francisco and were considered by both companies to be exceptionally gifted. They have rightfully earned the greatest of respect from all of their colleagues. There were also those artists who sang leading parts with these companies but made memorable some of the lesser important characters of Charpentier's *Louise*. The great bass Virgilio Lazzari consented to sing the part of the ragman, appearing only for a short time in the second act and again at the end of the third, after Louise runs away from her family to be with Julien. There he tells the story of the drama and of his own heartbreak, singing as he wanders off, "*Un père cherche sa fille qui était toute sa famille*" (A father seeks his daughter who is his whole family). "*Elle est partie dans la nuit*" (She went away in the night). Lazzari had a heartrending way of singing this part with a tremulous voice, and while I am writing about this wonderful artist, the picture of this bent old man comes to my mind.

The Metropolitan Opera had a fabulous backdrop for *Louise*'s third act, which set a truly romantic atmosphere. Louise and Julien are now living in a little house on the side of Montmartre. It is almost twilight as she enters the garden where Julien, sitting nearby, is apparently lost in pleasant meditation. This is the scene of the famous aria "Depuis le jour." Louise is no longer the naïve little girl, and here she reveals all the passion and mature love she has for Julien.

This lovely aria has been a particular favorite of mine, ever since the day I first sang it in Paris for Charpentier. Act III is probably the most joyous singing act of my repertoire. I have been asked to sing the aria on numerous occasions and it never fails to take me back to Paris. Technically it requires everything I have learned about singing, and I always enjoy the challenge.

The duet between Louise and Julien that follows is entrancing. As the sun goes down, the stage darkens. The backdrop of this act is a panoramic view of Paris as it was in early 1900. Ever so slowly one sees the lights begin to come on in the city. Watching it come to life they unfold their love, begging Paris to watch over them. "*Paris! Paris! O Paris! Cité de joie! Cité d'amour!*" (Paris! Paris! O Paris! City of joy! City of love). "*Sois douce à nos amour! Protège tes enfants! Garde nous! Défend nous!*" (Look kindly on our love! Protect thy children! Guard us! Defend us!). As they get more carried away in their ecstasy, the whole city begins to sparkle with lights and Paris seems to honor their love. Julien cries out, "*Libres! vous êtes libres! Nous crie la ville immense!*" (Free! You are free! The mighty town is crying). This sequence builds higher and higher as the lovers pledge their lives to each other and Louise exclaims, "*Vien, ô mon poète! sois ma conquête. Ah! viens mourir sous mes baisers!*" (Come, my poet, be thou my conquest. Oh come and die beneath my kisses).

A great celebration and carnival follows where Louise is crowned queen of Bohemia. But alas, amid all the gaiety the lovers are soon to be parted again. At the end of this act Louise's mother appears, suddenly interrupting the festivities, and pleads with Julien to let her daughter go. She explains that Louise's father is seriously ill and she alone can save him. Their great happiness suddenly turns to despair and finally Louise succumbs, torn between her love for Julien and her sense of duty to her father. Louise's mother gives her word that she can return, but that was never her intention, which she makes quite clear in the final act.

Louise's father makes every effort to regain his daughter's love but realizing that this was only a ruse to get her back, Louise is bitter and uncooperative. Sitting in his rocking chair he tenderly draws her to him and gently forces her to sit on his knee. While rocking her, he sings a touching lullaby, clearly revealing the fact that he still considers her a little girl.

The rocking chair scene worked out fine with Pinza as my father, because he was a big man. He behaved beautifully in the performance, but it was never beneath him to take advantage of our closeness with a more than "fatherly" caress in rehearsals.

Realizing her parents' real intention is once again to try to keep her from Julien, Louise becomes hysterical. The sounds of Paris are heard, and defying all their possessiveness, she flaunts her love for Julien by crying out, "*Julien! pour toujours prends moi*" (Julien, forever take me). Her enraged father goes to strike her but the mother restrains him. Instead, he furiously opens the door and orders her to go. Louise, terrified, hesitates but when he raises a chair and violently throws it crashing against the door after her, she screams and escapes.

The lights of Paris are suddenly extinguished. Louise is gone and her father, realizing he has lost her forever, pitifully calls after her. He pauses in the doorway as if prostrated by grief, listens to the sounds of Paris and, stretching his fist toward the city, cries, "*O Paris!*"

Pinza was so realistic in his action that there was never a performance when he did not warn me to duck that chair at the end. It was always smashed to bits and many times parts of it would follow me down the steps.

Charpentier was quite specific as to where he wanted me to scream. He wanted it to be exactly at the top of a descending scale in the orchestra that relates to her running down the steps. The throwing of the chair was probably Pinza's idea, for the old scores make no mention of it.

Louise is one of my favorite roles. What a pity this great opera is done so seldom in this country!

Mimi—La Bohème—
Giacomo Puccini

$\mathcal{P}$uccini had already been launched on the international scene with *Manon Lescaut* three years before he introduced *La Bohème* to the world. Since its 1896 première in Turin, conducted by Toscanini who was not yet thirty, *Bohème* has become one of the world's most popular operas.

Though it demands four good singers, it is not difficult to stage and can be produced with relatively little expense for both costumes and decor. For this reason this work is presented by even the most modest of opera companies.

Many people wrongly think of it as an easy score to sing. Gratifying, yes; but easy, no. It is sad that some singers do not bother to learn the infinite nuances of this score, so sure are they that it is an easy success with a few high notes, requiring very little effort otherwise. I never considered Mimi a simple role. Vocally, it is not as taxing as my other Puccini heroines; nevertheless, it does demand a well-focused and secure voice to deliver the long, floating phrases.

Curiously, the opera made its first appearance in the United States in Los Angeles in 1897; at the Metropolitan *La Bohème* was not given until three years later, on December 26, 1900. The New York *Times'* leading critic, Henry Edward Krehbiel, called it "foul in subject and fulfillment but futile in its music." Later he asserted that "Mimi is fouler than Camille, alias Violetta, and 'Pauccini' [*sic*], has not been able to administer the palliative which lies in Verdi's music." In addition he wrote, "Silly and inconsequential incidents and dialogues designed to show the devil-may-care life of artistic Bohemians, are daubed over with splotches of instrumental color without reason and without effect, except the creation of a sense of boisterous excitement and confusion."

I believe these incredible few excerpts from his review are sufficient to give one a pale idea of how completely off track he was. Such ill-conceived criticism, alas, has been repeated on many occasions by other critics who were unable to recognize a masterpiece when they heard it for the first time. It is gratifying in this case that an absurdly negative judgment did not influence the public in the least. Although I do not have the figures, I understand *La Bohème* is one of the most performed operas in the lyric repertoire.

The first interpreter of Mimi was Cesira Ferrani, a lyric soprano who also had been chosen by the composer to be his first Manon Lescaut. The Metropolitan's first Mimi was Dame Nellie Melba, who went on singing this role until her retirement in her mid-sixties. In fact, Puccini said, "She has sung it much too long," but she was universally recognized as a fine artist despite her size and limited acting ability in later years. On a vocal level Melba was the supreme interpreter of Mimi at that time. She began as a coloratura and later became a lyric; but eventually every type of soprano has sung this role, including coloraturas such as Sembrich, Galli-Curci, and Toti dal Monte. When I first began singing it with the Met, I recall that Sayão, Novotna, and Albanese all took turns at it; and later, a *spinto* such as Tebaldi, along with many others.

Leoncavallo's *La Bohème* premièred at the Metropolitan in 1897 but has never been performed there again, despite the fact that Caruso had made a great success of it abroad. This other version of the same story, but with Musetta having the lead over Mimi, was particularly successful in Geneva and the German cities. The libretto differs somewhat and it is interesting to know the background of how fate prompted the same subject to be used by two composers who had been great friends until then.

Leoncavallo had suggested the Murger novel to Puccini as a possible opera, but he turned it down. Then without ever advising his colleague, he changed his mind and set to work at it fast and furiously. In the meantime, Leoncavallo decided to set it to music himself and by the time he learned of the Puccini version, he was too far advanced to abandon his own. He never forgave Puccini, and many people sided with him. Suddenly there were two *La Bohèmes*, and considerable confusion ensued at first. Not long after, the Leoncavallo opera became a rarity and Puccini's advanced triumphantly, becoming a household name.

Mimi is close to my heart, for I sang this part with the Metropolitan for more than thirty years after my debut in the role with the company in 1945. The role is beautifully written for the voice, and the Illica-Giacosa libretto is so fine it could stand by itself as a work without music.

Rodolfo is a poet by profession, but Mimi is a poet in the way she expresses herself from the beginning until the end. She, like Violetta in *La Traviata*, is also affected by tuberculosis and dies young. But she is no courtesan, and it is only because of her impoverished state after leaving Rodolfo that she takes on an old viscount as a protector, though he never appears in the story.

Mimi's character is not like Violetta's at all. While the latter is sophisticated and disenchanted, Mimi is shy and at the same time in love with life; deeply aware of the joys that nature can give her, be it in a ray of sunlight or the perfume of a flower. The two women are conceived in different dimensions, Violetta being somewhat heroic in the renunciation of her profound love, Mimi a victim of her surroundings. Both are equally touching, but Violetta has more panache and is the more exciting character to me.

In the score there are several musical directions by Puccini which make all the difference in a successful interpretation. The words are of capital importance and Mimi's from the beginning are so tender and at times even fanciful that they immediately reveal the gentleness of her nature. Many sopranos tend to play her coyly and this is not right. She is too humble to be coy. On the surface Mimi appears as a complaisant role. It is not. Mimi must project a certain innocence all the way through the opera, though there is a deeply romantic side to her nature that dominates. Her character should develop slowly and move the audience with her fragility and inability to cope without true love.

The tenor's great aria in the first act, "Che gelida manina," is probably one of the most beloved in the repertoire. It is magnificent, long, and impassioned, with a triumphant ending. When sung well, with a good high C, it brings the house down.

I feel that Mimi is overwhelmed by Rodolfo's high-spirited outpouring about himself, and though her aria is beautiful, it is subdued and quiet in complete contrast. In order to bring the audience back to this mood, after Rodolfo's dramatic outburst, one must concentrate on control. The voice must be well supported to spin out lovely sounds in the many long phrases, starting slowly and increasing in volume as she gets carried away with the series of exquisite images that reveal her fanciful moods. It should be contained and not an overstated display of emotion.

From Mimi's first words, "Mi chiamano Mimì," I pour out my heart in this lovely aria and enjoy the simple, charming story she tells Rodolfo. But to me, the last phrase she sings has always been a letdown. Knowing how meticulous Puccini was in creating great dramatic scenes, the only excuse I can find for the "down beat" of Mimi's music here would be that he felt he needed a cooling-off period before the climactically beautiful duet we sing to close the act.

This love duet is a favorite and sung often in joint concerts. Its romantic ending is enchanting, for as Mimi and Rodolfo walk out of the garret they end their last phrase with a dramatic high C. Puccini actually wrote an E for the tenor, which harmonizes beautifully. But with time it became a custom for those who could sustain it to take the high note too, and the audience loves it. Many times, however, it has been a nervous experience for the tenor. With all the *Bohèmes* I have sung over the years, I have admired the few who sang the last phrase the way Puccini wrote it.

The second act is Musetta's big moment, but in the midst of all the confusion of the Café Momus, Puccini continues to weave the spell of Mimi and Rodolfo's love with some of his most enchanting phrases. The one I love most, *"Io t'amo tanto, e sono tutta tua"* (I love you so much and I am all yours), I had engraved on a gold tie clasp for my husband when we were married.

At the end of this act I have a bit of action that I feel is entirely natural. Mimi is already ill, and I begin to show her physical disintegration, due to the consumption from which she suffers, by a coughing spell during all the hilarity of the parade. She does not know yet that she is seriously ill, but it seems to me this sets up the third act when Rodolfo tells Marcello the sad story of her illness.

The third act is Mimi's, and her greatest chance to shine. First there is her tearful account to Marcello that Rodolfo loves her but his incessant jealousy is intolerable, and later the anguish suffered when she overhears Rodolfo telling Marcello that she is condemned by consumption. Mimi is crushed and decides she must leave him. Her loveliest aria, the farewell, "Addio, senza rancor" (Good-bye without regret), is one of Puccini's most inspired moments. The quartet closing the act is another gem with the intertwining voices of Mimi and Rodolfo with Musetta and Marcello. The soprano and tenor voices soaring above with long legato line and the choppy staccato sounds of the other two quarreling.

I find the role quite lyric until I reach this act, at which time the voice needs to be more *spinto* especially during the quartet as the orchestra increases in volume. Mimi has grown into a young woman and, though her voice must show suffering, it should not lose the innate sweetness that depicts her character.

The fourth act is a contrast of carefree gaiety and pathos. With Mimi's entrance the heartbreak is already in the score, and her death scene is a masterpiece. It is easy to be overcome with emotion by the extraordinary way in which Puccini has conceived it. She has but a few words to sing before Rodolfo helps her to the bed from where she sings the rest of the opera, including her beautiful aria which is demanding of the voice. I have often been asked how I manage to sing full voice while lying down. If you have learned how properly to support the voice, it matters not whether you are horizontal or vertical.

The aria "Sono andati?" (Have they gone?) should be started slowly and quietly, yet well projected to reach the last rows of the balcony. Each word should be clearly etched until, as though it were her last breath, she cries out, "*Sei il mio amor e tutta la mia vita*" (You are my love and my life), which is the climax and the end of her strength. From that moment it is downhill all the way as she becomes weaker and weaker with the voice showing that the end is near. My last words are always a breathy whisper.

There is a special place in the score where it is indicated that Mimi dies. I have always preferred to drop my hand to the side of the bed and allow my little white muff to fall to the floor. These are big enough gestures for the audience to see in the balcony.

As I went on singing this opera for more than three decades, I learned each time how far more difficult innocence and sweetness are to project than passion or anger. The only advice I can give young artists is to let the music and the text, one of the best marriages ever made in operatic literature, speak for themselves. To follow this counsel to the letter is a difficult task indeed.

The poignancy of Mimi's death scene is all the greater for me because each time I hold that little muff while singing those closing lines of Mimi's last scene I think of Grace Moore's thoughtfulness the night of my Met debut when she gave it to me.

Marguerite—Faust— Charles François Gounod

$\mathcal{B}$efore I began studying Marguerite I read Goethe's long poem from which Jules Barbier and Michel Carré extracted the text for the Gounod opera. Studying Gounod's life, I was intrigued to learn that he had studied theology for two years and had been deeply religious throughout his life. This is why he was fascinated with Goethe's immortal work, because it presented through the telling of the story the battle between evil and good, with the latter winning in the end (Dr. Johannes Faust had really existed in the sixteenth century in Württemberg). I also learned that at the time the opera was first performed in 1859, many music critics and literary figures did not understand why the composer had concentrated mainly on the Faust-Marguerite relationship. As far as I am concerned, what he did makes perfect sense because it is the part of the classic that is most adaptable to the lyric theatre.

The librettists were not only excellent writers with a formidable sense of theatre, but they remained close to the spirit of Goethe. Gounod was not the only composer to be attracted to this subject. Thirteen years previously Berlioz had written *La Damnation de Faust,* and later Boito was to produce his *Mefistofele* and Busoni his *Doctor Faustus.*

I am sorry I never had the opportunity to sing the Boito opera. It was in the Metropolitan's early repertoire for many seasons, but never appeared during my tenure. In this opera the role of Marguerite is shorter but more intense than in Gounod's version, and the well-known aria "L'altra notte in fondo al mare" (The other night at the bottom of the sea) is most affecting.

To take on Marguerite was a challenge I loved, for all the greatest lyric and *spinto* sopranos have sung it (hardly any of them escaped it), the opera having become tremendously popular all over the world. In Germany, curiously, it is called *Margarethe.*

The celebrated Swedish soprano Christine Nilsson inaugurated the

Thirty-ninth Street Metropolitan Opera House with this work in 1883. Among the supreme interpreters of Marguerite were Melba, Patti, Calvé, and Nordica. Later, other singers such as Eames, Farrar, and Rethberg were also famous in the role. It has been performed regularly since its inauguration of the house almost one hundred years ago.

In the beginning of my career *Faust* was in the repertoire of many opera companies, and I was singing it often. When I began to study the opera I was not much attracted to Marguerite's character. She seemed to me weak and dull. In fact the reason I performed her so often was that the ravishing music captured me, even if the character did not. The more I sang this opera, the more often I was asked to appear in it, making it difficult to turn down. *Faust* was perfect for my voice and when I sang it with a first-rate tenor, it was an exquisite vocal experience.

With great anticipation I first sang Marguerite at the Metropolitan on December 23, 1949, under the baton of Wilfred Pelletier, in a marvelous cast that included Giuseppe di Stefano, Italo Tajo, and the never-to-be-forgotten Leonard Warren. Later I performed it many times with Pinza as the Devil and Björling in the title role, and it was an unqualified joy in my early career to appear with these established giants of the opera world. Another artist most respected in the roles she did as a *comprimario* with the Metropolitan for many years was Thelma Votipka. She was unsurpassed in the short but vital role of Martha, and we did many performances together. Her antics with Pinza were hysterical. She was a great colleague with a beautiful voice that had a wide range, enabling her to sing soprano or mezzo and thus making her a valuable member of the company.

Melody reigns supreme in this score to depict each character. Immediately upon meeting Faust at the Kermesse and scorning his advances, Marguerite reveals what a naïve, unpretentious girl she is with the single phrase *"Non, monsieur, je ne suis demoiselle, ni belle"* (No, sir, I am neither a lady, nor beautiful). This is all she says before quickly disappearing. In her manner she is polite and shy, yet slightly brusque. It is a difficult first line because in the confusion of the popular fair it is not easy to make the needed impression with just one sentence, however pretty it may be.

At the Metropolitan her longest scene is in the second act. Marguerite is seated at the spinning wheel in the garden beside her house. She sings a charming song while spinning, but her mind wanders as thoughts return to her first meeting with Faust. This lovely theme leads into the well-known "Jewel Song." Here the soprano must have trills and a flexible voice that is pure in sound. It is quite exposed, for the orchestration is light. She must be played as a joyous young girl would be upon receiving unexpectedly a large jewel box filled with rings, bracelets and necklaces—with which she then adorns herself while singing and admiring her image in the mirror.

The music expresses her amazement and joy, with many phrases repeated to mark her exultation. Gounod wrote this long soliloquy to establish her youthful naïveté. The repetitions are effective, for they underline her innocence, almost childishness, as all bejeweled she asks the mirror, *"Est-ce toi? Est-ce toi, Marguerite? Réponds moi"* (Is this you? Is this you, Marguerite? Answer me). The end is infinitely touching for she is totally mesmerized and sings, *"Marguerite, ce n'est plus toi, ce n'est plus ton visage. C'est la fille d'un roi qu'on salue au passage"* (You are no longer Marguerite, it is no longer your face. It is the daughter of a king whom one greets at her passing).

The interesting way Gounod worked the interwoven action of his characters Mephistopheles, Martha, Faust, and Marguerite, coming in and out of the garden, is unique in the annals of opera. It is necessary for the quartet to be on its toes to time the continuous entrances and exits, for one tiny error could upset the whole scene.

The love duet that closes the long act is of unsurpassed beauty. Marguerite at first answers Faust's declaration of love with poetical expressions and then, building up slowly from *"Je veux t'aimer et te chérir"* (I want to love and cherish you), she realizes with sudden fear what this attachment may bring her and changes completely. With trembling voice she pleads with him, *"Partez, partez! oui, partez vite"* (Leave, leave, leave immediately), but it is too late. She is completely won over, and there is sensuousness in her voice as she opens the window, thinking she is alone, and sings, *"Il m'aime; il m'aime; quel trouble en mon coeur"* (He loves me; he loves me; how troubled is my heart). The tessitura climbs and when Marguerite sees Faust below, she ends with the voluptuous invitation, *"Cher bien aimé, viens, viens"* (Dearly beloved, come to me, come to me).

The church scene is short and somber. No indication is given as to how much time has elapsed since the preceding act, but it must have been months. To the majestic sound of the organ, Marguerite is deep in prayer and, although it is not specified here, fully conscious that she is with child. Here the voice must assume sheer fright, for upon hearing accusing voices she bursts into *"Je chancelle! Je meurs! Dieu bon! Dieu clément! Est-ce déjà l'heure du châtiment?"* (I am fainting! I am dying! Good and merciful God, is this already the hour of my punishment?). This anxiety becomes terror as Mephistopheles, usually hiding behind a column in the church, addresses her. The dialogue between them becomes increasingly frantic and here she loses her restraint. The unseen chorus of priests and boys lends a marvelous contrast to this scene as she sings, *"Ah! ce chant m'étouffe et m'oppresse! Je suis dans un cercle de fer"* (This singing stifles and oppresses me. I am in an iron circle).

In the following setting of the square, where her brother Valentine is killed by Faust, the structure of the action and music is curious. Marguerite is the cause of the crime and her brother curses her before dying; however, she has little to sing but *"Douleur cruelle! O châtiment! O châtiment!"* (Cruel sorrow! Punishment). Although it is not written in the score, before running off half-demented, I scream on seeing him dead. This always proves to be very dramatic. I felt that it was a natural way to express Marguerite's anguish.

One annoying thing about this opera is the necessity to wait in my dressing room long periods between appearances, and when a part of the Walpurgis Night episode is performed, it means still more time before the final act.

For all sorts of reasons too long to go into here, some opera houses switch the scenes around. Also, the short duet between Marguerite and Siebel before the church episode is often not performed at the Met, or anywhere in this country for that matter. This deprives the soprano of a lovely aria that explains many things. She laments Faust's disappearance, *"Il ne revient pas!"* (He does not come back), and we also learn here that she is expecting a child. It is for her unborn child, she tells loyal and understanding Siebel, that she will go to church and pray.

In the final act she is in prison for having killed her baby while in a demented state. When Faust appears, his presence and voice bring her back to reality. The music is a frenzied and happy sound when she sings, *"Oui, c'est toi, je t'aime"* (Yes, it is you, I love you), but her mind wanders as she repeats the lovely phrases they sang to each other on the day they met, recalling the past and briefly bringing back all the charm of that scene. But suddenly, when Mephisto appears, she goes from the sentimental recollections to facing the inexorable reality of her forthcoming death by execution and subsequent damnation. The impassioned cry, *"Mon Dieu, protégez-moi . . . Mon Dieu, je vous implore!"* (My God protect me . . . My God, I implore you!) must be delivered with total despair.

This is the beginning of the famous trio, and each one of the characters follows his or her own train of thought, with Marguerite interested only in her salvation. Here it is true *spinto* singing, with control and power gradually building the sound to a tremendous crescendo. For me the biggest thrill of the entire work comes at this moment. When the soprano sings with a great tenor and bass, this sequence virtually lifts the audience out of their seats. The tessitura for soprano is middle to high range, gradually climbing higher and higher with her voice floating above the others, and ending in a sustained high B natural. It must be one of the greatest trios in opera, and the trick in singing it well and having plenty of voice and strength to sustain it to the end is knowing how and when to save the voice.

Marguerite then turns on Faust and accusingly cries, *"Pourquoi ces mains rouges de sang? Va! tu me fais horreur!"* (Why are your hands covered with blood? Leave me, I despise you!), as she falls at his feet. This fall must be a slow, wilting one. It must not be overacted.

Little did I know that when I was to sing this opera in the Soviet Union there would be so many drastic changes in the way they interpret this opera. When I noticed at the Bolshoi that there was no spinning wheel for the second act, I was dismayed. To me it seems a charming addition to the scene when Marguerite spins while she sings the lovely ballad that precedes "The Jewel Song." I'm sure it was not easy but they did come up with one for me, and I hope they are still using it.

Fiora—L'Amore dei Tre Re— *Italo Montemezzi*

L'Amore dei Tre Re was given for the first time in this country January 2, 1914, with Toscanini in the pit. The text was by the well-known Italian poet and dramatist Sem Benelli, and the music by the practically unknown twenty-eight-year-old Italian composer Italo Montemezzi. Quoting *Musical America*'s review of January 10, the critic wrote, "Success unequivocal crowns *L'Amore dei Tre Re* in its first American performance. . . . One of the most deeply affecting and full-blooded scores since Wagner, thrillingly sung by Bori, Amato, Ferrari-Fontana and Didur."

Fiora was the second role I had the good fortune to study with the composer. The privilege of rehearsing a score with its creator is invaluable for many reasons, but most important is to learn firsthand everything there is to know about the character and how she should be interpreted. The role of Fiora was one of my first *verismo* parts and I came to love it very much. Working with Montemezzi was certainly another high point in my career. My debut performance was with the San Francisco Company in October of 1947, and in December 1948 I sang my first Fiora at the Metropolitan.

L'Amore dei Tre Re is an entirely symbolic drama. Fiora represents Italy, which in the Middle Ages was coveted by many surrounding powers. The blind King Archibaldo, Fiora's father-in-law; his son Manfredo, to whom Fiora was given in marriage for political reasons; and Avito, a young prince, are all in love with her. Fiora and Avito were once betrothed and their love remains evermore passionate. She shows great pity and respect for her warrior husband, but when all is quiet in the castle and Manfredo is away at war, the lovers meet secretly. All this precipitates the impending tragedy of the story.

My entrance in this opera was quite special. The beautiful light blue flowing gown, which ripples magnificently in the breeze atop the old castle's courtyard, was delightfully romantic. The lovers have been to-gether, and Avito precedes her to the courtyard to assure their soli-tude. Their fear of the old, blind King is temporarily forgotten while they profess their everlasting love for each other.

The second act of the opera is considered the greatest. Fiora's hus-band is about to return from battle. She appears in all her queenly robes and crown, and this is by far one of the most difficult costumes in my collection to manage. It is made of heavy ruby-red velvet. The wide yoke, which extends over the shoulders and the trim, completely encircling an enormous cape, is encrusted with stones resembling rubies, topazes, and emeralds. It weighs "a ton."

As the act opens, Fiora is seen on the parapet, looking out over the valley. One hears the music depicting so beautifully the sound of horses galloping toward the castle. Manfredo arrives, embraces his wife, and tries desperately to offer his love to Fiora. She tries but can only respectfully explain that she knows little of her husband. He is always far away, and when he returns, he says he must leave again soon.

When Manfredo leaves again for the battlefield after a short time, he begs Fiora to wave a long white veil in farewell from the parapet in order that he may see it as he gallops into the distance, *"che tu m'asciughi le lacrime sul mio cuore scoperto"* (and that you may dry the tears of my open heart). Fiora, touched by his devotion and trou-bled with remorse, fights with her conscience. The music at this point reveals the turmoil within her feelings, the passionate love theme inter-rupted by the sound of galloping horses' hoofs. But when the trum-pets are heard signaling Manfredo's departure, Fiora hurries up the steps to the parapet.

As she reaches the top and watches Manfredo preparing to leave, Avito appears. She begs him to leave, saying she can no longer see him, and pleads with him to leave her in peace. The noise of someone approaching interrupts them. Avito hides as Fiora starts down the steps. A servant enters the courtyard bearing a small chest and an-nounces that Manfredo has sent her a gift. Fiora orders the woman to leave it and dismisses her. As she slowly lifts the lid she is sadly re-minded of Manfredo's request, for there is the veil with which she had promised to signal him. Drawing it out of the chest, Fiora remorse-fully makes her way back to the parapet and begins to wave.

The waving of this long veil was a particular challenge for me. Montemezzi wanted it done to a certain tempo and also at special places clearly marked in the score. I tried different fabrics until I found one that floated in the slight breeze created by an electric fan placed behind the scenery. The fan kept the veil afloat against the sky for just the right number of beats before it was drawn back for another wave.

As Fiora is waving farewell to Manfredo, Avito returns. He again implores her to leave the castle with him. This glorious love duet is a highlight of the opera and a test of great vocalism. Fiora is up high on the parapet and far to the back of the stage, and she must be able to project her voice across an enormous distance, over a large orchestra, reaching the farthest corners of the theatre. The tenor's position is not much easier and with an extremely high and taxing tessitura for both singers, it would be easy to strain the voice.

Fiora is torn between Manfredo's undying devotion, her pity for him, and Avito whom she loves passionately. She struggles with her heart which aches to give in to Avito, yet there is also her promise to Manfredo. Finally, she drops the veil. "*Ahime! Si piega il voto mio, com'albero pietoso a chi muore di sete*" (Ah! It falls, the solemn promise of mine, like a piteous tree that dies of thirst). She descends from the parapet, throws off the crown, and drops her regal cape, falling into the arms of Avito in a passionate embrace. The lovers defy all danger of being discovered, professing their love forever until suddenly they hear the sound of the old King's groping footsteps as he enters the courtyard. Fiora insists Avito flee for his life. Flaminio, King Archibaldo's constant companion, who leads him in his blindness, is Avito's close friend and knows of his love for Fiora. When the old man comes forward Avito draws his dagger, but Flaminio intercepts and forces him to leave. Flaminio lies when the King asks him who was there, but Archibaldo's keen sense of feeling Fiora's presence tells him that she is still in the courtyard. When he calls for her the second time, she defiantly answers, "*Son qua*" (I am here). Groping blindly, he tries to follow the sound of her voice. When Virgilio Lazzari sang Archibaldo with me at the Metropolitan, his fantastic make-up was so realistic that even at close range it was hard to believe that he was not really blind.

Flaminio suddenly appears with the news that Manfredo is returning. Archibaldo orders him to meet his son and continues to demand of Fiora the name of her lover. When she tries to escape him, he blocks her way. Exasperated by his forcefulness, Fiora admits she was with her lover but refuses to name him. She arrogantly tells Archibaldo that she is no longer afraid of him and thinks only of her love. Infuriated by her refusal and admission of guilt, he grasps her by the throat, forcing her to her knees, and strangles her.

When Manfredo saw Fiora's veil disappear before he was out of sight, he was fearful that she had fallen over the parapet while waving to him and hurried back to the castle. Archibaldo hears Manfredo calling for Fiora and tries to hide her body from him. Desperately the old man attempts to comfort his son, but finally he admits that it was he who strangled her. He tells Manfredo that Fiora was no longer pure, that she had betrayed him in his own home. In disbelief the warrior weeps and, professing his great love for his wife, he pleads with his father, *"Dimmi tu chi era?"* (Tell me who it was?). The anguished Archibaldo exclaims, *"Sono cieco, cieco ma illuminato dalla mia vendetta"* (I am blind but he is illuminated by my vengeance). He then tells Manfredo of his plan to put poison on Fiora's lips as she lies in state.

The last act is quite short. Fiora's body is lying on a crypt in the church where the people come forward to pay their respects and pray for their adored princess. Avito enters as the people are leaving and when he is alone, approaches his beloved. He sings of their love and finally embracing Fiora, he kisses her, receiving the poison left on her lips by Archibaldo. As he is dying, Manfredo appears and, recognizing him, he questions, *"Tu ch'ella adorava?"* (Is it you that she adored?). Avito is hardly able to answer, and when he is told about the poison he replies, *"Questo facesti tu? Tu potesti in questo modo macchiare la sua bocca sacra?"* (This you did? You could in this manner mar her sacred mouth?).

Manfredo proclaims his innocence but tells Avito that it was his father, Archibaldo, who wanted to avenge their wrongdoing. Manfredo asks Avito, *"Dimmi t'amava ella?"* (Tell me, did you love her?). *"Come la vita. No! di piu, di piu"* (Like life itself. No! more! more!), responds Avito, barely alive. *"Se voi vendicarti non tardare che presto io muoio. Uccidimi"* (If you want to vindicate yourself, don't wait, for soon I will die. Kill me), he then says. However, Manfredo is deeply touched by Avito's plight and cries out, *"Dio mio, perche non posso odiare!"* (Dear God, why can I not hate him!). Avito dies and Manfredo, completely shattered by this confrontation, embraces the lifeless Fiora. He too kisses her, taking the poison, and soon falls beside Avito.

Archibaldo enters and making his way toward the crypt, he stumbles into the body of Manfredo. Believing he has at last caught Fiora's lover, he takes hold of the body, cursing it until he is shocked by the voice of his own son pleading, *"No, padre! Tu t'inganni!"* (No, Father! You are mistaken!). With Manfredo dying in his arms, the desperate old man cries, *"Manfredo, anche tu dunque senza rimedio sei con me nel l'ombra!"* (Manfredo, also you now, without remedy, you are with me in the darkness!).

Minnie—La Fanciulla del West— *Giacomo Puccini*

*I*t is a long way from the poetical antiquity of *L'Amore dei Tre Re* to the American story of *La Fanciulla del West*, but I love Minnie just as much as I do Princess Fiora. Being an all-American girl who adopted the West as her home for the past thirty years, I have always considered myself a natural for this character. It was fun to get out of the big, bouffant gowns I wore in most of my parts and swagger around the stage in a riding skirt and culottes.

I do not consider Minnie to be a rough-tough character, as some of my colleagues have played her. She must be strong-willed, able to handle a gun and defend herself, but soft as a kitten as well when she reads the Bible to the miners in the first act.

This Puccini opera, with the story by David Belasco, takes place in California during the gold rush days of the mid-nineteenth century. Minnie inherited a saloon from her parents and runs it with her good friend Nick, who is the bartender. The miners entrust her to keep their gold for them, and she faithfully guards it with her gun. Paul Franke, who regularly sang the part of Nick at the Metropolitan, was the best interpreter of this role. It is an important *comprimario* part in which he enjoyed a fine success.

The gun I used onstage was a real one. It had been my husband's service revolver, for which I had to carry a license. When I took the weapon across country I was asked to notify the airline in advance and generally it flew as a guest of the captain in the cockpit. I insisted on using an authentic one not only for the feel in handling it (stage guns are featherweight), but because I wanted the realism of smoke when the revolver was fired. When someone backstage fires a shot for a fake gun, the timing is frequently off, and I never wanted that horrible experience for my opening shot.

The sets we used at the Metropolitan Opera provided an exciting first entrance for Minnie. The saloon is two stories with steps leading up to Minnie's room and a small balcony from where she can observe the activity in the bar. When the miners start a fight, Minnie hears the noisy racket below and suddenly appears on the balcony. As one of the troublemakers draws his revolver, she shoots the gun out of his hand, causing the men to scatter. What could be a more dramatic attention-getter than that? The miners greet her warmly, calling, "Hello, Minnie," as she comes down the steps, and immediately you know who the boss is at the saloon the miners call the Polka.

Since this role can easily be a voice breaker, it should only be attempted by singers who are completely secure in their vocal production and have had experience in singing other *verismo* parts. To me it seems no more demanding than Puccini's *Tosca* or his *Manon Lescaut*. However, I had sung all of his popular operas before attempting Minnie and that could have been one reason why I found no difficulty in the role and instead thrived on it.

In the beginning Minnie was always sung by a dramatic soprano. Emmy Destinn, who created the role, had a heavy voice, large and dark-hued. Before I studied the score I thoroughly reviewed it with Fausto Cleva, the Italian conductor at the Met, who knew my voice and whom I trusted implicitly in judging my capability. A great deal can depend upon the conductor for this opera. The orchestration is frequently quite heavy in *Fanciulla del West*, and there is often a tendency for the conductor to enjoy the big sound and forget that the singers must reach the audience that came to hear an opera.

Minnie's softness and sincerity are shown clearly in the charming short aria she sings in the first act. She tells Rance, the sheriff who is deeply in love with her, of her youth and love for her parents who died when she was young. There are no big arias in this opera for the prima donna, but when Minnie enters she is the center of attraction and continually sings duets, trios, and ensembles. It is a considerably long role with little rest until the last act, when there is a short period before Minnie reappears.

Dick Johnson, the tenor, is a bandit who comes to the Polka in the first act to rob the miners. When he recognizes Minnie as a girl he had met in Monterey and was once in love with, he changes his plans. She accuses him of forgetting her and admits how much she has longed to see him again.

Having heard that the sheriff was tracking a suspect who had been seen in the vicinity, Minnie, not knowing Johnson's true identity, innocently tells him about the gold. Indicating the gun in her holster, she makes it clear that whoever tries to steal it will have to kill her first. Johnson is touched by her trust in him, and as they reminisce about their first meeting, Minnie invites him to her cabin, where they can continue their conversation.

The second act, like so many Puccini operas, is the tour de force; the meat of the drama. This act builds steadily using the full *lirico spinto* range of the voice to a high C sharp with heavy orchestral accompaniment.

Minnie arrives at her cabin, relieves herself of her gun, holster, and riding clothes. In preparation for Johnson's visit she dons her only dress, red shoes, places a flower in her hair, and puts on the gloves she wore more than a year before when she first met him. While they are enjoying this reunion, Johnson hears a shot and says he must go. Preoccupied about the sheriff who he knows is on his trail, he attempts to leave, but a raging snowstorm has developed and Minnie begs him to stay. When he asks her for one kiss, she falls into his arms and their love is fully reawakened. There is a short but passionate duet ending with Johnson singing, "*Non reggo più! Ti voglio per me . . .*" (I reason no more! I want you for me . . .), after which both exclaim, "*Eternamente!*" (Eternally!).

I will never forget the night of my San Francisco debut in this opera. When the tenor opened the door, an avalanche of tiny confetti used to resemble snow was blown by a fan backstage directly into our open mouths. It was a bit difficult to continue until we were able to swallow the paper!

Minnie persuades Johnson to stay and insists he sleep in her bunk. She explains that when it is very cold she often curls up on her bear rug before the fire. As they settle down and say good night, loud voices are suddenly heard calling from outside. She hides Johnson as Nick the bartender, Jack Rance, and the others burst into the cabin. The sheriff tells her that Johnson is the bandit, who has been identified by his old girl friend. Minnie vehemently denies this announcement to the men, but the minute they are gone she demands Johnson to come out. After accusing him, she desperately orders him to leave and then collapses in tears.

Johnson admits his guilt and, singing a beautiful aria, he tells Minnie the story of his life. His real name is Ramerrez and he was born the son of a vagabond. Like his father he became a bandit. When he first met Minnie he explains he was determined to change his ways to a life of work and love. He prayed that she would never learn of his transgressions, but after their initial meeting he never saw her again until he found her at the saloon. He professes his real love for Minnie and then leaves her cabin.

As he steps out into the storm, a shot is heard. Knowing he must have been hit, and struggling with hurt pride and deep love, Minnie rushes to the door. While she helps Ramerrez back into the room, he protests that he must go. Minnie passionately professes her love for him and helps the wounded man climb a ladder to the loft which is built over the entrance to the cabin.

The sixty-three bars of music we sing during this episode are frantic and probably rehearsed more than any other part of the opera. With all the action going on during our singing, and our backs to the conductor while we work far to the rear of the stage, we always have our fingers crossed and pray we get through without a fault.

After pushing Ramerrez into the loft to hide, Minnie quickly puts out of sight any evidence that she was not alone, just as the sheriff forces open the cabin door and enters with his gun drawn. Trying to look relaxed, but angered by his intrusion, Minnie then delivers a line which tickles me a bit because the translation makes it sound silly. *"Che c'è di nuovo, Jack?"* (What's new, Jack?). The sheriff searches every corner, demanding that Minnie swear she knows nothing of Johnson's whereabouts. However, finding himself alone with Minnie in her cabin, he feels his own ardor for her awakening, and while her back is turned, he grasps her and cries, *"Lo vedi! Son pazzo di te! T'amo, ti voglio!"* (You see! I am crazy for you! I love you, I want you!). Horrified, Minnie reaches back for his gun and frees herself from his embrace. She then turns his own gun on him and forces him back toward the door, crying, *"Vigliacco! Via di qua, esci, via di qua!"* (Villain! Away from here, out, away from here!).

The sheriff knows Minnie is serious, so he retreats, but warns her, *"Si, vado. Ma ti giuro . . . che non t'avra!"* (Yes, I will go. But I swear to you that he will not have you!). As he reaches the door a drop of the wounded Ramerrez's blood seeps through the floor of the loft above and drops on the sheriff's outstretched hand. When he shows it to Minnie she says, *"Forse v'avrò graffiato!"* (Perhaps I scratched you!), but as the second drop falls, he knows. Terrified, Minnie looks up. Rance lunges for his gun and wrestles it from her hand.

Puccini, with his great sense of drama, orchestrated three notes on the harp which beautifully designate the drops of blood and make us believe we actually see them.

Ramerrez, now very weak from the loss of blood, struggles down from his hiding place with Minnie's help and collapses in a chair at the table. Infuriated by Rance's remarks about Ramerrez, Minnie faces the sheriff over the table and sings a favorite arietta (short aria) which I have sung many times in concert. It begins with a typical Spanish motif which is quite compelling. I like to think that Puccini wanted this arietta to depict Minnie's love for the man whom she now knows as Ramerrez, the Spaniard. In it she proposes a game of poker. If the sheriff wins, he takes Ramerrez and she will be his. If she should win, Ramerrez is hers.

As they prepare to play, Minnie excuses herself, supposedly to get a new deck of cards. As she turns her back to Rance, she slips three aces and a pair in her stocking. Watching him carefully while telling how she always thought well of him, she manages to win the first game. The second game he wins, but before they finish the last hand, she suddenly pretends illness and begs him to get her medicine. While his back is turned she takes the winning hand from her stocking and when Rance jumps up joyously to say, "*So perchè sei svenuta, La partita è perduta!*" (I know why you fainted, you have lost!), she shows her winning hand. "*Vi sbagliate. È la gioia! Ho vinto io. Tre assi e un paio!*" (You are mistaken. It is joy! I have won! Three aces and a pair!). Rance slams his cards on the table and leaves. Minnie embraces her lover, takes the cards from the table, and tosses them into the air, singing, "*Ah! È mio! È mio!*" (Ah, he is mine, is mine!), and laughs hysterically.

The last act takes place high in the Sierras where the miners are gathered. Rance is bitter at the loss of Minnie and broods about the thought of her in the arms of Ramerrez. Ashby, the Wells Fargo agent who has also been hunting the bandit, brings word that they have found him. With this news the miners work themselves into a frenzy. Horses gallop across the stage and the men soon bring Ramerrez in, hands tied behind his back. The miners cry, "*A morte! A morte!*" (Death! Death!). As they prepare to hang him, Minnie's voice is heard in the distance. This act affords her another opportunity for a spectacular entrance. Minnie gallops in on her trusty pinto just in time to save her love, who already has the noose around his neck.

My experience with horses in this opera has been thrilling, funny, and sometimes frustrating. Thrilling in Hawaii when Mai Tai, a beautiful, spirited animal, galloped down a ramp and onto the stage at such a pace that we almost landed in the orchestra. When I sharply pulled him up, he didn't like the idea and backed into a rock made of Styrofoam, which exploded into a hundred pieces.

It isn't easy to get a horse to make a fast entrance from a few feet behind the curtain, and nice old Jordan, whom I rode at the Met, never could get off fast enough for me. His gallop was a decided trot. Then there was my appearance in San Francisco. My first performance there will long be remembered for "that horse." When the company went to Virginia City on a promotional trip with the Opera Guild, the horse I rode for the purpose of taking publicity pictures was frightened by a cameraman and took off with me holding on for dear life. I won, but Kurt Adler, our director, was terrified that he was about to lose his prima donna. Because of that episode I have always suspected that someone slipped my horse a pill on opening night. No way was that horse going to make an entrance. He was kicked, slapped, and pushed, but all the audience ever saw of him was his nose. Jumping off behind the curtain, I ran onstage to make my cue.

I have always liked to be mounted on the horse and ready to enter when I sing Minnie's entrance music offstage, because the cues are very close. The singing is quite high, urgent, and loud, which on one occasion excited the horse to such an extent that when the cue came to go on, he was hind side to and heading for the exit. That made for a few nervous moments.

When Minnie jumps off her horse and draws her gun on the sheriff who is demanding that the miners get on with hanging Ramerrez, everything stops. Standing in front of her lover, she defends him. *"Lasciatemi, o l'uccido, e m'uccido!"* (Leave me be, or I will kill him, and then kill myself!). Sonora, one of Minnie's best friends, comes to her aid, and the sheriff retreats. Here Minnie sings some of the loveliest music of the opera. Addressing them one by one, she chides the boys, reminding them that she has given them her youth. Ramerrez is now hers as God's will. He is no longer a bandit and they will leave to find new horizons. She recalls the times she comforted them when they were homesick and ill. Minnie has won them over completely. At this point they raise their voices to join her in singing together a magnificent ensemble, all wishing her happiness.

Minnie takes the noose from her lover's neck; they embrace and sing, *"Addio mia dolce terra, addio mio California!"* (Good-bye, my sweet land, good-bye, my California!). Their horses are brought forward and they ride off into the sunset.

Floria Tosca—Tosca—
Giacomo Puccini

The role of Floria Tosca is a dream come true for the singer who has the vocal technique to sing it and the dramatic ability to play the part. The opera *Tosca* is one of the most popular in the lyric theatre and continually stays in the repertoire at the Metropolitan year after year. The music is beautiful, exciting, voluptuous and at times violent. When the cast is right it can be a most thrilling night for both artist and audience.

The conductor is a major consideration. With a Fausto Cleva or Jimmy Levine in the pit, one hears clearly all the special nuances and dramatic expressions of Puccini. It is no wonder that this great opera was a sensational success from the beginning and how right the famous music publisher Ricordi was to insist that Puccini be the man to write the opera from Sardou's great dramatic play.

The world première of Sardou's tragedy took place in Paris in 1887 and was a triumph for both the dramatist and the great actress Sarah Bernhardt, who created the role. In fact, the play was performed for many years after the opera had already become successful. Several years ago my dear friend the Broadway producer Jean Dalrymple asked me if I would consider playing *Tosca*, the drama, on Broadway. Regrettably, it never developed, for that would have been a wonderful opportunity.

Puccini's opera was first performed in Rome in 1900 with the Romanian soprano Darclee as Tosca, and the eminent Italian conductor Mugnone in the pit. Toscanini took it to La Scala shortly afterward, and its great popularity began.

Before attempting the role of Tosca, I had already sung from other Puccini operas Mimi, Musetta, Manon Lescaut, and Cio Cio San, and by that time my voice had grown into the *spinto* range.

Floria Tosca is a beautiful brunette opera singer, and to play this role demands a fine singing actress. None of Puccini's heroines have quite the same dramatic opportunity as does Tosca to show her many moods. Easily she demonstrates her deep love for Mario Cavaradossi, her jealousy, suspicion, devotion to the church, her virtue and vanity. She is not heroic but quite capable of acting heroically. Her strength in defending her love and the impulsive decision to kill rather than be untrue express her remarkable character.

At her first entrance, Tosca reveals a certain impatience in her voice when she finds the door of the church locked. When Mario comes to receive her, refusing his embrace she hurries into the church and in a peevish manner asks, "*Perchè chiuso?*" (Why was the door locked?). "*A chi parlavi?*" (To whom were you talking?). She clearly shows her jealousy and accuses Mario of being with another woman, but, madly in love with him, she simply melts when he takes her in his arms. I like to play her petulant but never angry. When I raise my voice to say, "*Lo neghi?*" (You deny it?), I try to make it sound as though I were pleading with him to say yes. Tosca is as meek as a lamb with Cavaradossi. Never simpering or coy, she is too much of a woman for that, being instead proud and possessive. It is my feeling that Tosca is often played in too hysterical an attitude on her entrance and often loses the desired effect of a woman who is truly in love. Urgency in the voice, yes, but not hardness.

The lovely duets in the first act establish the passionate love Tosca and Cavaradossi have for each other, and the melodic Puccini line in the love music is quite lyric in this part of the opera. However when Scarpia, the police chief, enters, Tosca's part becomes quite dramatic. She shows a good deal of temperament in her responses when she allows her suspicious mind to be tortured by the police chief's accusations of Cavaradossi's unfaithfulness.

The second act is one of the most demanding in the repertoire. It can be exhausting physically and therefore treacherously dangerous vocally for a singer without a *spinto* voice and a solid thrust to sing over the surging orchestral accompaniment.

The second acts of Puccini's *Madama Butterfly* and his *Manon Lescaut* are also great challenges but of a different kind. These two operas are more like a marathon of constant singing. Though the tessitura is about equally high in all these operas, it is one thing to sing a love duet and another to sing at the top of the voice in anger while fighting all the way. *Tosca* is an opera which, because of the vocally difficult second act, should be well worked into the voice before singing it in a huge opera house. It is vital to learn how and where to save the voice so that when it must perform for a climax there is still plenty left to give.

The second act of *Tosca* is constant tension all the way through. When I play the part, I cannot relax for a moment, because from the time she enters, Tosca knows quickly that her lover will be tortured

Above left to right: With Eugene Conley, a fine Pinkerton. (Photo courtesy San Francisco Opera) Closing night at the old Met. Below left to right: *Bohème* with Pavarotti, the Met in Japan. (Credit: J. Heffernan, courtesy Metropolitan Opera) With my colleague Anselmo Colzani, a great *sheriffo*. (Photo courtesy Anselmo Colzani)

Above left to right: *Tosca* with Franco Corelli in San Francisco. (Photo courtesy San Francisco Opera) With Tito Gobbi—my thirtieth anniversary at the Met. (Credit: J. Heffernan, courtesy Metropolitan Opera) Below left to right: My twenty-fifth anniversary and James Levine's debut in San Francisco; Placido Domingo is gathering my flowers. (Credit: M. Norton, courtesy San Francisco Opera) San Francisco debut in *Tosca* with General Director Gaetano Marola. (Photo courtesy San Francisco Opera)

Above: Practicing my leap of twelve feet and . . . the real thing (*Tosca*). (Credit: Otto Rothschild) Below left to right: Great city-wide publicity with Barry Morell, Cesare Bardelli, and Salvatore Baccaloni. (Photo courtesy Foster & Kleiser, Division of Metromedia, Inc.) With William Tury and James Doolittle planning our opera production for the Greek Theatre, Los Angeles. (Credit: Otto Rothschild)

Working out with the horse that ran away with me! (Photo courtesy San Francisco Opera)

and she too is in grave danger. When the soldiers drag Mario out after torturing him, I fight them with everything I have, as if it was really happening. Though there is some difficult singing to do at that point, I never fake things on the stage. I live the part, crying, laughing, loving, or hating.

The lovely aria "Vissi l'arte" (I lived for art) comes directly after an extremely tiring duet with Scarpia. There are many ways to dramatize this aria. I have enjoyed dreaming up new ones, and I think with the hundreds of times I have sung this opera that I have played most of them. I used to have Scarpia push me down on the sofa as though he were going to attack me right there. With a good actor that worked, but with a poor one it was ridiculous and lost the whole point. Of course we all have to adjust to the furniture and setting, which may be totally different in every company. In my most recent performances, as Tosca struggles with Scarpia just before the aria, I had the villain catch me off center stage and, grasping me by the wrists, force me to my knees. Threatening Tosca, he tells her that for Mario there is little time left, "*si drizza un patibolo*" (they are raising the gallows), and with that he throws her to the floor. Though this is not exactly the most comfortable position in which to sing, this staging proved to be more dramatic, and I do enjoy the challenge.

Arrangements are always made in rehearsal with the conductor that when I begin to raise my head from where it rests on my arm after my fall, I am ready to sing. Puccini was considerate here, for the music quiets down quickly and finally dies out. Often I have wondered if this was not a purposeful effect by the composer. Considering the torture which Tosca has just experienced, I believe "Vissi d'arte" should begin quietly. I like to sing the aria as a prayer, for it should be remembered that in the first act Tosca reveals the fact that she has deep religious feelings. The score indicates *pianissimo, dolcissimo con grande sentimento* (quietly, very sweetly with great feeling). It would be far easier to "belt" it out as some do, but this is a great place to practice a bit of *bel canto* (beautiful singing) and remain in character as it seems obvious Puccini wished us to do.

The number of props important to Tosca's action in Act II are remarkable. I make it a point to check every one of them before the curtain, personally placing each where I need it to be. Checking the furniture too is important, so it will be in the position planned for our action.

Tosca has an opportunity to make a stunning entrance in Act II. The great couturière Valentina designed my lovely costumes for this role, and though I am now wearing my third set, they are all copies of her design except for one. The original gown she did for the second act was a beautiful Empire-styled white and silver-metallic creation, over which I wore an emerald green stole. With all the rough action in this particular act, the costume takes a beating. At Paramount Pictures I met Edith Head who designed a Tosca gown for the movie *Mr. Music* with Bing Crosby. I asked her to create my second one for the opera. This dress was made of a beautifully jeweled burgundy velvet and was complemented by a long stole of the same fabric but lined with a magnificent piece of gold cloth making it reversible. This was Edith's special gift to me. Then, for a new production in San Francisco, there was a third gown of royal purple velvet, embroidered in gold with topazes and other brilliant stones. For my wrap I had the same gold cloth lined this time with purple velvet. I designed my own Empire necklace, using topazes and rhinestones on a base of net, embroidering it on my trips from coast to coast.

I have spent a fortune over the years to have my own costumes created by top designers, but it is well worth it to know that every time I walk onstage I can be very proud. Fortunately, throughout my career I have retained approximately the same measurements and, more important, Vicki, my faithful friend, an all-purpose girl, has taken tender, loving care of my beautiful wardrobe.

For this great second act of *Tosca*, when I was beginning to learn the role, I studied Sardou's drama and adopted some of Sarah Bernhardt's moves. The way in which she handled the knife and Scarpia's murder interested me most. While Scarpia is writing the *permesso* (safe-conduct note) that he has promised Tosca, she goes to the table, turning her back to him. Seeing the glass of wine which he had offered her earlier and she had refused, Tosca now nervously drains it and, returning the glass to the table, happens to notice the fruit knife. Transfixed for the moment and shocked by her thoughts, she lifts her face to God as if to utter a prayer. But as Scarpia rushes toward her, crying, "*Tosca, finalmente mia!*" (Tosca, finally you are mine), she is horrified by his touch and suddenly grasps the knife, plunging it into his heart.

Puccini has indicated clearly in the music many interesting points where he wants special things to happen. For example, Scarpia bargains with Tosca that if she will give herself to him for one night, he will order only a mock execution for Mario. When he presses her for an answer, the orchestra plays the notes *la do*, which means in Italian, "I give," whereupon Tosca indicates "yes" by nodding her head. Afterward, while Scarpia is writing at his desk, there is a specific chord in the orchestration on which Tosca discovers the knife. Another chord that must be carefully timed is when he is stabbed, and one when she sees the note clutched in his dead hand. The most eerie sound of all is made by the orchestra when Tosca places the crucifix on his chest. Here the conductor waits for her cue as he had done with the action just before that, when Tosca arranges the candles. The composer has also made allowances for the timing in his score. Many larger sets require more time to do this action, and the music must then be slower.

Puccini was so expressive and knew what he wanted that he practically tells the entire story in his music. What a shame some people are not satisfied with this great work as it was written and originally directed. I remember with great disappointment the new production of *Tosca* directed by Jean-Pierre Ponnelle in San Francisco. His direction distorted the wishes of the composer in so many ways that the second act was hardly recognizable. The candles and the crucifix were simply eliminated. Tosca was asked to stab Scarpia in the back as he sat writing. After singing this role for two decades and having studied it thoroughly, I do not believe Tosca was capable of premeditated murder. Everything was so confusing in the Ponnelle production that I cannot remember what we did to fill the time before I had to exit.

In the last act Mr. Ponnelle had Mario tied to a post, which, when the soldiers shot him, made it impossible for him to fall. Consequently, all the words I say to him about falling carefully, and later when I beg him to get up and escape with me, did not make sense, because he was still tied at the post. Having read the notices of some of the other operas Mr. Ponnelle has directed, I know I am not alone in my feelings. It is a shame that with so much talent he feels he can ignore the text of the great composers. Poor Puccini!

Tosca is the subject of many questions in the minds of critics, artists, and others involved. There is one point that I have argued about for a long time and hope I can convince a few that my way is justified. The drama takes place in less than twenty-four hours. My critics believe Tosca goes directly to where Mario is prisoner after murdering Scarpia. This does not make sense to me. I contend that knowing she was last seen with the Baron Scarpia, his guards will soon look for her. She would not dare go to the castle dressed in all her jewels. The interval between her visit with Scarpia, his death, and just before dawn when she arrives at the castle is several hours. What did she do all that time? Anyone who knows Rome is aware that the distance between the Palazzo Farnese (Farnese Palace) and the castle is negligible. It has never been proven where she lives, but I believe Tosca goes to her home first, discards her jeweled gown, and dons a travel dress and cloak. After she arrives at the castle and explains to Mario what has happened, she says to him, "*Senti . . . l'ora è vicina; io già raccolsi oro e gioielli . . . una vettura è pronta.*" (Listen. . . . the hour is near; I have already collected money and jewels . . . a carriage is waiting). Her statement convinces me that she could not have gone directly from Scarpia's quarters to the castle, having made all of these preparations.

The tenor's aria in the third act, "E lucevan le stelle" (The stars were brightly shining), is one of the most popular and when beautifully sung is a showstopper. My favorite music of the opera comes with Tosca's entrance in this act, when she tells Mario the dramatic story of Scarpia's demands and how she finally killed him. Her excitement at bringing Mario the paper which supposedly would free them, and her beautiful music which follows, is climaxed by a stunning high C. The third-act music is much more lyrical and the text almost poetical in expressing Tosca's love for Mario.

I have sung *Tosca* more times than any other opera in my repertoire and have also directed this opera on several occasions. Historically, the action is based on real people and documented events, and perhaps this is why the story intrigues me.

Puccini must have truly loved Tosca, for he has provided her with some of the most exquisite opportunities to act and sing. This is the kind of opera I love best and the reason why I will sing this role until my career is through and the good Lord signals me that my time to sing is over.

Cio Cio San—
Madama Butterfly—
Giacomo Puccini

adama Butterfly is similar to *Tosca* in that it offers a wonderful role for a prima donna such as myself who prefers operas with excellent acting parts. As I have mentioned, this part is a marathon of singing. The second act is virtually a monologue for the soprano and one of the longest acts in my repertoire.

I began to dream about singing *Butterfly* long before my voice was sufficiently developed to sing it. The music and the character intrigued me so much that during my first visit to Italy to study, I picked up an old score of the opera in a tiny secondhand bookshop in Naples. Much to my astonishment I later noticed that it was dedicated by Puccini: "*A Sua Maesta La Regina Elena, reverente omaggio di Giacomo Puccini, Milano 5 2 04*" (To Your Majesty, The Queen Elena, reverent homage of Giacomo Puccini, Milan, February 5, 1904). How this precious volume ever found its way to such a shop and I was able to buy it for just a few lire remain a mystery. Victor Emmanuel III was still reigning with Elena, and their library, I understand, was one of the leading ones in Italy. *Butterfly* became one of my most successful roles, and it was from this score that I studied and worked for many years. It will always be one of my most treasured possessions.

I made my debut as Madama Butterfly in July 1946 at the Belles Artes Opera House in Mexico City. Later that year I sang my first performance of the opera at the Metropolitan and from then on I was singing Cio Cio San everywhere and often.

When I began to study this opera, Humphry Doulens asked me if I would like to meet the great former interpreter of Butterfly, Geraldine Farrar. Humphry lived not far from Miss Farrar in Connecticut, and, visiting her one day, he told her that I was studying the role. A few days later we were invited to tea with the famous star. Sitting in her chair, looking like a queen, her beautiful large eyes sparkling with obvious enthusiasm, she discussed this opera that was so closely identified with her during the early 1900s. Farrar knew my voice from all the radio I was doing and told me she was sure I would have a great success with *Butterfly*.

We talked a good deal about the second act and the amount of fortitude one needs to sing continually while so much action is also required of this role. It was interesting to learn where she had conserved her voice during this tour de force. Our visit was a fascinating afternoon which I shall never forget.

In the early stages of singing this opera I was forced to learn quickly the importance of controlling my emotions. Never have I sung Cio Cio San without shedding many tears. Weeping, however, can be dangerous while singing and interfere with voice production. Not only is it troublesome for the singer, but when working with the child in the opera, I have found it was so upsetting to them that they too began to cry. One dear little girl was so moved by my tears that she wiped them away with her sleeve, and the first few rows heard her say, "Please don't cry." That nearly threw me.

Madama Butterfly is a fine opera for getting lots of exercise. Cio Cio San is constantly moving, bowing, kneeling, and rising again. While I was relatively young it was very easy, but as the years rolled by I had to see to it that I kept in shape for this role. Walking eighteen holes on a golf course every chance I had was a great help and my favorite way to keep limber, though there wasn't always time for that. Knee-bending exercises were most important. Going from an upright position to one's knees, then rising in a graceful manner without helping yourself is not easy without practice.

There is a lovely Japanese gesture done with the hand while folding the kimono under the knees as one kneels. All of these typically Japanese mannerisms should be carefully studied by anyone who aspires to play the part of Cio Cio San or even Suzuki. Their movements are smooth and graceful, for example, the delicate way in which they handle a fan. And to walk as a Japanese woman does is a study in itself.

The wearing of the kimono is another consideration. Cio Cio San is fifteen years old. Most young Japanese women are diminutive and rather small-busted. In order to get this youthful look I used to bind my bosom, trying my best to look as oriental as possible. In comparison, American women are generally taller, and though I am by no means the tallest Butterfly to sing this role, I am always happiest when singing it with a tall tenor.

While I was working at Metro-Goldwyn-Mayer, making *The*

Great Caruso, the make-up man gave me some pointers on how to look Japanese. He used a pair of rubber pieces on my eyes which fitted over the lids. However, when I was singing this long opera they proved to be impractical as the perspiration began to pour off my face, and I never wore them again.

I will always remember the lovely Japanese woman with whom I was fortunate to work on my interpretation of Madama Butterfly. Hizi Koyke, a prima donna with the San Carlo Opera Company, was the most beautiful Cio Cio San I have ever seen. Vocally she gave it all, though there was not much there to give. But she was a consummate actress and a great example for a young and eager beginner such as I was at that time.

Puccini often introduced his leading ladies with an offstage entrance, but none had a more glamorous, melodious and lovely one than Madama Butterfly. It is a real test of *bel canto*, because the voice begins at the top of the scale and works up to a climactic high D. There is no easy singing on which to warm up. Not only is it essential to be ready when that entrance cue comes, but also to support an even scale and project the voice from backstage over the orchestra and a large chorus of women. As Cio Cio San enters, the sound steadily increases. The high D at the end of the entrance music is interpolated and not always sung. The score also shows a lower ending. Unless I was indisposed for some reason, I always sang the higher one, which invariably brought down the house.

It is easy to show Butterfly's tender age and innocence with the music which immediately follows. She tells of being a geisha girl to sustain herself. Her father is dead and her mother is very poor. Cio Cio San shows Pinkerton, her bridegroom-to-be, the simple belongings which she has brought with her. When he asks about the object in a sheath, she gently declines to comment, saying, *"C'è troppa gente"* (There are too many people), and excuses herself. But Goro, the marriage broker, explains that it is a dagger, a gift from the Mikado to her father, indicating that he had been asked to use it, and did.

In Puccini's *Madama Butterfly* there is a succession of arias, duets, and trios. The lovely, long, and lyrically beautiful duet that ends the first act is one of my favorites. Few in the lyric repertoire are as magnificently constructed or as gratifying, as it builds toward an exciting final high C. This time the tenor has his choice, either to join me in the high note or sing a lower harmonizing one, but when both voices soar to the top together, it is thrilling.

Suzuki, the maid, is quite insignificant in the first act but comes to life prominently for the second. The two lovely mezzos with whom I worked in *Butterfly* and remember as very special were Margaret

Roggero, who sang with me during my early days at the Metropolitan, and Shirley Love, who was my Suzuki later. Both are superb actresses and our work together was a joy.

The part of Sharpless is also one which can contribute enormously to an exciting and poignant performance. Among the many baritones with whom I have sung this opera, Frank Guarrera moved me the most. The tenderness shown in his voice was deeply felt and quite obvious. When he put the painful question to me, *"Che fareste, Madama Butterfly, s'ei non dovesse ritornar più mai?"* (What would you do, Madama Butterfly, if he should never return?), the manner in which he delivered that line was so full of compassion my stunned reaction was quite real.

While I was rehearsing *Butterfly* at the old Met in the late forties, I had an accident that was certainly untimely. We were well into the third act, and my next cue was the fast entrance when Cio Cio San comes into the house looking for Pinkerton. In this act I wear the indoor Japanese footwear called *tabi* which is like a cotton sock. As I ran across the stage my right large toe was caught in a hole in the flooring and I heard a "crack." I did not fall, and no one except my colleagues who heard the sound knew that anything serious had happened. Though my toe had been broken, I managed to finish the act, but the next day and several following days found me rehearsing for *Louise* in a wheelchair.

The old score of *Madama Butterfly* that I bought in Naples in 1939 has the opera printed in two acts. Instead of a third act, Act II is divided into two parts. At La Scala I understand they tried presenting the opera without the second intermission, and I have been told that in some German opera houses they too are abiding by the old score. I disagree with this concept. Though it does disturb the continuity of the play after the long, extremely emotional second act as we perform it here, I think the audience welcomes a respite. It does not make that much difference to the soprano, though Cio Cio San stands all during the vigil scene following that strenuous second act. After she takes her child offstage there is time to rest before she enters again. The humming by an unseen chorus, to my way of thinking, is a lovely way in which to finish the scene. Moreover, beginning the last act with the waiting scene and the sunrise seems to emphasize clearly the fact that Cio Cio San has been there all night.

My experience with children who played the part of Trouble, Cio Cio San's son, have been many; some great, some exasperating and some memorable.

When singing *Butterfly* with companies other than the Met and San Francisco, I was often asked if I would participate in choosing a local child to play the part of Trouble. The management would either put an item in the newspaper or contact the local children's ballet classes. This was good publicity for the opera and the public loved it. The response was always good but sometimes overwhelming. All the mothers would arrive with their little ones. I would usually narrow my choice down to five or six, hoping that two or three of them would be capable of learning the few important things they had to do. After we had a little talk (without Mommie present), all I needed do was lift them for weight and to see if they would either stiffen up or relax in my arms so I could comfortably carry them. If the child could not relax and pretend he was asleep, it was difficult to handle him while I sang the lovely lullaby of the last act and carried him out. I like to remain onstage for most of the singing and have someone waiting in the wings to take Trouble from me just before I have to hold a high B natural, letting it fade out as I disappear.

Little girls are almost always chosen for this part. I have found them more pliable and easier to handle. Furthermore, Trouble is really a three-year-old, blue-eyed, blond boy with curls, and few boys at the age of four or five are found still wearing curls. Three-year-olds are really too young for this assignment. I will always remember one little boy. Five-year-old Paul Sheehan played with me in Tulsa, Oklahoma, in 1958. Never was I hugged or kissed more by little Trouble. I wonder if he remembers!

At the Metropolitan we were required by law not to use any child younger than seven years old. Although one little girl we worked with was small for her age and a fine little actress, she looked much too big. Several of the other singers just would not attempt to carry her. It becomes somewhat of a shock nowadays when a big strapping young man or a mother of several children comes backstage to greet me with, "Remember me? I was your Trouble fifteen or twenty years ago!"

When I first sang *Butterfly*, we used to blindfold the child at the hara-kiri scene and have him wave a small American flag. Thank heaven that melodramatic action has been eliminated.

For several years now I have been using a doll onstage to give my son, gently sending him out into the garden to play before performing my tragic deed. This works beautifully and adds poignancy, because when Pinkerton arrives he finds the doll, and, bringing it into the house, speaks to Suzuki about the child.

Another badly staged part of the action was the way we used to do the scene of Cio Cio San's self-destruction. This was usually performed behind a tall screen on the far left side of the stage, where it was impossible for the entire audience to see it. In order to avoid that, when directing my own action I kneel before a Buddha in profile to the audience, close to the front of the stage so the hara-kiri scene can be seen by everyone. After the deed is done, ritual dictates that a scarf be tied through the mouth like a gag to alter the cries of pain. As Pinkerton's voice is heard calling, I rise and struggle to reach the *shosi* (Japanese doors). Climbing the steps, I pry the door open just a crack with my remaining strength and then drop to my knees. Collapsing on the edge of the landing, I fall backward and my body rolls down the steps.

The Met's version is slightly different. Using a short screen just high enough to hide Cio Cio San, she performs the hara-kiri center stage. As the last chords of the orchestra are played, I fall forward over the screen. The petals that were strewn in her ecstasy during the flower duet with Suzuki, when they decorated the room for Pinkerton's return, rise in a cloud only to float back down on the heroic little Japanese girl.

Manon—*Jules Massenet* and Manon Lescaut— *Giacomo Puccini*

he operas *Manon* by Jules Massenet and *Manon Lescaut* by Puccini, were adapted from the same romantic French novel of Abbé Prévost entitled *The Story of the Chevalier des Grieux and of Manon Lescaut*, a classic published in 1731.

Massenet was the first composer to finish his opera on the subject and simply called it *Manon*. It premièred at the Opéra Comique in Paris on January 19, 1884. Puccini, nine years later, introduced his opera about the same story on February 1, 1893, in Turin, Italy, titling his *Manon Lescaut*. The Massenet opera had already become renowned by the time the Italian composer started to write on the same subject. Puccini, however, had fallen in love with Manon, and it is said that he denied knowing the French version existed. Manon Lescaut was the first heroine in his family of "sisters": Mimi, Musetta, Tosca, Cio Cio San, and Liù.

The Italian operatic world was greatly influenced by Wagner while Puccini was at work on *Manon Lescaut*, and Verdi was the most revered Italian composer of the day. Not wanting to follow in those footsteps, Puccini endeavored to go his own way. It was at this time that young composers turned to the new school called *verismo* (realism). Opera at that point started to be based on a more realistic portrayal of characters, akin to real-life subjects and less poetic.

Puccini's *Manon Lescaut* was his first great triumph as a composer. At the première it was said to have ended in a feast of love and jubilation. The audience refused to leave until Puccini had made several appearances before them to thunderous applause.

I sang my first *Manon Lescaut* quite early in my career for the New York City Center Opera Company on November 9, 1944. Just four years before that date I had made my debut as an opera singer in Chicago. The Metropolitan Opera Company revived the opera for me in the 1949–50 season. This was my first performance of *Manon Lescaut* with the company and the first time my great colleague Jussi Björling and I sang the opera together. It was wonderful to go back to this opera which had opened the doors to the Metropolitan for me when Edward Johnson came to the City Center to hear me.

I find the character of Manon extremely interesting, whether in the French operatic version or the Italian. Having sung Puccini's *Manon Lescaut* more often, I can truthfully say I became more fond of that version. But this may also be because I began with her. The French *Manon* was better suited to my earlier voice when I was at ease singing the lighter roles. However, I do agree with many who believe that there is no scene in Puccini's opera to compare with Massenet's St.-Sulpice. I have recorded the duet in this magnificent scene with Richard Tucker, and it remains one of the best things we ever did together. Richard loved both *Manons*, and I enjoyed singing them with him, but he too preferred the Puccini opera. He was magnificent in both, as was Jussi Björling.

The libretto of Massenet's work proceeds more slowly than that of Puccini's, which is a great advantage. Manon's changing moods are too quick, and I have always felt the need of a scene such as Massenet's second act to explain what happened in the meantime. In the first act of the Italian opera, when Manon meets Des Grieux for the first time, there is too little dialogue to illustrate her character. It all seems too fast when we find the apparently naïve young girl of the first act separated without explanation from the boy she ran away with, already established as a courtesan and obviously bored at being the rich Geronte's mistress.

In the French opera the lovely second act takes place in an apartment in Paris where the lovers have been happily living together for a short time. As the story unfolds, Manon's love wanes when a rich suitor offers jewels and the glamorous life that she longs for. This libretto describes her capriciousness better.

Puccini's intermezzo, which is played just before the third act, is one of the most magical orchestral works I have ever heard in opera. Here his writing could well have been influenced by Wagner's soaring love music. As I stand offstage waiting to make my entrance, having hurried into my next costume so as not to miss a note, I am soon dissolved in tears by the beauty of the music. It's no wonder that we often hear this piece done by our great symphonies and finest conductors, and it was also said to be a favorite of the great Toscanini. The nostalgia it creates for my following scene is most appropriate.

The last scenes of these two operas are similar; however, in Massenet's work Manon dies en route to Le Havre, while in Act IV of Puccini's version she says her farewell in a vast plain on the borders of New Orleans where she has been exiled. The weary Manon soon collapses after the lovers enter the scene, and most of the act she sings from extremely awkward positions on a hard floor with an artificial rock put here and there to lean on. This scene is difficult to depict on the stage. The great aria "Sola, perduta, abbandonata" (Alone, lost, and abandoned) is decidedly *spinto* and quite dramatic. It demands flexibility, a wide range, and two well-sustained high B's projected over a heavy orchestration. It is a most gratifying aria, which I love to sing.

The final duet between Manon and her Chevalier is deeply touching, and her words at the end are more beautifully designed by Puccini. With her last bit of breath, held closely in the arms of her love, she murmurs, *"Le mie colpe travolgerà l'oblio ma l'amor mio non muor"* (My sins will be obliterated, but my love will never die).

In 1940 Grace Moore gave me her personal score of *Manon* by Massenet. In it she wrote these words:

To Dorothy Kirsten,
  With the hopes that "Manon" one day will be her greatest triumph.

Grace Moore
1940, NYC

Traveling Music

One place to which I have always enjoyed traveling is Hawaii. Most of the time my husband and I are on our way to Maui where we have a lovely apartment, twenty feet from the beautiful blue Pacific. The whales perform for us in the spring and the view of Lanai and Molekai is utterly spectacular. Here I paint with my friend and teacher Joyce Clark and play golf at the many excellent courses. I have also flown to the Islands many times to work with the opera company in Honolulu, which has been of special interest to me from its inception, when my friend Alice Taylor, who used to be the manager of the Los Angeles Symphony, and I dedicated ourselves to establishing a first-class company there.

On November 27, 1959, I was engaged to sing a concert with George Barati and the Honolulu Symphony to open a lovely new theatre which now also accommodates the opera. Alice was manager and worked hard to bring many of the finest singers to Hawaii, offering some excellent performances. In the early 1960s I was beginning to spend some of my time during the summer directing as well as singing. An invitation from the company in Hawaii to sing and direct my own production of *La Bohème* was extended to me in 1967. This was my first chance to put in play for this opera all the ideas I had gathered over the years. Alice engaged a fine cast for me and we used as much young, local talent as possible. The chorus was good, hard-working, and eager to please. Being preoccupied as I always am when working, I had forgotten we were in Hawaii, and when the company presented themselves ready for work in brightly colored muumuus and bare feet, the experience was new for me and amusing.

We did four performances of this opera; one in particular was very special. The symphony, which had never before traveled from the island of Oahu, was invited to bring the entire company to the neighboring island of Maui. We performed in their high school and nearly every living soul on the island turned out to greet us. The school was so crowded that all the doors and windows were opened wide. People sat in trees and on rooftops of nearby houses to get a glimpse of the stage. Many of these Hawaiians had never been off their beautiful island and few had ever seen a symphony orchestra or witnessed anything like an opera.

We wore make-up and costumes, and I had worked out a modest plan for light action so the audience had some idea of what we were doing. They were fascinated, laughing with us, and some even crying. Though they could not understand the Italian words we were singing, their reactions touched us so deeply that we outdid ourselves. I sincerely doubt we ever sang or played to a more appreciative audience.

Prior to that fun engagement I had had an opportunity, when George Kuyper was general director of the Hollywood Bowl, to sing *Madama Butterfly* in concert style with the Los Angeles Symphony. It always seemed to me so stolid to have singers just stand in a line and sing those passionately dramatic operas. An aria, duet or even trio possibly, but an entire opera of the romantic repertoire sung statically always bothered me. I suggested to George we revamp the whole opera-concert idea by designing two lovely small scenes, and appear in costume and make-up with modified action plus some spectacular lighting. Walter Hendl, associate conductor of the Chicago Symphony, was making his debut with the Bowl. The performance was so well received that I was engaged to do another opera the next Bowl season. I set to work as soon as possible on *La Bohème*, which, unlike the cut version we did of *Madama Butterfly*, I planned to be a fully cast, staged, and uncut version of the opera in three instead of four acts, eliminating the first intermission between Act I and Act II. I had been dreaming about this idea for theatres such as the Hollywood Bowl, and I knew it would work.

I still thoroughly enjoyed draftsmanship, and this was my golden chance to design two miniature stage sets, arrange the props, engage a good cast of my colleagues, work out the action for the production, direct, and sing it. I was fortunate in being able to find a good assistant to run the show for me while I sang. There was no pit at the Hollywood Bowl at that time, and we therefore had to arrange the musicians on the stage in a fan-shaped group, leaving enough space on each side for our two sets. Only the conductor's podium was placed far enough in front for contact with the artists. The musicians used lights on their stands, facing away from the audience, and only a few were dimly visible. The rest were behind the sets.

As the lights came up on Act I, the Bohemian garret in Paris was visible as well as its entrance, which plays an important part in the action but is generally hidden from sight in standard productions. I was anxious to change that and I think it added a lot.

As Rudolfo's friends call to him from the street below to join them at the Café Momus, a light comes on in the lamppost under which the boys are seen calling up to the garret. After Mimi and Rodolfo sing their lovely duet and prepare to leave, the light on the lamppost fades out and the lovers make their way out the door while singing the last few bars of that divine music. The Hollywood Bowl was bathed in bright moonlight that night. It was one of those spectacular evenings, achieving a romantic effect which I doubt had ever been obtained there before.

A spotlight picked us up as we left the set and followed us while we finished singing the climactic high ending of the duet. We walked across that huge stage, timing the music so that we arrived on cue in the second-act set. As we entered, the lights came on to introduce the Café Momus, and the chorus began their part. The reaction from the audience was tremendous and we were delighted.

For the third act, this set was reversible to a wintry scene, and since there was no curtain, the audience seemed amused to see the mechanics of setting it up. Of course we had no way of producing snow, which is always a lovely part of this scene, but I doubt that anyone missed it. The last act also takes place in the garret, the same setting we used for the first act. This made it simple to black out the second set and return to the first. The whole project was a most gratifying and enjoyable experience, truly a happy night at the Hollywood Bowl.

Traveling became a chore especially in the latter part of my career, when I began to do so much flying. In the earlier days I used to enjoy my trips from coast to coast by train, since I was always busy studying an opera, a script, or a show. It was an ideal atmosphere in which to work: no interruptions, no telephones.

In 1944 and 1945, I traveled for the first time to Canada on a War Bond show, which was quite a thrill, considering the artists with whom I journeyed. Bob Hope was our master of ceremonies; the great pianist Artur Rubinstein, Rosalind Russell, and Dinah Shore were the other stars, and for a debutante such as I, it was an exciting adventure. The Canadians showered us with beautiful mementos and were warm, generous hosts.

I later returned to Canada several times with the Metropolitan Opera when we used to tour there, and eventually sang in every major city of that country, including some not-so-major for concerts. Vancouver is one of my favorite places, and I have often returned to sing there for my dear friend of many years, Hugh Pickett, the highly regarded impresario who has brought so many of the greatest stars to his city.

I especially remember my trip to Canada in March 1966. This one was a long concert tour. Vicki; my accompanist at that time, George Posell; and I took off for Regina, our first stop. It was very cold and the air extremely dry. I immediately became aware that my throat and nose were becoming uncomfortable and I was experiencing difficulty in breathing. The concert was planned for the following evening, which hardly gave me time to adjust to this kind of climate. When we announced the emergency to our welcoming committee, they jumped to my aid, and I was surrounded with humidifiers that did wonders. I sang my concert, but that night a devastating snowstorm hit the area. We were to fly in the morning to Winnipeg, but all flights were grounded and the only transportation we could find was a bus. Concerned but not wanting to disappoint, we bundled up for the storm and, with only four or five other trusting souls, we boarded. The going was rough in the blinding snow, and our concern increased understandably when we continued to lose time. The roads became icy and the windows too. There was little heat and after a while my feet were freezing through my boots. Having had an early light breakfast as usual, I became ravenously hungry and longed for a hot drink. The driver was most accommodating, since we were brave enough to chance this wild weather with him, and agreed to stop at the first place he saw. It seemed like hours later, but eventually we found a tiny café where we gulped down terrible hamburgers and some very black coffee.

The storm was relentless and growing worse. When we returned to the bus the driver decided he had had enough. We had no idea how far we had yet to go, but by this time we were long overdue in Winnipeg and telephoned the reception committee. That city too was completely snowed in and my concert had already been canceled. Now what to do? There was no hotel, motel, or place to stay in sight. The bus was freezing cold and we were in the middle of nowhere. Realizing he too was in a spot, the driver said he had found out at the café that we were not too far from some railroad tracks and a small train station. He was not sure whether the train stopped there anymore, nor did he know where it went, but he would try to drive us that far. We made it, dragged our luggage to the platform, and waited for what seemed like hours, wondering what we would do if that train wouldn't stop. Suddenly the strangest sight imaginable appeared down the tracks. Slowly, in a cloud of steam, it was moving toward us. Waving madly to make it stop, we could not believe our eyes when the train appeared out of the snow, looking like one giant icicle with thousands of other icicles hanging all over it, and an enormous plow in front. That startlingly beautiful picture will remain with me forever. The train did stop and we gratefully climbed aboard. When the conductor told us they did not usually stop there and were on their way to Saskatoon, we knew our guardian angel was with us, for that was the city of our next concert!

A concert in Red Rocks at the natural amphitheatre just outside of Denver was another interesting engagement. I was singing a joint concert with Robert Merrill and the Denver Symphony. Most of the gowns I use for this type of occasion when there is a huge audience are designed with large, bouffant skirts, but this time I wished I had worn a slim one. The theatre is beautiful, but when the wind blows it seems to funnel its greatest strength directly onto the stage. It blew so hard into our faces that night that I had to cup my hand over my mouth to sing. I had sung there before but never experienced anything like this. When the weather is lovely and calm it is a magnificent place to sing in, and the voice easily soars out to the topmost seat, but this night we wondered how much was heard even though we were using a microphone. Most of the music flew off the musicians' stands with one of the stronger gusts, and my big skirt nearly blew over my head. Bob and I hung on and did our best, but it was the audience that was magnificent. They understood our predicament and still responded vigorously.

A trip to Stockholm in 1961 to open the newly decorated opera house with *Tosca* turned out to be a most successful visit. This was my first time in that country, and I'll never forget the hundreds of people who stood with little good-luck wooden horses tied to bouquets of flowers, waiting for me to come out of the artists' entrance. This was a welcome much appreciated. There were concerts too with the symphony, and a beautiful reception at our American Embassy.

While in Sweden I flew to Milan to discuss plans for my debut at La Scala as Minnie in *La Fanciulla del West*. Luigi Oldani was then the director of the company and this was the second time I was offered an opportunity to sing there. My good friend Mario del Monaco was my tenor, and I was thrilled, but once again it was not to be. The Met already had me engaged to sing several performances of this opera in the same period of time, and I was not free to accept.

Singing a great many operettas so early in my career was the most valuable experience I could have had. The more than five hundred performances of light opera represented the golden stairway to my success as an opera singer. It all started in 1942, just two years after I became a professional singer. My first appearance was as the Merry Widow at the famous Paper Mill Playhouse in New Jersey with the fine baritone Walter Cassel as an ideal Danilo. I remember going to Arthur Murray to learn how to look beautiful while waltzing. In 1943 I appeared in *The Only Girl* by Victor Herbert in Memphis. There is more acting than singing in this operetta, but one beautiful song called "When You're Away" is a standout. Then came seven weeks during 1944 of *The New Moon* by Romberg, in New York, with Earl Wrightson. At this same time I was also doing a radio show called "Keepsakes" for the diamond company of the same name, with Mack Harrell. That show went on every Sunday evening for more than two years, and the timing was so close for my entrance in *The New Moon* that I had a police escort from the radio studio to the theatre. On Sunday nights the dresser would spread my gown on the floor, ready for me to jump into while the orchestra began my entrance music. I used to make it only by the skin of my teeth!

The city of Dallas engaged me for two operettas in 1945, the year of my debut at the Met. These were *The Great Waltz* with music by Johann Strauss and *Countess Maritza* by Emmerich Kálmán. I did both shows with another good baritone, George Britton. In 1951 I returned to Dallas for *The Merry Widow*, when my handsome Danilo was John Tyers.

One of the best productions of operetta in which I have ever appeared was right here in Los Angeles for Edwin Lester in 1953. It was a brand new *Great Waltz*, with magnificent costumes by Adele Palmer, elegant scenery, and a stellar cast. The great baritone John Charles Thomas was charming as the elder Strauss, and Erich Korngold wrote some lovely duets for us. Florence Henderson, who has had a brilliant career, was the ingenue. Korngold also wrote a beautiful new waltz for me called "I'm in Love with Vienna," which I sang in a lovely ballroom scene. It was the highlight of the show. This operetta played for eight delightful weeks, four in Los Angeles and four in San Francisco.

In 1956 my California representative, Wynn Rocamora, presented me with a contract to make an appearance in Las Vegas. I knew that Wynn would never consider anything but the most dignified appearance for me, and having been to Las Vegas, I was curious as to how he intended fitting me into that kind of environment. It was promised I could sing anything I wanted, and the fee seemed like a fortune twenty-five years ago. My engagement was to be at the Hotel Tropicana which then had the only large stage and orchestra pit in the area. At the other hotels the performers worked on the main floor with the audience surrounding them. I agreed to consider the offer, and Wynn and I went to Las Vegas to check things out. I was satisfied we could have an exciting show and immediately arranged for a writer. David Rose was engaged to compose my musical arrangements, which were great. Edith Head of Paramount Pictures designed my beautiful gowns, and Fredrica, my furrier in New York, wrapped me in gorgeous Russian sables. It was all very elegant.

The first half of the show was Dick Shawn, the popular comedian. I opened my part with a grand fanfare and an orchestral arrangement from a number of the operas for which I am best known. We had eight male dancers for this big opening number, and I even did a dance routine with them. I sang everything from popular arias, to operetta, to show tunes. The waiters were mostly Italians and opera lovers. They stood in the back of the room like soldiers and refused to serve even a drink while I sang. There were many cries of "Brava," which were quite uncommon in Las Vegas.

I had promised myself that I would never venture into the gambling arena and I didn't. However, when Jack came for my opening night, he did. I'll never forget emptying his pockets of the silver dollars he won and sending him back for more. He couldn't lose that night and still believes it wasn't just luck or skill. The winning had been too easy. Could it have been that they were enticing him to spend my fee in the casino? Many entertainers leave every cent they are paid and more on the tables at Las Vegas. I'm glad I never had the urge to gamble except with the nickel machines.

When I think about concert tours and traveling, I cannot help but remember how fortunate I was to have Humphry Doulens of Columbia Concerts as my personal representative. Humphry had had great experience in managing three divas before me: Grace Moore, Lily Pons, and Gladys Swarthout. He also played a very important part in my career. He was so protective of me that at times I called him my own private eye. No one dared sneeze near me nor show the slightest signs of having a cold. He would quickly move me away as far as possible.

Humphry was a great front man in those days of community concerts. He would hustle off to the theatre immediately upon our arrival to check out the specific instructions that I had sent in advance and felt essential to my appearance. Poor lighting, an untuned piano, a dirty stage, or an unattractive background immediately create a poor atmosphere. I have always felt that we owe our audience something lovely to look at along with our vocal gifts. The first entrance on the stage, whether in concert, opera, or whatever, quickly establishes the authority of the diva and her personality.

I always dressed at the theatre and made it a rule to be there an hour before curtain time in order to prepare myself, vocalize, and relax. One of the most important requirements on my list was a floor runner, the kind used in churches for weddings, which would go from the wing of the stage to the piano where I stood. The theatrical value of this idea I found quite attractive. First, it made a more glamorous entrance and in a sense set the stage. Also, it kept my beautiful gowns clean! Next in importance was the lighting. I asked for a pink gel, a soft light which is easy on the complexion and not liable to change the color of my gown. All these things were just as important to me as my singing well. That was the only way I wanted to present myself. Whether it was on a huge stage in a big city like Cleveland, or a small one in a high school in Cinnaminson, New Jersey, I gave my all and was having a grand love affair with my audience.

Those were enjoyable touring days. Traveling today is different. Things have changed considerably since I was so busy in that phase of my career. When Humphry Doulens passed away in the early 1960s, there was no one to take his place. Since I had been completely spoiled by his attentiveness to my requirements, touring became more difficult. I remained at Columbia Artists with Michael Ries and Hattie Clark, and though I was fond of them both personally, the management business in general had changed a great deal. I continued to do short tours here and there, but being forced to depend on the local people to see that things I needed to be comfortable were there created problems in some instances. I soon became disenchanted.

I had beautiful gowns designed for my concerts and it disappointed me greatly when sometimes I found that the people responsible had neglected to check the facilities. On occasion they were so bad that the management should have been embarrassed. We arrived for one concert only to find that the dressing room which I was to use was flooded! I'll never forget that drafty enclosure we quickly improvised out of anything we could pin up to give me a minimum amount of privacy while I stripped to dress onstage.

One of the most unusual admirers to have ever attended a recital of mine turned out to be a resident of the auditorium. At my concert in Beeville, Texas, a rich oil city south of San Antonio, I began the evening with a group of difficult classical songs which required total concentration. Suddenly, I was aware of a strange whirring sound. Not wanting to distract the attention of my audience, I tried to ignore it until something whizzed around me and then disappeared overhead. I was really disturbed the second time it dived close, and the audience began to stir. As I paused to regain my composure I thought it must be a bird which had flown in an open window and became trapped in the theatre. Just then a young man in the front stood up and said, "Don't worry, Miss Kirsten, it's only a bat who lives up there. He doesn't come out for just anyone, only for special people." I appreciated his complimentary remarks very much, and everyone laughed. I started again, but not being fond of bats, I kept checking the rafters between selections. For the rest of the evening, much to my amazement, that bat sat on the proscenium and behaved like a gentleman. Maybe he did enjoy my performance.

Everyone who travels by air a great deal has had some nervous moments in the sky. On a trip to Miami for the opera, I recall flying from Los Angeles with a stop in New Orleans. As we flew South an electric storm developed and became more violent as we neared the airport. I was growing more tense with every passing minute, and as the lightning flashed all around us I began to help the plane land by sliding so far forward in my seat that I was nearly on the floor. The rain was pouring down in torrents and suddenly we hit the trees. The plane darted sharply up again and people screamed. We finally made a hard landing, and I'll never understand how that plane stayed together. It was a close call and I was determined never to fly again, as I had said several times before.

Vicki was with me as usual, and when we finally reached the airport in New Orleans, I refused to continue the trip. All I wanted to do was find a hotel out of the storm and away from airplanes! Having stayed for years at the Roosevelt Hotel in New Orleans, we immediately called my friend Seymour Weiss, who was the manager. When we told him our experience and that we needed lodging for at least the night, he blurted out, "But Dorothy, it's the first night of Mardi Gras and I haven't got a thing." After a few seconds he offered meekly, "But I'll find something for you." He did, and we were most comfortable in the President's Suite.

When I called Jack, needing to tell a kindred soul of our plight but hoping it would not worry him, he treated the incident lightly, as he has been known to do. "Go down to the oyster bar across the street," he said, "and have a wonderful oyster stew and a Sazarac. You'll forget all about it." How clever he was. He knew I had to continue in the morning and in order to meet my commitments I had to fly. I took his advice and we were on our way to Miami the next day.

There was another harrowing night on a plane which I shall never forget. This time we were flying over the lovely Blue Ridge mountain range on a concert tour. Again we were going through a storm of thunder and lightning, which was bouncing off the plane with sparks darting everywhere. The wings seemed to wave as we hit deep bumps, and suddenly we noticed that the man across from us was in trouble. We rang for the stewardess who crawled on her hands and knees down the aisle to him. He died of a heart attack before our eyes, and it's a wonder I didn't too, I was so frightened. It was difficult to continue flying again after that, but I did and still do, though the fear is always with me.

Traveling problems were quickly forgotten while I planned for my next tour. Whenever possible I really enjoyed trips by automobile because it was relaxing to drive through the beautiful countryside. I tried to schedule my dates with enough time to arrive at the city in which I was appearing at least by late afternoon of the day before. A nice quiet dinner and early to bed was our usual plan. Stopping at motels across the country had its attraction because they were mostly out of the city.

A concert tour we especially enjoyed began in Connecticut, went through Massachusetts and up to New Hampshire. Ralph Linsley, my accompanist and dear friend, was also an excellent driver. He is a fine pianist and a delightful person with whom to travel. Vicki was always with me and all I had to do was stay well and sing up a storm.

It had been a magnificent trip with superb weather. When we arrived in Nashua, New Hampshire, we checked into a charming motel. Though our rooms were separated from the main building where we dined, we thought little of it, had a good dinner, and retired early. Overnight, much to our amazement, we were completely snowed in. Our car had all but disappeared beneath an avalanche of snow, and we could not get out of our rooms. The concert had to be postponed. Fortunately I had an extra day and was able to stay over. We were finally rescued when everyone helped to shovel the snow away from our doors, making a path to the dining room.

The concert had been scheduled to be held at the local high school. Because of the storm there had been no classes, and when we arrived we were shocked to learn that the janitor had never shown up to turn on the heat. I sang that concert in my fur coat, and when I made my entrance I was not at all surprised to see my audience bundled up in their fur coats too.

Singing with the great symphony orchestras of the world and their famous conductors has been a special part of my career of which I am very proud. My first appearance with a major symphony orchestra was in Chicago, where I sang with Frederick Stock, who at that time was one of our country's major musical figures.

In 1944 I was engaged to sing with Dimitri Mitropoulos and the Philadelphia Orchestra and was thrilled by this dynamic conductor. Mitropoulos was best known in this country as a great leader of symphonic music, but my experiences with him much later when we recorded two operas were somewhat different. I gladly accepted when Mr. Bing asked me to record *Madama Butterfly* and *Tosca* for the Metropolitan Opera recording club under the direction of the Greek maestro. However, when the rehearsals began for *Butterfly*, I became most apprehensive. His approach to this delicate score was rigid and made it exceedingly difficult for me to express so many of the gentle nuances that are essential to this role. There was no freedom for my own interpretation and I was crushed. On the other hand, when we began to work on *Tosca* the music was far more suited to his flamboyant style, and I was much more comfortable.

I always found Eugene Ormandy to be a charming and warm human being. He was most considerate of the artist and always tried to control his superb orchestra so as not to cover the vocalist. I recall with much pleasure a concert with him at the Ann Arbor Festival in Michigan. I had requested a spotlight for my appearance in order to light my gown properly. When we began to rehearse, the spot was not there. I sweetly inquired of the light man, who informed me that such a light was annoying to the orchestra and was against Mr. Ormandy's regulations. During a break in the rehearsal I explained to the maestro how important the spot was to me. Offering to accept a softer one than usual, I begged him to make an exception. This dear man gave in to my request with humor and grace. In all his greatness, he was a joy to work with. After our confrontation he nicknamed me "the lioness," explaining that I always knew how to get exactly what I wanted.

Working with Erich Leinsdorf was always a pleasure. He too is a fine and considerate conductor and one of the few who can shift comfortably and expertly from symphony to opera. I have sung both with him and admire his talent greatly.

Sir Georg Solti is another with whom I enjoyed my work and whose directing is quite sympathetic to singers. I recall in particular a stirring Beethoven Ninth Symphony I sang with him and the San Francisco Symphony. The soprano part in this work is an especially difficult assignment because of its high, sustained tessitura.

The first time I ever sang this Beethoven masterpiece was with the New York Philharmonic under the direction of Artur Rodzinski at Carnegie Hall. Rodzinski chose me to sing Villa-Lobos' enchanting Bachianas Brasileiras No. 5 with him the next year and following that, Lukas Foss's cantata *In the Prairie*. He was a typical symphonic specialist who appeared to have little consideration for singers in general and operatic ones in particular. I became hopelessly entangled between his rehearsals and those to which I was committed at the Met, and it was obvious that he expected me to consider the symphony more important. Having admired this great conductor so much, at first I was quite disturbed by the situation, but obviously his attitude was not personal, for he continued to re-engage me.

Orchestral concerts in Washington and Baltimore with the renowned conductor and composer Georges Enesco was another wonderful experience. Enesco was a refugee and I think that is what brought such infinite sadness to his eyes. But the music had an enormously soothing effect on him the moment he stepped on the podium, and I shall always remember the emotional grandeur with which this small man conducted.

One of the most colorful characters of all was the immortal Arthur Fiedler, who passed away in 1979 at the age of eighty-five. I appeared with the famous "father" of the Boston Pops Orchestra in Boston and other cities when he was on tour. His idea of combining the classical repertoire with American jazz and lighter types of music was an enormous success, and it was obvious he enjoyed conducting for Ella Fitzgerald as much as for anyone else.

I will never forget the first time I met him when he appeared in his carpet slippers for our rehearsal. He was a dear, considerate old man and a fine conductor. It is no wonder that he was highly respected by the many artists with whom he worked. He was a disciplinarian too, and when his musicians did not respond to a jazz beat the way he wanted them to, they would rehearse it until he was satisfied. The city of Boston will never forget its beloved Fiedler.

I met André Kostelanetz at the beginning of my career and considered him a close friend until he died just a short time ago. My many concerts with him across the country will long be remembered as some of my most happy occasions on the stage. There was always collaboration with André, and he too was a conductor who could direct anything from a dramatic aria to a Gershwin tune or an art song. He breathed with the singer and never forced his own interpretation.

We had an especially lovely experience one night when I was singing at the Robin Hood Dell with the Philadelphia Orchestra under his direction. Unknown to me, someone had told him that it was my birthday. He knew I could not hear him when he announced it to the audience, because the dressing rooms were in the basement of the shell. When I made my first entrance and signaled André that I was ready, he abruptly turned around and directed the entire outdoor audience of thousands in singing "Happy Birthday, dear Dorothy." I was so touched that I forgot what I was to sing until I heard the introduction.

A glamorous but frustrating experience I shall never forget occurred when Richard Tucker and I were chosen to represent the Metropolitan Opera at a huge telecast benefit to raise funds for the Kennedy Center in Washington. This affair was held at the National Guard Armory in the nation's capital and brought out President and Mrs. Kennedy, as well as the elite of Washington. I have always found these colossal fund-raising affairs a cross to bear because of the confusion, the late hours of waiting to go on, and often a distracted audience. There was a large dais at which the President and his wife sat through the interminable evening. I was seated between Stewart Udall, Secretary of the Interior, who was good company; and Orville Freeman, Secretary of Agriculture, who smoked one big cigar after another. As more and more time elapsed, the air was getting thicker with smoke, and I thought our turn would never come. Finally, Richard and I were announced and walked to the improvised stage where the National Symphony Orchestra and Leonard Bernstein were waiting for us. We sang our operatic duet with Leonard accompanying us beautifully. When I returned to the dais Secretary Udall escorted me directly to the President, who immediately rose from his seat. We talked, and he was most complimentary of our singing. Like so many others, I became quite aware of his considerable charm.

New Orleans had one of my favorite opera companies, for which I sang just about everything in my repertoire. I celebrated a twenty-year anniversary with them and that day was declared by the mayor to be "Dorothy Kirsten Day." The second key to the city, and all kinds of commemorative gifts, were presented; and the company gave me a beautiful gold bracelet with inscribed charms for each opera I had performed there.

An incredibly funny and embarrassing moment which almost stopped the show happened in New Orleans while I was singing Marguerite in Gounod's *Faust*. Customarily she sings a lovely aria in the garden scene while seated at her spinning wheel. I was surprised when there was no such prop for me to use. With all the antique shops in that city, one was located without too much trouble, and we were assured it would be in place for the performance. When I came to the theatre that night, I was shocked to find an odd-looking piece with an extraordinarily large wheel. It did work, however, and though I was half-hidden sitting behind this monster, it was too late to make a change. When the time came for me to sing and spin, I ever so nonchalantly seated myself and putting my right hand on the top of the wheel, I gave it a turn. After barely getting started, the big wheel fell off, rolled across the stage and kept going right into the wings. I was in shock and missed a few notes, but hardly a soul knew, for the audience covered everything with its laughter.

One of my most exciting trips to London was with Frank Sinatra; it was arranged by our friend John Haskell of Hollywood. We went over to participate in a royal command performance for Prince Philip, the Duke of Edinburgh. The proceeds were to go to the Duke's favorite charity at that time, American-styled playing fields for British children. The entertainers were both American and British and we performed at the London Coliseum. The list of celebrities was long, and as the only opera singer invited I was asked to sing an aria and did the popular one from *Madama Butterfly*, "Un bel dì." The reception was marvelous. I took my applause bowing to the royal box, and when I came offstage for the last time I was informed that the Queen was requesting I sing again. Quite surprised, because this had not happened to the others, I looked in dismay at my old friend Jimmy Van Heusen, the songwriter who was there to accompany Frank Sinatra. The program was so long that we had been asked to prepare only one number, therefore the orchestra could not accompany me. Jimmy gallantly came to my rescue by offering to play for me. "Just name it, Dorothy, and I'll follow you." He did beautifully while I sang an old favorite of mine, Noël Coward's song from *Bitter Sweet*, "I'll See You Again."

Following the performance the Duke gave a dinner, and I was tickled pink to find myself honored by being seated at his left. He was a real Prince Charming and a delightful dinner partner. When he asked me to have the first dance with him I could not have been more pleased. Humphry Doulens had accompanied me to London, and when he saw the Duke escorting me to the dance floor his face just beamed.

Before publishing in my book the picture of us dancing together, I wrote to his personal secretary. A quick reply said that His Highness was delighted to be reminded of our meeting in 1951 and was "entirely content" that our photograph be included in my book.

A unique singing experience occurred during an official visit to China in 1979, representing the city of Los Angeles. Our close friends Howard Edgerton and Charles Luckman were instrumental in arranging this exciting trip through the mayor of Los Angeles, Tom Bradley. The seven couples going to China were chosen because of distinction in their representative fields. Jack represented medical science, and I the arts. Before leaving I was asked what I wanted to see and hear. I responded that I was interested in hearing their symphony orchestra and observing the opera. However, I soon discovered the Chinese had no notable orchestra of their own, and what they called opera had absolutely no similarity to what we know of this art. I understand that one or two of our major symphonies have visited China since then and they are now definitely training their young to play instruments. I was delighted to find that in some schools there were courses in musical education, and one in particular was a joy to visit. A string orchestra of children, ranging in ages from four to eight, with instruments made to fit their tiny hands, played a Mozart piece for us and several interesting Chinese selections unbelievably well. We were enchanted.

In a vocal class of about one hundred children, at a school in Shanghai called The Children's Palace, our guide introduced us to the teachers and told them I was a great American singer. The head instructor begged me to sing something for them. When I hesitated, wondering what I could do without accompaniment, she said, "The children would like you to sing 'Home on the Range.'" We all nearly collapsed. My friends who were sitting behind me, and not being of any help at all, were playfully nudging me. I carefully tried to explain, hoping not to embarrass them, that this was a man's song and I did not know the words to it. Struggling to be serious, I told them I would sing something very special just for them. In operatic tones, high and low, making up the words as I went along, I let out my voice. The look of amazement on those lovely little faces with big round eyes was even more thrilling than the effort they made to applaud with their little hands. Though I heard no music in China that thrilled me, the nearly three hundred colored photographs I took of the children and countryside are being used as the inspiration for a series of oils I am doing for my next exhibition now that I have a new career in painting.

Afterthoughts

Having had no experience as an author I never dreamed I would write my own book. Doubleday had approached me at least fifteen years ago, but at that time I was too busy with my career.

One evening while discussing the subject with the great author Irving Stone, I was telling him of the difficulty in finding the right co-author when he completely surprised me by saying, "Dorothy, why don't you write your own book?" I have always loved a challenge, and decided to try. It has certainly been an exhilarating experience.

As I began to write, exercising daily to keep fit and checking on my vocal powers became the only escape from my writing pad. Once I was into it, I could concentrate on nothing else. Time passed so quickly I found myself annoyed by having to stop for any small interruption. My enthusiasm gathered momentum with Jack's encouragement and his valuable help in editing the first drafts.

Our social life was set aside and my painting and golf were sadly neglected, but I had never before realized how rewarding the feeling of accomplishment would be. There were no singing engagements for over a year and I often dreamed of performing again.

The book was nearly finished when the usual invitation arrived to play golf with the lady professionals in the Dinah Shore Pro-Am Golf Tournament at Mission Hills in Palm Springs. This was the tenth anniversary of the Colgate affair and I had been a regular from the beginning. I couldn't miss this one.

Off to the practice range, a fast boning up of my golf game, and I was on my way to Palm Springs and the tournament. Before I was able to unpack my golf clubs and say hello to old friends, there was a message from Dinah. This being a special occasion, would I please just sing "something" at the gala celebration? After being introduced at the tournaments for several years as the great Metropolitan Opera star, I knew I would be expected to share a few high notes with my Colgate friends. I was already committed to play golf for two days, but this was an opportunity to express my pleasure at being a part of these exciting tournaments.

The evening affairs had been quite informal and consequently I had nothing with me which would be appropriate for such an appearance. After a few calls to Los Angeles the music I needed and my brand-new Pauline Trigère creation were hurried to Palm Springs. Sheri Sheridan, my friend and fan of many years, once again came to my rescue.

After the golf game, a quick run-through of my music with Dinah's conductor John Rodby, a bite to eat, a few notes in the shower and it was time to dress. When I stepped into my gown, I was shocked to discover that someone had forgotten to shorten the skirt. It was at least four inches too long! Since it was a slim one and much unlike my usual bouffant concert gowns that I can daintily raise to make a grand entrance and then let fall around my feet, there was no way I could walk in this one unless we shortened it somehow.

A few minutes before I was due to appear, we were able to round up several safety pins. Rolling the belt over and over and pinning it in place adjusted the length, but now the waistband was so tight I was fearful that with my first big breath to reach a high note I would find my skirt around my knees.

The show had already begun when I joined my friends Bob Hope and Andy Williams to salute Dinah and Colgate for their generous contribution to women's golf. The music was decidedly upbeat as I entered and I wondered about singing opera. Would they listen to "Un bel dì" from *Madama Butterfly?* Indeed they did, with a standing ovation. All went extremely well. My gown was a smash; I was back in form and feeling great.

As for my golf? I helped my team with a few birdies and had a wonderful time as usual but when I goofed a shot, I remember muttering, "Thank God I can sing."

Singing is an expression of the soul, more completely fulfilling than anything I know. There is no greater reward.

Now that my book is finished and my story has been told, it will be a joy to get back to the work for which I was born, and the gift of song I hold so dear.

Appendix

AWARDS, DEGREES, CITATIONS, ETC.

1944 Three Awards in silver, from the Canadian Government (in rec-
–45 ognition of War Bond Shows)
1951 Doctor of Music, Ithaca College, New York
1955 "Woman of the Year" Los Angeles *Times* (for outstanding achieve-
ment)
1962 Awarded one of the original stars by the Chamber of Commerce to
be placed in the "Walk of the Stars" on Hollywood Boulevard
1965 "Silver Clock," Metropolitan Opera, Twentieth Anniversary
1970 "Silver Bowl," Metropolitan Opera, Twenty-fifth Anniversary
1970 "Silver Medallion," San Francisco Opera, Twenty-fifth Anniversary
1971 Citation from City of Los Angeles (in honor of Silver Jubilee)
1971 Citation from County of Los Angeles (in honor of Silver Jubilee)
1971 Doctor of Fine Arts, Santa Clara University, California
1971 Handel Award, City of New York (Mayor Lindsay)
1975 "Gold Bracelet," Metropolitan Opera, Thirtieth Anniversary
1975 Citation from City of New York (Mayor Beame) (commemorating
Thirtieth Anniversary at the Metropolitan Opera)
1977 "Commendatore," Italy's highest cultural award, presented by
Italian Consul General Alessandro Cortese de Bosia, in recognition
of contribution to United States–Italy relations
Keys to many cities too numerous to mention

DISCOGRAPHY
by Stanley A. Bowker

Mi chiamano Mimì, *La Bohème*, Puccini.   RCA 11-9694 (78)
Mimi's Farewell, *La Bohème*, Puccini.   RCA 49-0387 (45)

OPERETTA

THE DESERT SONG, Romberg.
  Dorothy Kirsten and Gordon MacRae.
  Van Alexander conducting   ANGEL 37319*

KISMET, Wright and Forrest (adapted from Borodin).
  Dorothy Kirsten and Gordon MacRae   ANGEL 37321*

THE MERRY WIDOW, Lehár.
  Dorothy Kirsten, Robert Rounseville,
  Genevieve Warner, Clifford Harvuot,
  Wesley Dalton   COLUMBIA ML 4666

THE NEW MOON, Romberg.
  Dorothy Kirsten and Gordon MacRae.
  Van Alexander conducting   ANGEL 37320*

ROSE MARIE, Friml.
  Dorothy Kirsten and Nelson Eddy.
  Leon Arnaud conducting   COLUMBIA ML 2178

SHOW BOAT, Kern.
  Dorothy Kirsten and Robert Merrill.
  John Scott Trotter conducting   RCA DM 1341

THE STUDENT PRINCE, Romberg.
  Dorothy Kirsten and Robert Rounseville.
  Lehman Engel conducting   ODYSSEY Y 32367

THE STUDENT PRINCE, Romberg.
  Dorothy Kirsten and Gordon MacRae.
  Van Alexander conducting   ANGEL 37318*

FAVORITE SONGS FROM FAMOUS MUSICALS
  Dorothy Kirsten and Felix Knight.
  Wanting You, Thine Alone, Will You
  Remember, Sweethearts, Ah! Sweet
  Mystery of Life, One Alone, My Hero,
  Serenade   RCA P 133

DOROTHY KIRSTEN SINGS VICTOR HERBERT
MELODIES
  Kiss Me Again, Moonbeams, A Kiss in the
  Dark, Indian Summer, 'Neath the Southern
  Moon, Romany Life   RCA DM 1069

* Originally issued on Capitol.

POPULAR

*DOROTHY KIRSTEN SINGS SONGS OF
GEORGE GERSHWIN*
  Mine, Someone to Watch over Me,
  Love Walked In, Do-Do-Do,
  Embraceable You, I've Got a Crush on You,
  Our Love Is Here to Stay, Soon   COLUMBIA ML 2129
                                                 MM 929

*DOROTHY KIRSTEN SINGS SONGS OF
JEROME KERN*
  All the Things You Are, Dearly Beloved,
  Don't Ever Leave Me, Yesterdays,
  I've Told Every Little Star, I'm
  Old Fashioned, Long Ago and Far Away,
  Look for the Silver Lining.
  Percy Faith conducting   COLUMBIA ML 2175

TROPICAL LOVE SONGS
  Flamingo, Orchids in the Moonlight,
  Sleepy Lagoon, Temptation,
  Poinciana, Jealousy, The Breeze and I,
  Brazil.
  Russell Case conducting   COLUMBIA ML 2212

MR. MUSIC
  Dorothy Kirsten and Bing Crosby.
  Accidents Will Happen, Milady
  Music by James Van Heusen   DECCA 9-101

78/45 RPM RECORDINGS

You Go to My Head, Gillespie-Coots.	RCA 10-1499 (78)
More Than You Know, Vincent Youmans.	RCA 49-0721 (45)
The Man I Love, George Gershwin.	RCA 10-1497 (78)
Why Was I Born? Jerome Kern.	RCA 49-0697 (45)
Wanting You, Sigmund Romberg.	RCA 10-1423 (78)
When I Grow Too Old to Dream, Sigmund Romberg.	RCA 49-0677 (45)
I'll See You Again, Noël Coward. Why Do I Love You? Jerome Kern.	RCA 10-1398 (78)
April in Paris, Vernon Duke. The Love I Long For, Vernon Duke.	RCA 10-1137 (78)
Every Time We Say Goodbye, Cole Porter. Only Another Boy and Girl, Cole Porter.	RCA 10-1156 (78)

COLLECTIONS*

DOROTHY KIRSTEN IN OPERA AND SONG
  Depuis le jour, *Louise*, Charpentier;
  Un bel dì, *Madama Butterfly*, Puccini;
  In quelle trine morbide, *Manon Lescaut*, Puccini;
  Mi chiamano Mimì, *La Bohème*, Puccini;
  Gavotte, *Manon*, Massenet;
  Chi il bel sogno di Doretta, *La Rondine*, Puccini;
  Wanting You, *The New Moon*, Romberg;
  Death of Thaïs, *Thaïs*, Massenet;
  You Go to My Head, Gillespie-Coots;
  More Than You Know, *Great Day*, Youmans;
  The Man I Love, Gershwin;
  Why Was I Born? *Sweet Adeline*, Kern   RCA 1552

BY POPULAR DEMAND
  Vissi d'arte, *Tosca*, Puccini;
  Ore dolci e divine, *La Rondine*, Puccini;
  Excerpts from *Manon Lescaut* (with Richard
  Tucker), Puccini; Un bel dì, Tu, tu,
  piccolo iddio, *Madama Butterfly*, Puccini;
  O mio babbino caro, *Gianni Schicchi*, Puccini;
  C'est des contrabandiers, *Carmen*, Bizet;
  La mamma morta, *Andrea Chénier*, Giordano;
  Do-Do-Do, *Oh, Kay!* Gershwin;
  Love Walked In, *Goldwyn Follies*, Gershwin   ODYSSEY Y 31737

DOROTHY KIRSTEN IN SONG
  Colombetta, A Southern Song,
  My Curly-Headed Baby, Annie Laurie,
  So in Love, I Love Thee, The Man I Love,
  If I Should Lose You, Comin' Thro' the Rye,
  My Ideal, My Man's Gone Now, Take Me in
  Your Arms, Les Filles de Cádiz, Since
  First I Met Thee, Czardas (from *Die Fledermaus*),
  All the Things You Are.
  Kraft Music Hall Broadcasts, 1948–49   PELICAN LP 2005

PRIVATE RECORDINGS

Dorothy Kirsten's all too limited commercial recording career may be
supplemented by the following selection of private or "pirate" recordings,
most of which are unfortunately out of print. All of these recordings,
though, may be found at the Rodgers and Hammerstein Collection of the
New York Public Library at Lincoln Center.

---

* Reissued to commemorate Dorothy Kirsten's twenty-fifth anniversary with the
Metropolitan Opera.

FAUST, Gounod.
  Kirsten, Björling, Siepi,
  Guarrera. Fausto Cleva
  conducting. Metropolitan Opera,
  December 23, 1950   UORC-110

FAUST, Gounod.
  Selections.
  Kirsten, di Stefano, Warren,
  Tajo. Wilfred Pelletier conducting.
  Metropolitan Opera, 1949   UORC 144

MANON LESCAUT, Puccini.
  Kirsten, Björling, Valdengo.
  Giuseppe Antonicelli conducting   UORC 207

L'AMORE DEI TRE RE, Montemezzi.
  Selections. Virgilio Lazzari, Robert
  Weede, Charles Kullmann, Dorothy Kirsten,
  Leslie Chabay, Paul Franke, Thelma Altman,
  Paula Lenchner, Claramae Turner.
  Giuseppe Antonicelli conducting.
  January 15, 1949   EJS 241

MANON LESCAUT, Puccini.
  Selections. Björling, Kirsten,
  Valdengo, Baccaloni.
  Antonicelli conducting.
  December 10, 1949   EJS 251

In addition to the above operas, one may also listen to Dorothy Kirsten's "Farewell to the Met radio audience," an intermission feature of the December 27, 1975, Metropolitan Opera radio broadcast.

For those who require still more Kirsten recordings, the answer lies in tape. Various companies (their names may be found in opera magazines and the back of the Schwann catalog) possess extraordinary collections of operatic performances and are prepared to sell taped copies to the public. As an example, *La Fanciulla del West*, one of Kirsten's most famous roles and an opera which was otherwise totally unrecorded by her, may be found in performances with tenors as diverse as Sándor Kónya, Richard Tucker, and Franco Corelli. Similarly, if one is dissatisfied with the casting in the recorded version of *Tosca*, one can find in the tape catalog such rarities as a December 13, 1952, performance with Ferruccio Tagliavini, as well as additional performances with Placido Domingo, Franco Corelli, Sándor Kónya, and Richard Tucker.

Index